Globalization and Military Power in the Andes

Globalization and Military Power in the Andes

William Avilés

GLOBALIZATION AND MILITARY POWER IN THE ANDES
Copyright © William Avilés, 2010.

First published in 2010 by
PALGRAVE MACMILLAN®
in the United States—a division of St. Martin's Press LLC,
175 Fifth Avenue, New York, NY 10010.

Where this book is distributed in the UK, Europe and the rest of the
world, this is by Palgrave Macmillan, a division of Macmillan Publishers
Limited, registered in England, company number 785998, of Houndmills,
Basingstoke, Hampshire RG21 6XS.

Palgrave Macmillan is the global academic imprint of the above companies
and has companies and representatives throughout the world.

Palgrave® and Macmillan® are registered trademarks in the United States,
the United Kingdom, Europe and other countries.

ISBN: 978–0–230–10387–0

Library of Congress Cataloging-in-Publication Data

Avilés, William, 1971–
    Globalization and military power in the Andes / William Avilés.
        p. cm.
    Includes bibliographical references and index.
    ISBN 978–0–230–10387–0 (alk. paper)
    1. Civil-military relations—Andes Region. 2. Democracy—Andes
Region. 3. Globalization—Andes Region. 4. Political culture—Andes
Region. 5. Andes Region—Politics and government. 6. Andes Region—
Armed Forces—Political activity. 7. Andes Region—Economic conditions.
    I. Title.

JL1856.C58A85 2010
322'.5098—dc22   2010019213

A catalogue record of the book is available from the British Library.

Design by Newgen Imaging Systems (P) Ltd., Chennai, India.

First edition: December 2010

10 9 8 7 6 5 4 3 2 1

Printed in the United States of America.

To Susan

CONTENTS

List of Tables and Figure   ix

Acknowledgments   xi

Introduction   1
1   Military Power and Capitalist Globalization   13
2   The Erosion of Military Prerogatives:
    The Cases of Peru and Colombia   43
3   "Radical Populists" and Military Prerogatives in
    Venezuela and Ecuador   83
4   Low-Intensity Democracy, Popular Resistance,
    and Military Power in Bolivia   123
Conclusion   151

Notes   161

Bibliography   167

Index   191

TABLES AND FIGURE

Table 1.1   Global Competitiveness, Selected Years   38
Table 1.2   Index of Economic Freedom, Selected Years   38
Table 3.1   U.S. Military and Police Aid to the Andes
              (in millions of U.S. dollars)   93
Table C.1   Military Prerogatives in the Andes, 1998–2010   158
Figure I.1   Military Prerogatives and the Interaction of
              Global/Domestic Factors   7

ACKNOWLEDGMENTS

The history and contemporary politics of the Andes continues to illustrate states and societies in conflict. In particular the struggle over capitalist globalization, whether to embrace economic liberalism and market democracies or reject this model for nationalist/statist alternatives, has been central. The militaries of the region have often been at the center of these conflicts, expanding and losing institutional power, depending on a combination of domestic and international factors that have structured the level of influence the armed forces will possess. The findings of this book demonstrate that the existence of substantive internal security threats, which have been a part of violent conflicts in Colombia and Peru, has not led to the expansion of military power and in fact has aided the consolidation of low-intensity democracies with the political role of the military circumscribed to maintaining order and repressing anti-capitalist globalization movements. Militaries have not only been central to the struggles over capitalist globalization, but have witnessed their role shaped by those political actors and social forces who ultimately wield power within the state.

I would not have been able to complete this book without the departmental and institutional support from the University of Nebraska at Kearney (UNK). I thank my colleagues for their friendship and camaraderie, factors that have been central to creating an environment conducive to writing and research. I would like to thank my partner Susan Honeyman who has provided me with excellent feedback to different parts of my work and even joined me on a research trip to Venezuela. I would like to thank the Research Services Council at UNK which helped to finance field study work in Venezuela as well as provided me the financial support for a course release so that I could complete this manuscript. I am also grateful for the research and editorial assistance of Jorge Mora and Viridiana Almanza Zavala. I greatly appreciate the indexing work completed by Collin Grimes. I would also to like thank the different military officers and former members of defense ministries in the Andes for their time and information regarding their respective countries. I am also grateful for the helpful comments from outside reviewers on the original draft of this book as well as the support and advice I received from my editors at Palgrave Macmillan, Robyn Curtis, Joel Breuklander, and Rohini Krishnan. Finally, my gratitude to Blackwell Publishing and the Taylor and Francis group for permission to reprint portions of my earlier work as follows:

"Despite Insurgency: Reducing Military Prerogatives in Colombia and Peru," *Latin American Politics and Society*, Spring 2009, vol. 51, no.1, pp. 57–85 (Copyright 2009, Blackwell Publishing).
"Policy Coalitions, Economic Reform and Military Power in Ecuador and Venezuela," *Third World Quarterly*, vol. 30, no. 8, pp. 1549–1564 (Copyright 2009, Taylor and Francis Group).

Introduction

The conflicts and struggles over capitalist globalization in the Andes are intricately connected to the political power and influence of the military in the region. Many have viewed the use of military power as essential in creating the stability and order necessary to facilitate economic investments from transnational corporations as well as to ensure open trading regimes (see O'Donnell 1973; Petras and Morley 1992; Harvey 2005). Others have pointed to the pressures that economic liberalization has placed upon military budgets or examined the extent that regional integration has worked to lessen external military threats (Mares 2001). While these issues are all relevant to understanding military power and influence in the region, and are addressed in this work, I submit that the relationship between capitalist globalization and civil-military relations is not simply a reflection of budgetary pressures or the basic prerequisites of corporate investors, but also reflects a set of ideological, political processes and norms associated with capitalist globalization.

The inclusion of global processes allows us to explain the various counterintuitive outcomes of civil-military policies in the Andes during the 1990s and 2000s. Specifically, the reduction of military prerogatives in Colombia, Peru, and Bolivia during intensive counter-insurgent or counternarcotic conflicts while countries such as Ecuador and Venezuela have witnessed the expansion of military prerogatives despite the lack of substantive internal threats. How can one explain that the two Andean countries experiencing the greatest internal security threats in the region have made the greatest progress in maintaining and strengthening civilian authority over the armed forces in the last twenty years? Why has the military's role and prerogatives expanded or been maintained in countries such as Venezuela and Ecuador despite the absence of such internal security threats?

These questions are answered by examining the influence of political struggles associated with the economic and political integration of these national economies into global capitalism. Differences in political control over the military and military prerogatives are related to the capture of national states by neoliberal policy coalitions. These coalitions consist of technocrats, politicians, and members of the military high command and sectors of the national/transnational business community committed to the integration of their economies into capitalist globalization. In Peru, Colombia, and Bolivia neoliberal policy coalitions came to power in the late 1980s and early 1990s focused primarily upon accelerating the internationalization of their respective economies as well as reforming their civil-military relations as a necessary element in the modernization of their respective states. By contrast, in Ecuador and Venezuela this process has been disrupted. Neoliberal policy coalitions have either been unable to consolidate their hold upon political power or been directly removed, or as in the case of Bolivia, are witnessing the reversal of their previous success. The existence of internal security threats has worked to strengthen the hand of neoliberal policy coalitions, creating the justification to repress a political opposition associated with challenges to neoliberalism and capitalist globalization. The military's emphasis upon counterinsurgency has worked to unify these armed forces against these internal security threats and marginalize a potential source of opposition to capitalist globalization—nationalist factions within the military.

What this illustrates is that the spread and institutionalization of capitalist globalization in Latin America has not only meant the decentralization of capitalist production, increasing foreign direct investment, the expansion of free trade and the diffusion of neoliberal economic policies,[1] but it has also meant the reconfiguration of nation-states (Cox 1981; Robinson 1996, 2001; 2004; Sklair 2002; Gills et al. 1993). To borrow from Robert Cox, an emerging "historical structure" can be identified that represents a "particular configuration between ideas, institutions and material forces" (Cox 1981) or a "framework of action which constitutes the context of habits, pressures, expectations and constraints within which actions take place, but which does not determine actions in any direct, mechanical way" (Hoogvelt 2001, p. 11). Increasingly from the 1970s and into the present day the political regime viewed as best equipped to integrate Latin America into capitalist globalization has been a type of elite democracy sometimes referred to as "polyarchies," "market democracies," or "low-intensity democracies." Low-intensity democracies are limited democracies in that they achieve important political changes, such as the reduction of the military's institutional prerogatives, greater individual freedoms, and electoral competition, but stop short in addressing the extreme social inequalities or broadening popular political participation in a meaningful way within capitalist nation-states (Gills, et al. 1993). Power is often concentrated in the hands of executive offices as technocratic elites implement policies with greater autonomy from the public. In these regimes the armed forces are *generally* allied with the neoliberal government, maintaining domestic order and preventing radical efforts to extend democracy beyond the formal political process.

The United States has played (and continues to play) a central role in the construction and strengthening of low-intensity democracies consistent with capitalist globalization (Robinson 1996; Gilly 2005). The promotion of market democracies, or low-intensity democracies, was deemed preferable to authoritarian regimes in maintaining the legitimacy and stability necessary to preserve U.S. interests and capital accumulation (Robinson 1996, p. 148). Military-led authoritarian regimes, military-controlled state companies, and extensive military budgets are all counter to the democratic civil-military relations being promoted, one in which free markets and trade are directly tied to the establishment of formal liberal institutions, including the subordination of military power to civilian authorities. The internationalization of capital markets and the monitoring of economic behavior by international financial institutions have reduced the necessity of military rule to ensure economic strategies amenable to the interests of international economic elites.

When one examines contemporary politics of the Andean region, social protests, military coups, armed insurgencies, corruption scandals, poverty, and economic inequality as well as an entrenched drug-trafficking industry have all been prominent (Burt and Mauceri 2004; Crandall, Paz and Roett 2005; Drake and Hershberg 2006; Mainwaring and Bejarano 2006). Political party systems throughout the region are decaying and/or have collapsed. In addition, there has been a resurgence of "populist," leftist, and nationalist movements that have attempted to fill political vacuums by promoting new forms of political relations and/or developmental strategies. Between 1990 and 2010 three different presidents in Ecuador were removed from power by combinations of social protests and military rebellion, between 1992 and 2002 three military coups were attempted in Venezuela, and the militaries of both Peru and Colombia have fought guerrilla insurgencies while regularly committing human rights violations throughout the 1990s and 2000s.

In Bolivia, massive social protests forced out the president in 2003, after failed attempts to militarily repress these movements, while regional elites have engaged in political violence to obtain greater autonomy. In many of these conflicts, the question of capitalist globalization has been central, with the vicissitudes of the global marketplace often undermining economic growth and contributing to political instability. In addition, the implementation of a set of neoliberal economic policies has also triggered political reaction and resistance. The direction and shape of civil–military relations has not and is not disconnected from these conflicts.

Traditional indicators of civilian control include the appointment of civilians at the head of defense ministries and domestic intelligence services, civilian determination of budgets, security missions being established by elected leaders or their appointees, and a promotion process that allows congressional or presidential control over the appointments of the high command. In addition, the military's role in maintaining internal security is curtailed or absent, allowing for civilian police forces to wield that responsibility. The military's institutional prerogatives are limited in a manner that expands the authority and influence of civilian policymakers. Stepan suggests that the military's institutional prerogatives include those sectors where "the military as an institution assumes they have an acquired right or privilege, formal or informal, to exercise effective control over its internal governance, to play a role within extra-military areas within the state apparatus, or even to structure relationships between the state and political or civil society" (Stepan 1988, p. 93).

Democratic civilian control also includes the noninterference of the military into domestic politics, with the military maintaining an apolitical orientation. Trinkunas has argued that as military involvement in policy areas such as leadership selection, public policy, and internal security expands, the greater threat to civilian control, especially if such actions are undertaken independent of civilian authorities or direction (2001, pp. 164–5). David Pion-Berlin (2005, p. 28) concludes that while Latin American governments still have challenges with complete civilian control, they have largely established "political civilian control," which he defines in part as the avoidance of "…undesirable military behavior, be it intense pressure, provocation, coup threats, or actual coups."

Three Andean countries that have made significant progress in the 1990s and 2000s in not only maintaining relative political civilian control, but in also reducing the military's institutional prerogatives, have been Peru, Colombia, and Bolivia. Civilian authorities have not only avoided military coups, but have eroded military prerogatives over defense budgets and defense ministries and military promotions, as well as in the development of security strategies since 1990. In the case of Colombia and Peru, this has been accomplished despite the existence of internal armed threats to state authority that have included the Fuerzas Armadas Revolucionarios de Colombia (FARC) and the Shining Path in Peru. Bolivia also faced internal security threats, though not to the same extent as Peru and Colombia, with its struggle against coca growers and anticapitalist globalization movements that required the militarization of specific regions of the country. The existence of such internal security threats has long been viewed as central to the expansion of military prerogatives (see Stepan 1986; Desch 1999; Fitch 1998), *not the erosion* of military prerogatives that took place in these three countries.

During the period in which neoliberal policy coalitions controlled the state, Colombia, Peru, and Bolivia largely limited their militaries to external and internal security roles. In contrast, in Ecuador and Venezuela, the military has steadily expanded its jurisdictional boundaries, while Bolivia's military has expanded its boundaries with the coming to power of the Morales administration. Again, the expansion in the military's role has happened in those three countries facing relatively weak or nonexistent internal security threats in comparison to the armed insurgencies that challenged different Colombian and Peruvian governments during this period. These are the types of security threats that have long been associated with the expansion of jurisdictional boundaries, not their erosion.

An understanding of this unexpected outcome requires attention to the interaction of domestic and global factors. As mentioned earlier, neoliberal policy coalitions have been important actors in furthering civil-military reforms. These coalitions have internalized many of the economic and political norms disseminated globally through their educations in U.S. universities, their interaction with international financial institutions and transnational policymaking bodies, and/or through their deference to more powerful actors or forces in the global system (such as the United States, transnational corporations, or capital markets) that expect a certain set of political and economic arrangements in exchange for their continued support and/or investments. While this process took place during the 1980s and 1990s in most of Latin America, it progressed in Colombia, Peru, and Bolivia despite the existence of growing and substantial security threats to the state—internal threats that historically had led to the expansion of military prerogatives or even direct military rule in the region.

Within a context of neoliberal policy coalitions in power and U.S. pressures for civilian control, the military's confrontation and autonomy over internal security threats has mitigated the likelihood of military political intervention as the armed forces have committed to the immediate security mission of defeating/containing internal threats. Their role in internal security has expanded in line with the conception of low-intensity democracies; however, other institutional prerogatives, such as their control over military budgets, military training, or control over defense ministries, have been eroded. Furthermore, in none of these three countries did we witness direct attempts by the military to remove civilians from power despite deteriorating security situations or expand their role in other policy arenas (such as public policy or leadership selection of the state). These counterinsurgent wars have undermined nationalist/statist factions within the armed forces who might directly challenge the authority of neoliberal policy coalitions, strengthening those actors in the military and prioritizing the successful repression of such an insurgency and their alleged allies. The military's role has not only been instrumental against armed insurgents, but in also repressing anticapitalist globalization movements within civil society[2] throughout this period. Figure I.1 helps to illustrate my argument.

In Venezuela and Ecuador, nationalist and populist forces have successfully resisted or turned back the influence and power of neoliberal policy coalitions, with factions of the armed forces instrumental in this resistance, undermining the ability of domestic or international political actors to institute democratic reform of civil-military relations. In both Ecuador and Venezuela, sectors of civil society have worked with sectors of the military to either resist specific neoliberal governments (e.g., Ecuador's 2000 coup, Venezuela's 1992 coup attempts) or in the development of antineoliberal movements (e.g., the Movimiento Bolivariano 200 in Venezuela). Relatedly, the absence of significant internal security threats created greater institutional space for nationalist, antiglobalization military factions to attain greater influence within the armed forces. Nationalist/populist factions within the military have allied with elements of civil society in supporting the coming to power of political movements critical of capitalist globalization and traditional conceptions of liberal democracy. The existence of such divisions within the military was not something anticipated or examined by proponents of the conception of low-intensity democracy, who typically viewed the armed forces as a monolithic force buttressing elite interests

GLOBAL FACTORS

SPREAD AND INSTITUTIONALIZATION OF
CAPITALIST GLOBALIZATION AND LIBERAL DEMOCRATIC NORMS

(e.g., U.S. DEMOCRACY AND HUMAN RIGHTS PROMOTION,
THE OAS, AND THE DEMOCRATIC CHARTER, PRESSURES FROM INTERNATIONAL
FINANCIAL INSTITUTIONS)

Balance of
prerogatives
between civilian and
military authorities
within the state

DOMESTIC FACTORS

(e.g., BALANCE OF POWER BETWEEN POLICY COALITIONS,
THE EXISTENCE OF INTERNAL SECURITY THREATS)

Figure I.1   Military Prerogatives and the Interaction of Global/Domestic Factors

(Gills and Rocamora 1992).[3] The recent history of the Andes clearly demonstrates the inadequacy of such a view.

The case of Bolivia shares elements from all four cases with neoliberal policy coalitions obtaining success in wielding national power and the military oriented toward internal security missions in counternarcotics. For much of the 1980s and 1990s neoliberal policy coalitions successfully reduced military prerogatives while the armed forces committed themselves to the domestic mission of establishing internal order and repressing coca growers and antiglobalization activists. While the Bolivian military often violently responded to this threat, with the support of neoliberal policy coalitions and the United States, the extent of this threat and level of military support for repressive strategies never matched the intensity and commitment present in the Peruvian and Colombian militaries. For example, the Bolivian armed forces did not face guerrillas with operational control over major regions of the country as faced by the Colombian and Peruvian armed forces since the 1980s. Thus, space continued to exist for political action and resistance within civil society while the military's counterdrug mission was not institutionally embraced, with elements of the military openly expressing solidarity with antiglobalization and nationalist causes during this period. Ultimately the failure of neoliberal policy coalitions to obtain hegemonic rule led to the successful presidential election of the leftist and anticapitalist globalization leader Evo Morales in December 2005. Morales has steadily reduced U.S. influence on the Bolivian military and has committed the armed forces to an expanded developmentalist role. This political shift in Bolivia remains unconsolidated, as neoliberal policy coalitions and the United States have sought to frustrate the establishment of an anticapitalist globalization regime. What the Bolivian case illustrates is the nonstatic nature of these political developments and the ongoing conflicts over the state and civil–military relations taking place throughout the Andes. In the end, military factions, struggles between nationalist/populist and neoliberal movements in civil society, and the pressures of the United States, intergovernmental organizations, and/or international financial institutions have all played a role directly and indirectly in expanding or reducing military prerogatives within these specific states. This argument runs contrary to the various institutionalist approaches that have long dominated the study of civil–military relations.

Civil–military studies have often restricted analysis to specific key decision makers, such as defense ministers, congressional committees, presidents, and military officers, with little attention to the policy networks linking these actors to socioeconomic groups outside of the state within national or global societies, or little to any attention to the dominant values, ideas that legitimize state behavior beyond specific military doctrines or perceptions of immediate institutional threats. The civil–military relations literature has long argued that the corporate interests of the military, the institutional power of civilian authorities, the electoral incentives of individual legislators, and/or the level of domestic/external threats to the state are central to understanding successful civilian control over the military or even civilian attention to defense policies (Trinkunas 2002; Pion-Berlin 2001; Diamint 1998; Pion-Berlin and Trinkunas 2007). The focus has been upon the state, specifically upon the interactions/rules/beliefs that structure the relationship between civilian authorities and military officials.

In order to understand the variation in civil–military relations in the Andes, analysis needs to complement the institutionalist/nation-state emphasis of traditional civil–military studies with attention to the societal and global context. Neoliberal policy coalitions have represented one part of a transnational process in which international financial institutions, transnational corporations, and the United States, as well as policy planning groups, have collectively worked to construct the conditions necessary for capitalist globalization. Neoliberal policy coalitions have faced not only the economic necessity of free market reform, but also the political necessity to demonstrate to extranational audiences their equal commitments to both free market principles and democratic governance. For example, both the militaries of Colombia and Peru have allowed greater authority to human rights authorities from within their governments in response to conditions placed on U.S. military assistance while also acquiescing to budgetary limits set by neoliberal technocrats over military spending. The armed forces in Bolivia, Colombia, and Peru have also been recipients of relatively significant amounts of military aid and training from the United States, tying them closer to the globalist camp of capitalist globalization and low-intensity democracies.

However, as Ecuador, Venezuela, and more recently Bolivia have demonstrated, the integration and identification with the global system is increasingly being rejected and/or openly challenged in favor of various nationalist/populist policy agendas. The top-down imposition of neoliberal economic reform has created a number of rationales for the public to mobilize and resist this agenda (Arce and Bellinger 2007). In these three countries, leaders have come to power promoting economic policies critical of free markets and open trade as well as of U.S. foreign policy. Venezuelans elected Hugo Chávez in 1998, while Bolivia and Ecuador witnessed the elections of Evo Morales and Rafael Correa in 2005 and 2006, respectively. In each case nationwide social movements, protests, and/or military movements in opposition to capitalist globalization have preceded and contributed to these elections. In 2004, the head of the U.S. Southern Command, General James Hill, referred to these movements and political leaders as "radical populists" and an "emerging threat" in the region, complementing the threats of "terrorism" and "narcotrafficking" (Gilly 2005). Hill argued that "some leaders in the region are tapping into deep-seated frustrations of the failure of democratic reforms to deliver the expected goods and services. By tapping into these frustrations, which run concurrently with frustrations caused by social and economic inequality, the leaders are at the same time able to reinforce radical positions by inflaming anti-U.S. sentiment" in which the "democratic process is undermined" (as quoted in Gilly 2005 and see also Barry 2005).[4] The challenge for U.S.

policy is to reduce the threats to "market democracy" or "low-intensity democracy," maintaining a political system "... tightly bound by the restraints of the global market economy and monitored by military-security forces still ready to combat the 'threat from below' " (McSherry 1996, p. 27).

These "radical populists" consist of movements, leaders, and parties attempting to implement a mixture of nationalistic/social democratic measures inconsistent with the free market principles of neoliberalism that have suffered from a crisis of legitimacy within these nations. The relative success of "radical populists" in these countries has roughly coincided with the expansion (or maintenance of an influential role) of the military's power within the national state and society. In both Ecuador and Venezuela the military's role has consisted of not only an emphasis upon external security, but also a direct role in economic and social development. Since 2006, this has increasingly been taking place in Bolivia as Morales consolidates his political/economic project.

In contrast to traditional conceptions of liberal democracy that require the subordination of the military to civilian authorities and their restriction to primarily security affairs (see Karl 1991 and Diamond 2000; Trinkunas 2001), these radical populists have allowed or extended military authority in the economic and social realm as part of an overall strategy to extend the role of the state in economic matters. Civil-military scholars generally view the expansion of these prerogatives as potentially threatening to the maintenance of liberal capitalist democracy and as inconsistent with democratic civil-military relations, given the potential consequence that the military's involvement in political or economic matters will lead to greater demands for political power and control. However, the record so far is quite mixed regarding the consequences of expanded military prerogatives and the democratic behavior of states. Colombia has arguably gone the furthest in reducing the military's institutional power, yet political assassinations, the displacement of communities, and the killing of civilians to substitute for dead guerrilla fighters continues to take place in the country. In contrast, while legitimate concerns exist regarding presidential power in Venezuela and Ecuador, the expansion of military prerogatives has coincided with a general expansion of political participation and substantive experiments with participatory democracy. The Andean region clearly demonstrates that there is no linear relationship between a decline in military prerogatives and the overall democratic behavior or institutionalization of states.

Overview of Book

Chapter 1 presents the central argument of this project and the theoretical framework that guides it. It speaks to how the interaction between global and domestic factors can explain the variation of civil-military relations in the Andes as well as how such an approach fills gaps left by institutionalist-centered analyses. This chapter also presents the methods that I employ in this book as well as a brief introduction to the five cases. Chapter 2 compares and contrasts Colombia and Peru, the two cases that I view to have had success in maintaining political civilian control over the armed forces and effectively reducing their institutional prerogatives within the state despite the existence of antistate guerrilla armies. This chapter outlines the role of neoliberal policy coalitions and global factors in implementing civil-military reforms, as well as the influence of the counterinsurgency war upon the level of unity within the military and strength of civil society. Chapter 3 explores similar issues in Venezuela and Ecuador, detailing the relative failure of neoliberal policy coalitions in these two countries as well as the strength of nationalist and reformist faction/movements within the military and civil society to resist capitalist globalization. In both countries the struggle between nationalist and globalist sectors of civil society is ongoing, but the strength of anticapitalist globalization movements has forestalled economic reform, contributing to the maintenance or expansion of significant military prerogatives. Chapter 4 explores the intermediate case of Bolivia, one in which civil-military relations have represented an example of successful political control in the 1980s and 1990s as well as reduced military prerogatives. However, Bolivia's low-intensity democracy has been buffeted by nationalist/ populist movements in the 2000s with important consequences for the power and influence of Bolivia's military. The case illustrates a middle ground with the existence of neoliberal policy coalitions in power and internal security threats greater than what existed in Venezuela and Ecuador, but not to the extent present in Colombia and Peru. Also, unlike Colombia and Peru but like Venezuela and Ecuador, neoliberal policy coalitions have been displaced by a nationalist/populist movement. This suggests that the level of internal security threat in the context of an ongoing struggle between globalist and nationalist policy coalitions can have important consequences to the ultimate success of that nationalist/antiglobalist movement. The absence of real military threats to state power undermines the legitimacy of repressive tactics against these types of movements, allowing them greater space to challenge state power while simultaneously creating opportunities for those in the military open to alternative uses of the armed forces. Furthermore, the degree that the military viewed U.S. pressures to take on a fight against coca growers and antiglobalization protesters as reflecting genuine security threats or simply the imposition of the United States is also important to understanding how far the armed forces will go in repressing these actors. Finally, the national strength of Bolivian social movements relative to the power of Bolivian security forces must also be considered in understanding the limits to the widespread repression that has taken place in Colombia or Peru.

The final chapter concludes the book with a brief discussion on alternative forms of democracy and military power in a context of continuing struggle over capitalist globalization as well as suggestions for future research. The formal subordination of the military to elected civilian authorities has long been considered a central prerequisite to the establishment of democracy. This chapter illustrates the disconnect between institutional change and the democratic behavior of states, as human rights violations and military impunity for such violations persist in those countries that have ostensibly made the most progress in democratic civil-military relations. In the end, the five cases illustrate the degree that military power and influence reflect larger national and global conflicts that exist not only outside of the armed forces, but ones in which the military often plays an active and sometime decisive role.

CHAPTER 1

Military Power and Capitalist Globalization

"[military officers] are not outside the social and economic life of
the country"
— Former Venezuelan president
Carlos Andres Pérez (cited in Rouquié 1987, 200)

The reduction in military prerogatives in Colombia, Peru, and Bolivia
runs contrary to the expectation of civil-military scholars who posit
that domestic security threats to state authority should worsen the ability of civilian authorities to establish political control over the armed
forces and reduce military prerogatives. Yet different Colombian governments have faced multiple guerrilla armies and drug cartels since the
early 1980s and proceeded to expand civilian authority over the armed
forces in the early 1990s *and* maintain their political authority over the
military to the present day. In the case of Peru, different civilian-led
governments confronted the Shining Path guerrilla movement during the 1980s and 1990s, a movement that achieved a level of military
influence that at one point undermined state authority and control in
Lima; however, significant reductions in the institutional prerogatives
of the armed forces were achieved during the late 1980s through the
1990s and 2000s. Finally, Bolivia during the 1980s and 1990s waged a
U.S.-driven counternarcotics struggle against coca growers requiring
the militarization of regions of the country, yet governments reduced
military prerogatives over budgets, the defense ministry, and security
strategy. Governments in Venezuela and Ecuador have not faced armed
guerrilla insurgencies, nor have they engaged in highly militarized
campaigns to repress antigovernmental social movements, but their
militaries have challenged civilian political control while maintaining
or expanding military prerogatives.

This variation in military power and influence has occurred in a roughly similar political context. The region has been wracked by the deterioration of political institutions (such as political parties), increasing economic inequality, and poverty. This has most especially been the case since the 1980s debt crisis, which thrust Latin America into economic turmoil and created the political basis for the neoliberal reorientation of these economies by international financial institutions dominated by the United States. The neoliberal economic reforms of the 1990s and 2000s have largely failed to provide formal, stable employment or increasing incomes for the majority of the populations in the Andes, and have been met with substantial social resistance. This economic crisis has undermined the legitimacy of established political parties and national governments in all five countries. Traditional parties in the countries have been frustrated by declines in state resources and the inability to find economic solutions that simultaneously abide by the demands of international actors while addressing the domestic issues of social inequity. Neoliberal economic policies worked to weaken the state, undermining its ability to not only offer patronage, but also to fulfill essential state services (providing social welfare, reducing crime, or providing education) that citizens depend upon (Mainwaring 2006, pp. 25–6). By the end of 2004 more than 40 percent of Latin Americans lived in poverty, almost 50 percent continued to work in the informal sector, and the region remained well above the world average in income inequality (Roberts 2007, p. 10). The 1990s and 2000s also witnessed attempted coups in Venezuela and Ecuador, the politicized use of domestic intelligence agencies and paramilitary repression within Colombia and Peru, and violent attempts at regional autonomy in Bolivia, including the removal of two sitting presidents. However, within this context three countries have made considerable progress in reducing the political prerogatives and influence of their armed forces, while two others have clearly failed. This variation in military power has reflected the interaction between the spread of capitalist globalization and market democracies regionally with domestic struggles over the political and economic direction of the Andes.

Theoretical Context: Traditional Approaches

For too long the examination of civil–military relations in Latin America has been wedded to different variants of institutionalist approaches that focus primarily on national-level variables in explaining civilian control (Trinkunas 2002; Pion-Berlin 2001; Diamint 1998). The existence of electoral competition (Hunter 1997a), the relative power between civilian authorities and the military (Stepan 1988; Aguero 1995), or the corporate interests of the armed forces (Nordlinger 1977) are viewed as central in understanding the extent of civilian or political control within a respective nation-state. For example, Wendy Hunter's analysis of civil-military relations in Brazil utilizes a "rational choice institutionalism" that focuses upon the "strategic choices" of civilian and military authorities (1997a). Changes in institutional structures (i.e., the introduction of elections) changed the incentives and choices available to civilian authorities, which led them to erode military prerogatives. David Pion-Berlin (1997) has argued that the degree that power is concentrated in the hands of civilian authorities within a specific agency, as well as the degree that the military can influence the direction of a specific issue, contributes to success or failure in eroding military power. Increasingly, research focuses upon how much civilian authorities should know about military affairs and whether this knowledge actually contributes to civilian control over the armed forces (see Bruneau 2005 and Pion-Berlin 2005). Felipe Aguero (1995) posits that the balance of power between civilian and military authorities within the state is a consequence of the prior balance of power in democratic transitions that established an institutional path, which permeates present-day civil-military relations. In addition, he suggests that a process of socialization and reorientation for the armed forces is important to civilian control, such as establishing meaningful pursuits and missions and modernizing military equipment. However, like others, Aguero argues that the military's reorientation should be focused upon an external defense role (1995, p. 117).

As Aguero highlights, an important element in understanding the success or failure of civilian control has rested upon the specific missions assigned to the armed forces and security threats facing the state. Desch's attention to the global context examines how a country's "international threat environment" (1999, p. 2) conditions the degree that civilian preferences will prevail over military ones. Desch argues that "... it is easiest for civilians to control the military when they face primarily international (external) threats and it is hardest for them to control the military when they face primarily domestic (internal) threats" (1999, p. 6). These threats work to shape the behavior and organization of the military, state managers, and society—directly influencing civilian control (Desch 1999, p. 11). According to Desch, "... domestic threats divide the state and focus everyone's attention inward" and a military is more likely to intervene in politics given their role in internal repression and the failure/incompetence of civilian leaders to maintain internal order, while "the smaller the domestic threat to the military institution and its interests, the stronger civilian control will be" (Desch 1999, pp. 13–5, 98; see also Hunter 1996). Fitch argues that internal wars "...generally inhibit *overt* military takeovers for fear that a military coup might trigger a defection of the nonviolent left and the loss of U.S. aid" (1998, p. 164, emphasis mine), but the military will maintain a "tutelary" role, one in which the "...armed forces participate in the policy process and exercise authority over civilian authorities" (Ibid, 38). This is consistent with Alfred Stepan's conception of a "new professionalism" in which he argues that military involvement in internal security inevitably leads to military role expansion and the need for military "managerialism" in the political sphere (see Stepan 1986, p. 138). Institutional contexts and strategic decisions, the balance of prerogatives within the state, and civilian/military perceptions of threat or doctrines have all been utilized in civil-military studies in order to explain shifting patterns of civilian control and military autonomy.

This institutional and national focus is illustrated in the various arguments that have been applied to civil-military relations in the Andes. In the case of Venezuela and Ecuador, a great deal of attention has been focused upon the corruption and factionalism of the countries' politics, the decline in the legitimacy of dominant political parties, reductions in personal benefits for the armed forces, economic crises, and/or the failure of specific institutional arrangements designed to control the armed forces (Rivera 2001; Bustamante 2003, p. 95; Trinkunas 2005; Aguero 1995; Manrique 2001). These analyses have contributed to our understanding of these two cases, but problems remain. For example, how much weight should we place on the influence of democratic transitions, when Venezuela's transition to democracy preceded Ecuador's by twenty years and civilian authorities largely dominated the process, yet both countries have experienced episodes of military intervention and the expansion of military prerogatives? In addition, how much weight can we place on party deinstitutionalization and the weakness of civilian institutions? Party deinstitutionalization has not only been a problem in Ecuador and Venezuela, but also in countries such as Colombia, Peru, and Bolivia where civil-military relations have not been marked by either successful coups or coup attempts (Mainwaring and Scully 1995, p. 17). In other words, the failures or weaknesses of democratic institutions have not led the military to intervene in politics to the degree that they have repeatedly done so in Ecuador and Venezuela.

In studies examining civil-military relations in Peru and Colombia, the focus upon state interests and/or domestic politics is central. For example, Obando argues that the power of the military in Peru was at very low levels in the mid-1990s because of the country's economic crisis, which led to fewer benefits for the military rank and file and lower military budgets (1994, pp. 116–7). In addition, the Alberto Fujimori administration's (1990–2000) use of co-optation and control over promotions and the granting of specific benefits/resources to loyal sectors of the armed forces also contributed to ensuring greater civilian authority and the ultimate loss of military power/prerogatives (1998b, p. 193). In partial contrast to Obando, Rospigliosi (2000) concludes that Peru was governed in the 1990s by a partnership between the military and civilian authorities, with the military often in a dominant position (pp. 147–9). In addition, Rubio stresses that the military retained power due to their centrality to public order, but concedes their power had been reduced because of U.S. opposition to military coups in the region (Rubio 1994, pp. 130–1). However, it is not clear from Rospigliosi or Rubio how the military steadily lost important prerogatives over budgets, promotions, and institutional benefits if it maintained such a leadership position within the state, or from Obando why this historical period of intense internal security threats would coincide with the reduction of military prerogatives.

In the case of Colombia, Francisco Leal Buitrago explains the civil-military reforms of the early 1990s as reflecting a greater willingness to accept a diminished role among military leaders (Leal Buitrago 1994, pp. 135–7). Though both Andrés Dávila and Eduardo Pizarro discuss the changes to Colombian civil-military relations, neither specifically explains why the changes occurred when they did, other than representing the general democratic reform process symbolized by the 1991 constitution (Dávila 1998 and Pizarro 1995; a point shared by Leal Buitrago 1994). Ortiz comes closest to my argument, stressing the increasing centrality of the U.S. "war on drugs" in the late 1980s and early 1990s, which led to demands from the United States for greater respect for human rights as well as professionalization in the armed forces and national police. In addition, Ortiz argues that the breakdown in social and political order in the 1980s and 1990s created incentives for civilian state managers to become more involved in security issues and strategies (Ortiz 2005, pp. 57–9).

This analytical focus upon domestic institutions and national politics has been maintained despite the spread of global capitalism in the international economy, shifts in U.S. foreign policy (varying levels of "democracy promotion"), the emergence of globalist or neoliberal regimes that came to power throughout the region during the 1980s and 1990s, or the recent populist resistance to the "Washington Consensus" in the 1990s and 2000s. These types of political and economic developments are often viewed as peripheral to the historical or institutional frameworks that structure the decisions of key civil-military actors within the state.

International Attention in Civil-Military Studies

The work of Bruneau and Trinkunas (2006, 2008a), Mares (2001), and Desch (1999) represent important exceptions to this domestic-level focus. For example, Bruneau and Trinkunas find that global democracy promotion efforts by the United States and the European Union have privileged civilian control over other potentially important issues to democratic civil-military relations, such as defense efficiency and military effectiveness (2006, p. 776). They find evidence to support that global democracy promotion has contributed to a greater willingness by governments to challenge the military overbudgets as well as to creating an environment conducive to civilian control (Bruneau and Trinkunas 2006, p. 787). In the introduction to their 2008 edited book *Global Politics of Defense Reform* they conclude that "globalization has created a world of 'softened sovereignty' wherein states are much less capable than ever before at shielding their institutions and citizens from the transnational diffusion of norms, ideas, practices, legal understandings and knowledge that alters how they perceive themselves" (2008, p. 6; see also Clunan 2008). Cross-national military training, human rights norms promoted by nongovernmental organizations, as well as international treaties promoting regulations about military behavior (such as bans on the use of landmines) are all working to promote democratic conceptions of civil-military relations, conceptions that states find difficult to resist (Ibid, pp. 6–8). Clunan suggests that states will sometimes adopt certain norms about the military's role because they believe it will serve their interests and/or they fear the consequences of not adopting specific norms, especially if powerful states are promoting them (Clunan 2008, p. 30). She writes that the spread of certain norms can sometimes reflect a type of "coercive isomorphism" with states adopting a set of norms because of the

"...threat of punishment or the denial of benefits from more powerful actors" (Clunan 2008, pp. 30, 37). Bruneau and Trinkunas cite countries like Colombia as being particularly "vulnerable to global trends" because of their weak governing structures and dependence on U.S. foreign aid, which allows the United States greater ability to influence defense reform (Ibid, p. 17). However, Bruneau and Trinkunas argue that more attention should be paid to the "...ideas and attitudes that reformers [economic reformers] develop toward defense" (Ibid, p. 8), a central objective of this book.

Mares (2001) has also examined international factors in his analysis of civil-military relations. He suggests that economic integration between nations (such as customs unions or free trade agreements) may work to mitigate external threats and contribute to democratic civilian control, which contrasts with Desch's expectations that external threats actually *contribute* to civilian control (Desch 1999, p. 14). Ultimately, Mares's analysis finds that the "...rationales for economic integration are not clearly supportive of greater democratic civilian control of the military," as Mares concludes that despite regional economic integration threats still exist that can undermine this control. While Mares prioritizes regional economic integration, he de-emphasizes or ignores how the individuals promoting economic integration may themselves be carriers of norms that conceptualize the reduction of military prerogatives as consistent with democratic societies. We need to recognize the role that global capitalism, and the politics that has coincided with it, plays in contextualizing/influencing governmental relationships traditionally understood as disconnected from the global economy. A "transnational" or "global" perspective, one that does not limit our analyses solely to the "key decision-makers" or "central policy decisions" within governing institutions of the state, but integrates actors outside of nation-states is necessary.

Capitalist Globalization, Hegemony and Civil-Military Relations

For some time the study of civil-military relations has represented a version of "problem-solving" theory within comparative politics. To cite Robert Cox, "problem-solving" theory "takes the world as it finds it, with the prevailing social and power relationships and the institutions into which they are organized, as the given framework for action. The general aim of problem solving is to make these relationships and institutions work smoothly by dealing effectively with particular sources of trouble" (1981, pp. 128–9). Traditionally, the "sources of trouble" that have been at the center of civil-military studies have been the study of military coups, military autonomy deemed "undemocratic" and/or threatening to democratic consolidation. The ability or inability of civilian authorities within a democratizing state to wield effective control over the armed forces and to erode their prerogatives has also been the subject of academic attention. The goal of much of the literature has been to ascertain the factors that might work to prevent military coups, or establish civilian control within an overarching framework of liberal capitalist democracy.

This work seeks to employ a form of "critical theory" (Cox 1981), examining the forms of domination and conflict within and outside of states, and assessing how these frame and structure civil-military relations. As Deborah Yashar (1999, p. 79) argued scholars "need to *analyze* democratic politics in the context of *state-society relations* by evaluating the reach of state institutions and assessing the broader social forces that surround, support, and oppose the terms of democracy's new institutions [italics in the original]." Or as David Mares suggests, a central determinant of civil-military relations is found in ". . . the constitutive rules that arise out of the struggles among its principal political forces to create a governmental structure" (1998, p. 2). These struggles are fundamental to my analysis. However, I am not only interested in the struggle to create "governmental structure," but also in the struggle over the developmental and economic strategies that these governments will pursue. The acceptance or rejection of the various policies associated with capitalist globalization.

The term "globalization" has long been subject to debate as to the extent that it represents a genuine new stage in capitalist development, or simply the continuation of a process that has been going on for hundreds of years. In Latin America there is little debate that in the last three decades there has been a shift away from state-led development strategies and an expansion of neoliberal economics and international trade. Furthermore, this dramatic shift in economic policy has often been led by political elites, businessmen, and technocrats dedicated to integrating their respective economies into a global economy. Central features of globalization have included:

- An intensification of flows in which there has been an expansion in the interaction and interconnectedness between peoples, economies, and nations (Cochrane and Pain 2004, p. 16);

- Increasing interpenetration involving the exchange and adoption of cultures and norms across borders—for example, the spread of Western notions of "market democracy" as the model for countries in Latin America as opposed to nationalist or populist forms of governance.
- Global infrastructure. These include intergovernmental organizations such as the Organization of American States, the United Nations, the World Bank, the International Monetary Fund, and the World Trade Organization, or policy-planning organizations, such as the World Economic Forum or the Interamerican Dialogue, the "... basic infrastructure for governing the global system" (Cochrane and Pain 2004, p. 17).

The integration of Latin America into capitalist globalization has not represented a linear and smooth process, but has been associated with conflict. Often conflict emerges between those actors wedded to a nationalist orientation and/or a rejection of capitalist forms of globalization versus those coalitions very much committed to a globalist perspective. Neoliberal policy coalitions consist of those politicians, economic elites, bureaucrats, social movements, intellectuals, and factions within the military that enjoy important ideological, material, and/or political links/sympathies with the processes and political actors promoting capitalist globalization and market democracies. These neoliberal/globalist policy coalitions have often shared the economic and political goals promoted by the United States, such as the U.S. "drug war" and "war on terrorism." When examining the spread of these economic and political ideas, they clearly have been facilitated by the diffusion and internalization of these norms by elites within Latin America convinced that this model is consistent with democracy.

Neoliberal policy coalitions are largely made up of individuals referred to as "technopols" (Domínguez 1997), domestic actors committed to freer markets as well as modern states and politics. The "technopols" embrace democratic politics because, according to Dominguez, "democratic regimes" provide assurances that the rules and institutions that guide economic policies will endure over the long term (Ibid, p. 13). Of course, this only works if both "government and opposition are committed to the same broad framework of a market economy" (Ibid). Technopols are part of various institutes, policy-planning groups, and economics teams in which they work to develop and transmit their ideas, as well as to colonize state agencies in order to establish the transnational agenda of market democracies (Ibid, pp. 19–20).

The neoliberal policy coalitions that technopols have led represent an important domestic element to the institution of a market democracy being promoted globally. This model includes the erosion of military prerogatives.

Solingen (1998) and Harris (2005) argue that internationally oriented policy coalitions have regularly competed with nationally based coalitions resistant to economic globalization and supportive of various developmentalist/state-directed strategies of development. Statist/nationalist policy coalitions consist of those politicians, social movements, factions of the armed forces, intellectuals, sectors of the business community, and bureaucrats that resist the integration of their respective economies into a global system and accept various import substitution, nationalist economic strategies while seeking alternative forms of democratic politics. Historically and globally the armed forces have played a prominent role in the latter coalition (Solingen 1998, p. 33). Military–industrial complexes and military establishments are frequently at odds with efforts to streamline budgets with greater transparency or to give up national sovereignty in the face of greater economic integration (Solingen 1998, p. 57). In contrast to the neoliberal/globalist policy coalitions, the statist/nationalist coalitions have often represented significant opposition to U.S. policy objectives in the region. Intergovernmental and transnational social movement organizations have emerged to represent an array of groups and states seeking alternatives to capitalist globalization, including the World Social Forum, the Bank of the South, and the Bolivarian Alternative for the Americas (ALBA).

The capture of national states and leading sectors of the economy by neoliberal policy coalitions contributes to pressures for a leaner, more modern state in which a developmentalist role for military authorities, military autonomy over the determination/administration of state resources, and "managerialism" in the political sphere are viewed negatively. Mares argues in one of his "rationales for integration" that "domestic actors who favor liberalizing integration gain powerful international allies to use at home against the influence of the nationalist military and their civilian allies....military autonomy at home is undermined because the international context is perceived as conducive to national welfare rather than as a threat" (Mares 2001, p. 228). Of course this process has not represented a linear one, as neoliberal/globalist policy coalitions have confronted resistance throughout Latin America, and increasingly this resistance has been able to obtain state power. As William Robinson argues, contemporary class and social conflicts as well as political change have reflected:

1. struggles between descendant nationally oriented and ascendant transnationally oriented elites. When we cut through the fog of ideological discourse we find that political competition among elites in the late twentieth and early twenty-first century often broke down along this fault line; and
2. struggles waged by popular sectors against global capitalism and neoliberal restructuring. Earlier struggles against dictatorship and for an extension of the Keynesian or developmental state have given way to new mass struggles against neoliberalism, or have been combined with them, and are often led by emergent subjects (indigenous, women, etc.) (Robinson 2008, pp. 169–0; see also Harris 2005).

The success of one coalition in establishing a hegemonic position over the state and civil society is central to understanding the varied direction that military prerogatives and civilian control has taken in the Andes.

Hegemony and Low-Intensity Democracy

Augusto Varas (1989, p. 8) has argued that "... civilians will be able to dominate the armed forces to the degree that political groups and *social classes establish hegemony over the state*" (emphasis mine). I would argue that not only is this hegemony necessary, but that the character of civil-military relations will vary depending on the type of political groups and social classes (nationally and globally) wielding and maintaining this hegemony. This hegemony is established through consensual (elections, interest group competition, or the dispersion of dominant ideologies) means, as a variety of social forces (such as intellectuals, party leaders, or factions of the military) within and outside of the nation-state come together to maintain a particular order (Gramsci 1971).

Antonio Gramsci (1971) argued that "hegemony" is a relation between social classes in which one class takes a leading role by gaining the willing consent of other classes and groups. The schools, the churches, political parties, and the media are examples of institutions that socialize the consent of subordinate classes, establishing a specific "historic bloc" or social order. This social order is internalized by subordinate actors who accept the prevailing economic and political institutions as the norm, as "common-sense." This hegemony is obtained and maintained through both coercive and consensual mechanisms, though coercive power is not regularly required, given that subordinate groups have come to accept the nature of things. The establishment of hegemony does not simply take place through state institutions, but through an "integral state" that includes civil society (unions, social movements, the media, and/or interest groups). In an era of capitalist globalization, the growing internationalization of production and exchange represents the potential material basis for a transnational historic bloc, hegemonic relations between social groups and political elites that transverse the borders of nation-states (Cox 1981, 1987; Gill 1994; Robinson 1996).

Central components to establishing a historic bloc that furthers capitalist globalization are the various neoliberal or globalist policy coalitions that successfully obtain and maintain power within specific national governments. Leslie Sklair argues that this elite or class "consists of those people who see their own interests and/or the interests of their social and/or ethnic group, often transformed into an imagined national interest, as best served by an identification with the global system" (2002, p. 9). As Sklair argues "Everywhere, we find corporate executives, globalizing politicians and professionals, and consumer elites (merchants, marketers, advertisers) telling us in public and doing their best to ensure in private that the globalizing agenda of contemporary capitalism driven by the TNCs [transnational corporations] and their allies is inevitable and, eventually, in the best interests of us all" (Sklair 2002, p. 171).

These globalist policy coalitions operate with a great deal of ideological and material legitimacy, with international actors (the United States, international financial institutions, and transnational corporations) actively supporting their policy agenda. One senior International Monetary Fund (IMF) official, speaking of the connections between the IMF, the World Bank, and the individuals who run the finance and economic ministries in Latin America, stated that "We are all the same—people who come and go through the Bank, the Fund, and Finance Ministries and Central Banks of Latin American countries. We all study at the same universities; we all attend the same seminars, conferences....we all know each other very well. We keep in touch with each other on a daily basis" (as quoted in Faux 2006, p. 170). These are norm or policy entrepreneurs promoting a set of globalizing ideas in line with this agenda, one that includes challenging certain military prerogatives and modernizing the national state along lines consistent with a low-intensity or market democracy.

Low-intensity or market democracies are elite forms of democracy that generally uphold political rights and market principles while social reforms to broaden popular participation or reduce social inequities are marginalized (Gills et al. 1993). Gills and Rocamora argue that this democratic model should be viewed "...as an integral aspect of the economic and ideological restructuring accompanying a new stage of globalisation in the capitalist world economy," a regime in which civilian-based governments are prioritized over military ones (Gills and Rocamora 1992, p. 502). In the present conjuncture, military rule is viewed as problematic in maintaining stability within specific nation-states, while liberal civilian rule is to be prioritized, given its ability to more effectively co-opt radical opposition while more efficiently adapting to a more globalized environment. Carl Gershman, a former president of the U.S. National Endowment for Democracy (NED) suggests "traditional autocrats...simply cannot adapt to the pace of change and conflicting political pressures of the modern world" (as quoted in Robinson 1996, p. 67). Greater military power and military regimes may engender "...mass-based political changes that threaten perceived core and local elite interests...The purpose of promoting polyarchy [low-intensity democracy] is to remove dictatorships *and* to pre-empt more fundamental change" (Robinson 1996b, p. 626).[1]

In these regimes coercive structures (including the military) are utilized to maintain order and prevent radical efforts to extend democracy beyond the formal political process (McSherry 1998, p. 16). Civil-military relations within low-intensity democracies do not reflect classic conceptions of objective civilian control where the military's role is focused upon external defense, but one in which important internal security roles are maintained to narrow the space for political opposition and marginalize/repress radical opposition to capitalist globalization. The erosion of military prerogatives (through their institutional subordination to elected officials, such as civilian defense ministers) does not necessarily translate to the democratic behavior of a nation's armed forces. Certain military missions, models of civil-military relations, and/or forms of military professionalism are being promoted that work to reinforce the power and influence of transnational corporations specifically and more generally the smooth workings of capitalist globalization.

Global Democracy Promotion and Civil-Military Relations

The transitions to democracy in Latin America during the 1970s and 1980s represented part of a global trend that began in the Iberian region in the mid-1970s and in Latin America with Ecuador's transition in 1979. The literature examining these transitions stressed the role of political actors and institutions. The *Transitions to Democracy* volumes stressed the importance of the specific choices of political elites (military and civilian) in understanding the success or failure of democratic transitions. The competition between "hardliners" and "softliners" within the state and/or "radicals" and "moderates" within the opposition during specific periods were given important power in explaining democratic change. These works complemented various structural explanations that stressed the influence of large middle classes and/or the outcome of class conflicts which could be conducive or ill-conducive to democracy. Regional and global factors have also been cited as being important to this "third wave" of democracy. Wiarda (2003, pp. 313–4) stresses the role of a "demonstration effect" set off by Portugal and Spain's democratic transitions as well as Ecuador's democratic transition in 1979, which provided a model for democratic change in the region. In addition, the region-wide debt crisis of the 1980s worked to effectively undermine the developmentalist legitimacy that military regimes had developed during the 1960s and 1970s as well as disrupting coalitions the military had maintained with economic elites (Conaghan, Malloy, and Abugattas 1990). Democratic transitions were also aided by important changes in U.S. foreign policy.

The United States has played (and plays) a central role in promoting low-intensity or market democracies (McSherry 2000, pp. 26, 34; Robinson 1996; Smith 2000; Gills et al. 1993). The establishment of these elite democracies reflected an important shift in U.S. foreign policy in the late 1970s and early 1980s away from a long tradition of propping up authoritarian regimes in Latin America during the Cold War (Robinson 1996, pp. 74–83). The Carter administration's foreign policy was strongly influenced by transnational policy-making bodies such as the Trilateral Commission (which much of his foreign policy cabinet came from) as well as the Council on Foreign Relations that increasingly developed a consensus around the importance of promoting democratic institutions alongside economic globalization (Ibid, pp. 75–76. In particular, the Linowitz Report from the Center for Inter-American Relations played an important role in Carter's Latin American policy, concluding that the United States would benefit from promoting human rights, fearing that military regimes could lead to greater societal opposition and instability (Robinson 1996, p. 148).[2] As Robinson has found, "Political aid [to promote democracy] has become an efficacious instrument of the United States, in the context of the transnationalization of political processes, in its effort to establish control over transnational politics and to reconfigure a new "historic bloc" over which the transnational elite exercises hegemony" (1996, p. 85).

In 1983 the NED was established through National Security Decision Directive 77 (NSD 77), which directed a series of political operations in U.S. foreign policy to influence international public opinion, covert operations, and the creation of the NED (Robinson 1996, pp. 91–2). The NED emerged from the work of the American Political Foundation (APF) that was established with U.S. funds in 1979 and was chaired by Allen Weinstein, the NED's first president.[3] The APF was a working group made up of top leaders from business, labor, and the foreign policy community that recommended that the Reagan administration examine how the United States could promote democracy abroad. This recommendation was accepted, and Walter Raymond Jr., a CIA propaganda expert, supervised the *Project Democracy* program within the National Security Council, which would later recommend the creation of the NED as a vehicle to promote overt political action to achieve U.S. aims in the world (Robinson 1996, pp. 89–92). NED's public documents state that its goals include strengthening democratic institutions, pluralism, and open economies, arguing that "...an open market economy is a prerequisite of a democratic political system" (NED 2010).[4] The United States Agency for International Development (USAID)[5] has also been involved in democracy promotion, and specifically in civil-military relations. Between 1986 and 1998 the USAID promoted a region-wide collaboration among scholars, practitioners, and governmental officials to discuss the role of the military within newly elected civilian governments, establishing the basis for "engagement between civilian and military actors" throughout the region (Center for Democracy and Governance 1998, p. 21).

The Clinton administration (1993–2001) was a vocal supporter of "democracy promotion," arguing that the spread of capitalist markets and economic globalization would provide the basis for democratic politics (McClintock and Vallas 2003, p. 39). The administration's stated goals of "democratic enlargement" to, according to his national security advisor, "foster and consolidate new democracies and market economies where possible," (Brinkley 1997, p. 116). Clinton argued in 1996 that "...democratic states are less likely to threaten our interests and more likely to cooperate with the United States to meet security threats and promote free trade and sustainable development (Clinton 1996). The Bush (2001–9) and Obama administrations (2009–present) continued to maintain a commitment to the promotion of democracy, though with variation in emphasis and application (Traub 2010; Blair 2010). The promotion of democracy and human rights simultaneously with free markets and trade works to provide capitalist globalization with greater legitimacy. However, the actual implementation of policies associated with this rhetoric has been quite uneven, though U.S.-Latin American relations increasingly stressed the subordination of the armed forces to civilian authorities. The general goal of democracy promotion has been complemented with specific efforts by the United States to ostensibly advance human rights and civilian control of the military. (Bruneau and Trinkunas 2006, p. 777). In 1997 the U.S. Congress passed the Leahy Law, which requires that no assistance can be "provided to any unit of the security forces of a foreign country if the Secretary of State has credible evidence that such unit has committed gross violations of human rights" (Center for International Policy 2003). The Leahy Law was first established for narcotics control assistance and later expanded to include all security assistance programs and military training programs (in 1998 and 1999, respectively), though the application of these conditions has been inconsistent. In 1995 the U.S. Southern Command (U.S. SOUTHCOM[6]) commander argued "that increased economic integration, the prevalence of 'market principles,' democratization, and cooperative security arrangements were the wave of the future in the region" (Loveman 2006, p. 6). In fact, U.S. SOUTHCOM mandated human rights training for its Latin American trainees and established a human rights division within the command focused upon promoting human rights in training, civil-military relations, and doctrine (Laurienti 2007, p. 2). The Human Rights Division was established in 1994 by the then-head of SOUTHCOM General Barry McCaffrey, who also developed a human rights steering group dedicated to ensuring that human rights were fundamental to all Command components, as well as raising the status of the Human Rights Division commander (Ibid, p. 43). McCaffrey would later go on to lead the Clinton administration's Office of National Drug Control Policy and subsequently would take a position with the international advisory board for Fleishman-Hillard, a communications consulting firm that advises corporations on their investment strategies in the United States and throughout the world, including Latin America (Fleishman-Hillard 2008).

At the first gathering of the region's civilian and military leaders at the Defense Ministerial of the Americas in 1995 the U.S. Secretary of Defense, William Cohen, announced that "the bedrock foundation of our approach to the Americas is a shared commitment to democracy, the rule of law, conflict resolution, defense transparency, and mutual cooperation" (Loveman 2006, p. 6). After leaving the Clinton administration Cohen would take a position on the board of American International Group, a transnational financial and insurance firm (Rothkopf 2008, p. 150). The goal of the U.S. military for Latin America was clearly stated by General Charles E. Wilhelm, commander-in-chief of U.S. Southern Command from 1997 to 2000, when he wrote that his aim for the region was a "... community of democratic, stable, and prosperous nations...served by professional, modernized, *interoperable* security forces that embrace democratic principles, demonstrate respect for human rights, are subordinate to civil authority, and are capable and supportive of multilateral responses to challenges " (as quoted in Addicott and Roberts 2001, emphasis mine).

An element of U.S. commitment to these objectives has been the International Military Education Training (IMET) grant program. IMET was established in 1976 to provide professional, leadership, and management training for senior military leaders and mid-grade officers with leadership potential. In 1991, the U.S. Congress dedicated $1 million to an expanded-IMET program (E-IMET) that included training courses on defense management, civil-military relations, law enforcement cooperation, and military justice. This program would also be available to foreign civilians as well as military personnel (Center for International Policy 2006a). These programs complement the decades-long training that Latin American officers have undergone at the Western Hemisphere Institute of Security Cooperation (formerly the School of the Americas).[7]

The U.S. Department of Defense has also been active in promoting democratic civil-military relations through the creation of regional institutions such as the Center for Hemispheric Defense Studies for Latin America. The Center for Hemispheric Defense Studies (CHDS) developed out of the annual Defense Ministerial of the Americas, beginning in 1995, in which defense ministers from the Western Hemisphere began to come together on a regular basis to discuss security issues and civil-military affairs, specifically focusing upon the lack of civilians with appropriate knowledge of defense/security topics. From these discussions the U.S. Department of Defense and the National Defense University, with consultation from other defense ministries, established the CHDS in 1997. The mission of the CHDS includes promoting "...effective civil-military relations in democratic societies" and contributing to a "...cooperative international security environment and mutual understanding of priority U.S. and regional defense and international security policy issues" (CHDS 2008a).

With regard to the political consequences of military training and assistance, there has long been a debate as to the effect of such assistance upon the likelihood of military coups, military autonomy, and/or the development of pro-U.S. political/economic philosophies. Wolpin has found that U.S. military aid was conducive to marginalizing radical/nationalist sectors within the military (Wolpin 1975, p. 266), and Baines concluded that U.S. military assistance did not promote undemocratic regimes (Baines 1972), while Fitch (1979) finds that U.S. military assistance often led to greater military professionalization (such as greater levels of efficiency and improved training and technological expertise). Finally, and important for this analysis, Mertus finds that the substantiveness of U.S. human rights training should be questioned, given the failure to effectively maintain these standards within the U.S. military itself, as illustrated in a number of cases of torture and abuse committed by U.S. military personnel in the Middle East and Central Asia or the ongoing use of double standards when applying these values in its international relations (Mertus 2008, p. 227). The fact that the largest recipients of U.S. military assistance and training in South America in the last two decades (Colombia and Peru) have also been the sites of extensive human rights violations by state security forces should also give us pause in the effectiveness of such assistance. However, all of this assistance represents important components in a larger process of transferring elite democratic norms of civil-military relations.

The recipients of U.S. military assistance and training in the Andes have increasingly reflected the dynamics of the U.S. "drug war." U.S. counternarcotics policies have been focused upon the militarization of supply-side strategies of crop eradication and the dismantling of drug cartels. The Andean region is the principal source of the cocaine and much of the heroin that enters the United States. The first major program for the Andes began in the George H. W. Bush administration with the Andean Initiative. This program provided approximately $2.1 billion in U.S. economic, military, and law enforcement aid to Peru, Colombia, and Bolivia (Congressional Budget Office 1994). The U.S. State Department believed "drug war" aid would further democracy by actively engaging the military in a constructive mission and in ensuring that U.S. assistance was coordinated and directed by civilian authorities (Call 1991, pp. 119–20). In addition, various human rights provisions were included in antinarcotics agreements, such as the 1990 Declaration of Cartagena—an agreement between the governments of the United States, Colombia, Peru, and Bolivia—which required that all "parties act within the framework for human rights" (Youngers 2004, p. 135).

The "drug war" was also directly tied to U.S. economic objectives of market reform for the region. The Andean Trade Preferences Act (ATPA), adopted by the United States in 1991, reduced tariffs upon goods exported from Andean nations, which expanded trade between the United States and Andean countries, in the hopes of increasing the incentives for legal trade while decreasing the incentives for illicit trade. U.S. exports to the Andean region increased by 65 percent between 1991 and 1998, and exports from the Andes to the United States increased by 98 percent during the same time period (Williams 2005, p. 164).

The promotion of democracy has also been advanced by intergovernmental organizations such as the Organization of American States (OAS), the World Bank, and the Andean Community. Following the end of the Cold War, the OAS endorsed the Santiago Commitment in support of democratic government in the hemisphere at its General Assembly meeting of 1991 (Shaw 2003). This commitment required that the OAS mobilize its members in response to an unconstitutional disruption of democracy in a given country in order to adopt measures to address the political crisis. In 2001 the OAS incorporated the "Inter-American Democratic Charter," which declared the unconstitutional interruption of the constitutional order will lead to the suspension of member states from the organization. The constitutional order being protected is one in which the military is subordinated to at least the political control of civilian authorities.

Regarding military roles in Latin America, the OAS adopted the Declaration on Security in the Americas in October 2003, which promoted a type of hemispheric security that calls for the involvement of the armed forces in the "wars" against drugs, crime, and/or "terrorism" to be defined in the manner that governments deem fit (Chillier and Freeman 2005). Thus, the use of the military to put down protesters in Bolivia in 2003, instead of the police, is in line with this idea in which radical social movements are equated with terrorism (Chillier and Freeman 2005, pp. 5–6). This broader conception of security, consistent with the National Security Doctrine of the Cold War period, complements the objectives promoted by the United States, which has for decades urged a greater role for Latin American militaries in internal security. However, since the late 1970s this internal security role has been administered or directed by elected civilian elites governing low-intensity democracies. The OAS, like the United States, also actively promotes the economic integration of the region, backing the Free Trade Area of the Americas and working closely with the World Trade Organization, the World Bank, and the Inter-American Development Bank in establishing open, neoliberal economies in the region (Organization of American States 2006).

The Andean Community has committed to strengthening democracy in the region as well. In February 1989 the Andean presidents met in Caracas and collectively posited that "the existence of democratic regimes in all the Member Countries makes it possible to advance the subregion's integration on legal bases," and in 1999 the Andean Community made a democratic government a requirement for membership in the group (Wagner 2005, p. 6). In 2005 the Andean Community's secretary general declared that "...[economic] integration must be considered, at the same time, a process of democratic consolidation in the Andean region" (Wagner 2005, p. 6).

The promotion of democracy and democratic civil-military relations by the United States, the OAS, or the Andean Community takes place within a supportive economic context for reducing military prerogatives. The internationalization of capital markets and the monitoring of economic behavior by the International Monetary Fund, the World Bank (two institutions dominated by the United States and its European allies, given their level of contributions to these organizations), and/or the U.S. Treasury have reduced the necessity of military rule to ensure economic strategies amenable to the interests of international economic elites. The IMF's conditions upon loans to Latin America have created budget-cutting pressures upon governments, pressures that have increasingly led to reductions in military spending often viewed as wasteful. Demands for transparency in governmental spending have also affected the armed forces, an institution long accustomed to exclusive control over how defense funds are utilized with little public accountability.

Throughout the 1980s and 1990s these global processes created the necessary structural conditions for the successful reduction of the military's institutional prerogatives and political power by neoliberal or globalized policy coalitions that increasingly captured national states in Latin America. While multiple global and domestic actors have been involved in the establishment of market democracies, increasingly the progress of these regimes is being undermined by nationalists within the military and anticapitalist globalization movements within civil society.

Radical Populists, Counterhegemony, and Civil-Military Relations

In 2005 U.S. SOUTHCOM commander Lt. General Bantz Craddock testified to the U.S. House Armed Services Committee that "anti-U.S., anti-globalization, and anti-free trade demagogues" were the causes of political instability in the region (Barry 2005). Craddock also warned that "We cannot afford to let Latin America and the Caribbean become a backwater of violent, inward-looking states that are cut off from the world around them by populist, authoritarian governments" (Barry 2005). He justified increased U.S. military spending in Latin America, arguing that a "... secure environment is a non-negotiable foundation for a functioning civil society" (Barry 2005) presumably in contrast to the nonfunctioning civil society that produced various nationalist and populist movements opposed to capitalist globalization. In 2006 Craddock informed a group of Latin American cadets at the Western Hemisphere Institute of Security Cooperation that they should be wary of populists who criticize free trade and who "incite violence against their own government and their own people" (as quoted in Grandin 2006). Max Manwaring of the U.S. Army War College stresses the importance of subnational threats to democracies in the Western Hemisphere that include "... terrorists; insurgents; narcotraffickers; and other organized criminals, *populists*, warlords, and gangs (2005, p. 15, italics mine). Manwaring concludes that U.S. inaction in the face of these threats "... could destroy the democracy, free market economies, and prosperity that has been achieved, and place the posterity of the hemisphere at risk" (2005, p. 20).[8]

Populism has many definitions and historically has varied in the policies and actions promoted by populist regimes. John Crabtree submits that populism's "core characteristic" is the "... attempt to channel and direct mass political participation in such a way as to absorb pressures from below" (2000, p. 164), while Kenneth Roberts refers to populism as a "... top-down political mobilization of mass constituencies by personalistic leaders who challenge elite groups on behalf of an ill-defined *pueblo*, the 'people'" (2007, p. 5). Individuals such as Hugo Chávez, Evo Morales, and Rafael Correa have definitely reflected the political style and mobilizing capacity of populism and have also promoted policies traditionally associated with this concept. However, in contrast to the populism of the past, the rise to power of Correa and Morales in Ecuador and Bolivia, respectively, has been associated with powerful mass indigenous rights movements that have sought various ethnic rights while also resisting capitalist globalization. In addition, all three leaders have sought to establish or utilize participatory democracy (such as referendums or community councils) to strengthen the legitimacy of their respective projects. Finally, in the case of Venezuela especially, there has been progress toward the establishment of an alternative model of socialism, one that Chávez and Correa refer to as "Bolivarian Socialism." These factors all differentiate these leftist leaders from classical populists.

The factors underlying the emergence of these leftist movements and governments of today do share important elements of classical populism's history. Classical populism has been associated with responses to economic downturns, the deinstitutionalization of established political parties, the support from important mass-based social movements, and/or the loss of legitimacy of traditional political leaders. As Kenneth Roberts has pointed out, the re-emergence of "populism" at the end of the twentieth century is "... rooted in the institutional frailties and market insecurities of contemporary Latin American democracies, conditions that have made the region prone to new patterns of social and political mobilization" (2007, p. 3). All of these governments were preceded by major and recurring struggles against capitalist globalization. These included the periodic mass mobilizations of the Confederation of Indigenous Nationalities in Ecuador (CONAIE) during the 1990s and 2000s, the nationwide protests and riots of the 1989 *Caracazo* in Venezuela, or the water and gas "wars" in Bolivia that sought to resist privatization and foreign control of natural resources in 2003. The legitimacy of neoliberalism, and the leaders that promoted such policies, had been under continued assault in the years prior to these leaders coming to power. In these countries, low-intensity democracies in the Andes have been unable to channel and/or co-opt the popular mobilization and resistance that has emerged, creating space for new leaders and parties to channel and represent that resistance within the state.

In all three cases some combination of these factors has been the context for the emergence of "outsider" candidates, who have successfully used the delegitimation of the previous political order to come to power on antineoliberal/antitraditional party platforms. These presidents have all presented some variant of economic populism by enlarging the role of the state in the ownership of specific industries, in the regulation of capital, and/or in the expansion of redistributionist policies. As in populist periods in the past, the leaders of these different governments have embarked on efforts to centralize political power in their hands while often increasing the overall level of participation of groups previously disenfranchised.

The emergence of this left in Latin America has not taken place with the armed forces watching from the sidelines. Far from being a unified actor, the armed forces have often reflected the various divisions and struggles that are salient within the larger society. Rosengo Fraga has found that capitalist globalization has contributed to a "profound crisis for the military, since the existence and *raison d'être* of the armed forces is intimately tied to the existence of the nation-state" (as quoted in Zibechi 2005a, p. 6). In the case of Argentina, Fraga has concluded that "nationalism and patriotism, which used to represent the symbolic wealth of oligarchies and the right wing, are now more represented by popular sectors and even the left" (as quoted in Zibechi 2005a, p. 6). This changing relationship between nationalism and leftist/anti-establishment movements has influenced the attitudes of soldiers throughout Latin America, who increasingly come from lower middle-to-low income positions, thus making them more susceptible to nationalist/populist movements in civil society (Zibechi 2005a, p. 6).

Fitch's analysis of ideological role beliefs within the armed forces finds considerable evidence that militaries in Latin America are often segmented by how officers/soldiers view their role within a democratic system, the centrality of civilian authority, and relations with the United States, as well as the necessity of neoliberal economic reform. Both Fitch (1998) and Norden (2001) find that military factions and movements in Ecuador and Venezuela, respectively, have prioritized the centrality of national development and the need to protect a country's economic sovereignty from the pressures of capitalist globalization. However, this use of the armed forces is viewed as suspect by the United States and neoliberal elites. As the Latin American military analyst Fernando Bustamante observes "... military developmentalism and civic action are under heavy attack from policymakers who support neoliberalism, which in turn is encouraged by many institutions seen as connected to the U.S. government; nation-building from the barracks is suspect..." (1998, p. 355). In the cases of Peru and Colombia, the emergence of influential leftist/nationalist movements during most of the period that I examine has largely not taken place. Throughout most of the 1990s and 2000s those sectors of the political and economic establishment sympathetic with global capitalism have successfully held leadership positions on a national level.

The consolidation of their power has been facilitated by the relative weakness in popular resistance from civil society and opposition from within the state to globalization. Internal wars have reduced the space for antiglobalization groups in civil society, thereby marginalizing a potential instigator of military political intervention. In a similar vein, the centrality of the counterinsurgent war has undermined nationalist/ statist factions within the military that might directly challenge the authority of neoliberal policy coalitions, strengthening those actors in the military and prioritizing the successful repression of such an insurgency. The existence of a very real *raison d'être* for these militaries, one that has been financially and militarily supported by the regional hegemon, has created greater unity around an explicit security mission. The mission has involved regular campaigns of state and parastate repression against socialists, trade unionists, indigenous communities, and other individuals/groups perceived as sympathetic with the armed insurgents. Not only have these popular sectors had to face violence from the state, but they have also faced attacks from the armed left that has often demanded their subordination to the armed movement. The absence of such internal wars in other countries has contributed to the existence of greater space for resistance to neoliberalism/capitalist globalization within the military and civil society.

In both Ecuador and Venezuela, sectors of civil society have worked with groups within the military to either overthrow specific neoliberal governments (e.g., Ecuador's 2000 coup) or spark antineoliberal military movements (such as the 1989 *Caracazo* riots in Venezuela). The integration of their economies has been "forestalled" as representatives of neoliberal policy coalitions have been displaced (Venezuela) or frustrated (Ecuador) in their efforts at reforming their respective economies (Burt and Mauceri 2004). Neither Colombia nor Peru has witnessed the level of resistance that Venezuela and Ecuador have experienced during their respective periods of market reform (Colombia, 1988–present; Peru, 1990–present), as the integration of their economies has progressed without the level of national protest and resistance that has appeared in other countries.

For much of its postauthoritarian period Bolivia shared with Colombia and Peru a series of neoliberal governments that successfully reduced military prerogatives. However, the late 1990s and 2000s have been a period of increasing unrest as nationalist/populist social movements demonstrated their power to oppose capitalist globalization while avoiding the level of repression from the government or armed insurgents that movements in Colombia and Peru faced. In fact, governmental repression in the Bolivian case only strengthened the legitimacy of anticapitalist globalization movements, setting the stage for the election of Evo Morales in 2005.

In Venezuela, Ecuador, and Bolivia, factions of the armed forces supportive of a nationalist, developmentalist, and progressive conception of politics and security have allied with these respective governments while maintaining or expanding important military prerogatives. This role for the military is not unprecedented. In the history of military governments in Ecuador, Bolivia, and Peru, populist or reformist regimes have held power at different times, promoting nationalistic foreign policies and extending state control/regulation over the economy while seeking to redistribute wealth. The Peruvian military regime of General Velasco Alvarado (1968–75) sought the establishment of "revolutionary nationalism" and the transformation of "... social, economic, and cultural structures" (Rouquié 1987, pp. 310–2). These inclusionary regimes were often short-lived and/or achieved few of their stated goals; however, they did represent an ideological orientation that is still present in some Andean militaries.

Coinciding with these counterhegemonic models of economic and political development has been the emergence of a broader conception of national security beyond simply military security that includes such challenges as environmental destruction and extreme poverty. Venezuela, Ecuador, and Bolivia have expanded or maintained the use of their militaries in tackling these challenges rather than solely relying upon nonmilitary actors to address these issues. Finally, these governments have been at the forefront of reducing/eliminating ties with the U.S. military while increasing connections to other governments viewed as rivals to the United States (such as Russia or Iran), or within Latin America, such as in the South American Defense Council, which excludes U.S. participation.

The Andean Context and Methodology

The Andes has reflected the emergence of different "forms of state," variants of neoliberal and state capitalist forms that have been developed by "... specific historical circumstances, shaped by particular combinations of pressures, and have performed [and are performing] different functions in relation to the world orders within [which] they exist" (see Cox 1987 on forms of states). These variants in how states in the Andes have resisted and/or embraced the neoliberal economic order of global capitalism in the past two decades are reflected in Tables 1.1 and 1.2. Table 1.1 presents the ranking that the five countries achieved on selected World Economic Forum's "Global Competitiveness Reports,"

Table 1.1   Global Competitiveness, Selected Years

	Ranking/total number of countries evaluated that year					
	1999	*2000*	*2004*	*2005*	*2006*	*2007*
Colombia	4	3	1	1	1	1
Peru	1	1	2	2	2	2
Bolivia	5	2	5	4	3	3
Ecuador	3	5	4	5	4	4
Venezuela	2	4	3	3	5	5

Source: World Economic Forum, "Global Competitiveness Report."
Notes: 1 = *Most globally competitive*; 5 = *Least globally competitive*

Table 1.2   Index of Economic Freedom, Selected Years

	Ranking/number of countries evaluated that year			
	1995	*2000*	*2005*	*2008*
Colombia	1	3	2	2
Peru	4	1	1	1
Bolivia	5	2	3	4
Ecuador	3	4	4	3
Venezuela	2	5	5	5

Source: World Economic Forum, "Global Competitiveness Report."
Notes: 1 = *Most market reform*; 5 = *Little to no market reform*

which are based on those policies, institutions, and factors deemed central to economic productivity and growth, such as the security of private property rights, the avoidance of "excessive" regulation, and low governmental deficits and inflation—the fundamentals of economic neoliberalism (World Economic Forum 2008, p. 4). Colombia and Peru consistently ranked higher on this index than Venezuela or Ecuador, with the exception of 1999—the first year of the Chávez presidency, indicating a more globally competitive business environment. Bolivia's rankings illustrate a degree of inconsistency, with some years representing a more globally competitive tendency than others.

Table 1.2 presents data from the *Index of Economic Freedom*. Since 1994 the conservative think tank the Heritage Foundation and *The Wall Street Journal* have published this yearly index in order to document "...the link between economic opportunity and prosperity," specifically the degree of economic freedom in a specific country (Miles, Feulner, and O'Grady 2008, p. 1). The ranking focuses on such factors as a country's level of protectionism, governmental intervention in the economy, budget deficits, and capital controls. The country with the highest ranking (#1) in 2004 was Hong Kong, and the country with the least amount of economic openness was North Korea (#155) (Miles, Feulner, and O'Grady 2004). Table 1.2 ranks the five Latin American countries in order of their relative placement on the Heritage Foundation table.

The variation in their level of economic integration has roughly corresponded with their variation in accommodating the political institutions associated with market or low intensity democracies, as well as the level of military prerogatives and political control over the armed forces.

Research Hypotheses

The theoretical framework that I utilize allows us to understand why countries facing substantial internal security threats successfully reduced military prerogatives while countries lacking such security threats witnessed repeated moments of military political intervention and the expansion of military prerogatives. I hypothesize that the capture of national states by neoliberal policy coalitions within the context of global promotion of market or low-intensity democracies by the United States and central international financial institutions (IFIS) and intergovernmental organizations (IGOS) is central to the reduction of military prerogatives within a specific country. The existence of internal security threats reinforces this political and economic agenda rather than undermining it. Armed insurgencies have created greater justification for the repression of antineoliberal/globalization actors in civil society while marginalizing those nationalist/populist factions within the military interested in an active political/developmentalist role within the state. It is expected that the existence of an armed insurgency should weaken the political space for groups in civil society. In contrast to the expectations of the traditional literature, the existence of internal security threats *within* a context of the global promotion of market democracies and the capture of national states by neoliberal policy coalitions were fundamental to the political control of the armed forces and the reduction of military prerogatives in Colombia, Peru, and Bolivia before Evo Morales came to power in 2005.

The military's institutional prerogatives within the national government include extensive representation on national security councils and other decision-making bodies; the ability to avoid civilian administration or oversight in military justice, budgeting, or promotions; and the autonomy to establish national security missions with little to no civilian input (see Stepan 1988). Stepan argues that the military would constitute having a "low" prerogative if de facto and de jure control is exercised by civilian officials, and a high one when the military enjoys effective control over responsibilities such as military budgets, promotions, and the defense ministry (Stepan 1988, 93). Stepan finds that it is conceivable for the military to go from high prerogatives to low prerogatives without contestation or conflict "...if such a pattern of low prerogatives were seen as an integral part, by both the military and civilian leaders, of the overall model of governance and civil-military relations that is being restored" (Stepan 1988, p. 98). The interaction of a global effort to promote low-intensity democracies, with the emergence of neoliberal policy coalitions confronting internal security threats, has created the conditions for a model of governance and civil-military relations that militaries in Colombia, Peru, and Bolivia have conceded to, often with little contestation.

Cases

In a broad sense the five countries represent "most similar" cases. The five countries all represent a part of the Andean region, located along the Andes mountain chain and sharing a political and economic situation that some view as in "peril" (Council on Foreign Relations 2004, p. 7). In addition, the region contains strong cross-national influences and demonstration effects, which have been reinforced by an array of regional organizations that have sought tighter connections. These have included the Andean Parliament, the Andean Tribunal of Justice, and the Andean Corporation of Promotion (Mainwaring, María Bejarano, and Pizarro Leongómez 2006, p. 7). Between 1987 and 2003 the World Bank classified all five countries as "middle-income countries," with Colombia, Bolivia, Ecuador, and Peru falling in the "lower-middle income" category and Venezuela in the "upper middle income" category.[9] By July 2009 these classifications had changed some, with Colombia and Peru entering the "upper middle income" category. Between 1995 and 2005 economic growth for the five Andean countries was lower than the average for the region (Solimano 2005, p. 16). In all five countries in 2002, poverty was near or surpassed 50 percent of their respective populations, with rural poverty regularly surpassing the poverty levels for the overall population (Council on Foreign Relations 2004, p. 112; Soliman 2005, p. 34). In 2003 the richest 10 percent of the population received at least 36 percent of the total income (over 44 percent in Colombia and Ecuador) and the bottom 10 percent received no more than 1.3 percent of the total income (with the poorest 10 percent receiving less than 1 percent in Peru, Colombia, and Ecuador) (World Bank 2003).

Compounding these economic problems are weak political institutions and uneven control over national territories. An ongoing internal war in Colombia that regularly involves the public security forces of other Andean nations and an entrenched narcotrafficking industry with operations throughout the region further complicate the political and economic situation. All five countries have been governed by electoral regimes since at least 1982. However, all five have been viewed as suffering crises of democracy related to a "dissatisfaction with democratic representation," with citizens throughout the region having low levels of trust in agents of democratic representation (Mainwaring, María Bejarano, and Pizarro Leongómez 2006, pp. 1, 5). These governments, often unstable, have at different times been engulfed in corruption scandals and/or directly challenged by social protests, sectors of the armed forces, and/or armed insurgents. Political parties in each of the governments have undergone various levels of de-institutionalization, while "outsider" movements and personalist politics have predominated. According to the World Bank, in 1998 and 2001, the Andean countries ranked lower on different governance measures (such as rule of law, political instability, and violence or corruption) than the Latin American and Caribbean average (Soliman 2005, pp. 28–9). Finally, since 1979 the region's governments have proceeded with the implementation of at least some neoliberal economic measures, with certain countries going further than others in their implementation. Importantly, they differ on the dependent variable that I am examining—the reduction of military prerogatives and continuous political control of the military by civilian authorities.

The policy periods that I examine are the periods in which significant efforts were made to "modernize" the state politically and economically along the lines of "market democracies" between 1980 and 2010. I specifically focus upon the policy coalitions behind such efforts, examining the degree that such coalitions pursued changes in the arena of civil–military relations. The approach that I will employ to examine these questions and cases is a "comparative historical approach." I seek to identify specific patterns in the development of policymaking in civil–military relations as well as resulting outcomes in state behavior. This approach will be applied to these five Latin

American republics. The detailed, qualitative analyses will compare the emergence of specific policy coalitions and their conflicts with competing ones in an effort to understand differing policy outcomes. A comparative historical analysis is most appropriate, given that it generally aims to explain "substantively important outcomes," is concerned with a causal analysis, and stresses processes over time, as well as the "use of systematic and contextualized comparison" (Mahoney and Rueschemeyer 2003, p. 6).

The purpose of this book is to employ an emphasis upon policy coalitions and international variables in the analysis of civil-military relations, a topic that traditionally eschews such analyses. This book will trace the intellectual and political origins of attempts to reduce military prerogatives of the armed forces, their relationship to changes in the ideological and political makeup of different national governments, and the factors (global and domestic) that affected their implementation or prevented them from ever becoming a part of the policy agenda.

CHAPTER 2

The Erosion of Military Prerogatives: The Cases of Peru and Colombia

Demagogues at the service of terrorism, who, like cowards, wave the banner of human rights in an attempt to bring terrorism back into spaces from which the armed forces and the public have expelled it. Every time a security policy aimed at defeating terrorism appears in Colombia, every time the terrorists start to feel weak, they send their mouthpieces to talk about human rights.

> —Colombian president Álvaro Uribe providing
> his opinion of human rights organizations while
> speaking at a military ceremony on September 8, 2003

We know that the terrorists and their front organizations, or useful idiots, will not give up and will use all possible resources to harm the image of Peru by alleging that the Peruvian armed forces systematically violate human rights.

> —Peruvian president Alberto Fujimori while
> speaking at a military ceremony on September 24, 1991.[1]

In the cases of Peru and Colombia, civilian authorities have not only avoided military coups in the 1990s and 2000s, but also have made progress in managing the size of defense budgets, influencing military promotions, and playing a greater role in directing security policy. Civilian appointees have headed defense ministries and intelligence services, and prerogatives over military training and budgets have been eroded by civilian authorities. The reduction in military prerogatives coincided with the coming to power of neoliberal policy coalitions that maintained power and pursued economic reform in a region that increasingly has been shifting away from market solutions to development. This has been accomplished despite the existence of internal armed threats to state authority and stability from guerrilla armies such as the Fuerzas Armadas Revolucionarios de Colombia (FARC) in Colombia and the Shining Path and the Túpac Amaru Revolutionary Movement (MRTA) in Peru. By the end of the 1990s the Shining Path had been substantially weakened from its peak of approximately 10,000 guerrillas, but in 2008–9 there was evidence of a resurgence of the group as they engaged in weekly ambushes on army/police patrols operating in the Apurimac Valley and attacks that led to the deaths of 22 soldiers during 2008 (*The Canadian Press* 2008; Romero 2009). The Colombian state faced multiple guerrilla armies during this time—most importantly the FARC and the National Army of Liberation (the ELN) ranging in their numbers from 10,000 to 20,000 since 1990. By 2008 both guerrilla armies, though militarily weakened, continued to engage in attacks against military/police units, key parts of the country's infrastructure, as well as kidnappings of the civilian population. How could these governments reduce military prerogatives in the context of such internal security threats? How could neoliberal policy coalitions survive and successfully implement their agenda in this context?

The answers to these questions rest, in part, on the respective internal wars in Colombia and Peru. Opposition from civil society to these neoliberal policy coalitions was weakened by their respective internal wars, which reduced the space for antiglobalization groups in civil society (such as trade unions, indigenous rights organizations, and leftist political parties). The centrality of the counterinsurgent war has undermined nationalist/statist factions within the military that might have directly challenged the authority of neoliberal coalitions and/or allied with sympathetic sectors in civil society. This has strengthened those actors in the military, prioritizing the successful repression of the insurgency and its alleged allies. While the military's internal order mission remains prominent, other military prerogatives are inconsistent with the "market democracies" or "low-intensity democracies" being established by these neoliberal/globalist policy coalitions. These include military control over defense budgets, direct control over governmental agencies, or the existence of military-run industries inconsistent with the privatization direction of neoliberalism. The erosion of military prerogatives and the promotion of capitalist globalization have been reinforced and legitimated by a global process of democracy promotion that has stressed the centrality of civilian control and market reform.

The following examines how national and global processes have interacted with and contributed to civil-military reforms in Colombia and Peru. These two cases are important because the reductions in military prerogatives took place within political environments ostensibly not conducive to such progress. In the case of Peru and Colombia, the erosion of military prerogatives has occurred with relatively little contestation and coincided with a new "model of governance" led by neoliberal policy coalitions that governed during the 1990s and 2000s.

Colombia

The National Front, Narcotrafficking, and CounterInsurgency, 1958–90

Colombian politics throughout the twentieth century were synonymous with the electoral, and sometimes violent, conflict between the Liberal and Conservative political parties. The appeal of these two parties has declined among Colombians in the last two decades, with increasing rates of abstention being only one of the many indications of this decline.[2] Their historically elitist nature has also contributed to an increasingly alienated polity. Economic elites have traditionally enjoyed greater access and influence among Colombia's political establishment (Hartlyn 1985; Peeler 1992). Colombia's politics have also been associated with extraordinarily high levels of political and social violence related to the development of a narcotrafficking industry as well as a four-decade-long internal war.

Beginning in 1958 and continuing into the 1980s the political system operated under the rules of the National Front (formally until 1974 and informally until 1986) in which the Liberal and Conservative parties rotated control of the presidency while allowing the opposition party to obtain representation in the bureaucracy and the national legislature. This agreement settled most of the issues at the heart of a ten-year civil war between the parties that took place between 1948 and 1958 while replacing the military regime of General Gustavo Rojas Pinilla, who governed between 1953 and 1957. Rojas Pinilla was supported by most of the political and economic establishment, which hoped to see an end of the partisan civil war.[3] However, this establishment became alienated from the general when he sought to prolong his rule through the development of a personalistic political movement. Military and party leaders came together to remove Rojas Pinilla from power with the support of a broader societal movement that was resisting the authoritarian regime.

The two-party system that replaced this military regime governed during the next several decades with a high level of consensus. Both parties maintained a moderately nationalistic economic policy with protectionist and state subsidies for domestic industries, but with a significant role for exports in coffee and agriculture. By the end of the twentieth century exports such as cocaine and oil would complement these traditional exports. During the post-1958 period issues such as the limits upon political representation, land reform, and economic inequality were largely not addressed. The failure to address these problems contributed to the emergence of a variety of guerrilla armies directly challenging the state from the 1960s to the 2000s, with the FARC and the ELN representing the two largest movements.

Civil-military relations in Colombia prior to the late 1980s and early 1990s were marked by a largely unspoken agreement between civilian authorities and the military leadership, in which the military was excluded from politics while it retained autonomy over public order/security, specifically its counterinsurgency mission (Dávila 1998; Blair 1993). The general counterinsurgent strategy pursued was a militarized one, a strategy that emphasized repressive measures over social development strategies. The army was central to securing the continuity of the two-party system, working to eliminate those political alternatives refusing to be co-opted by it (Rouquié 1987, p. 213). Throughout the 1950s and 1960s the United States played an important role in influencing the country's national security doctrine through the interaction between Colombian and U.S. troops in the Korean War (Colombia was the only nation in Latin America to send troops to this conflict) or U.S. military advisory teams on counterinsurgency. Colombia's campaign to wipe out the FARC in the 1960s was aided by the largest U.S. military aid package in Latin America until the Central American wars in the 1980s (Rochlin 2007, p. 7). During the nation's partisan civil war, and in the decades that followed, this counter-insurgency strategy involved the use of paramilitary units, armed civilians that supplemented the actions of public security forces. In fact, the use of civilians in the nation's internal defense had been a legal part of Colombia's counterinsurgency for the two decades prior to the formal ending of this policy in 1989.

The national security doctrine promoted in Colombia (and in the rest of Latin America) by the United States during the Cold War oriented Latin American militaries to focus on internal threats and suppress the possibility of "revolutionary" change. For example, U.S. military advisor General William Yarborough led a U.S. Army Special Warfare team in 1962 to assess Colombia's counterinsurgency strategies and recommend changes. Yarborough concluded that the Colombian army should "select civilian and military personnel for clandestine training in resistance operations . . ." and that they be used "to perform counter-agent and counter-propaganda functions and as necessary execute paramilitary, sabotage and/or terrorist activities against known communist proponents" (Human Rights Watch 1996, p. 12). According to Michael McClintock, "the framework of the doctrine developed by the end of 1963 would provide the foundation of counterinsurgency and unconventional warfare into the 1990s" (1992, p. 228).

Colombia's militarized strategies did complement efforts to win the "hearts and minds" of the rural population through civic action programs, which were regularly funded by the United States Agency for International Development (USAID) and U.S. military aid programs, but these efforts were often inadequate and subordinated to a military focus. In fact, military leaders who voiced skepticism of the repressive bias of Colombian counterinsurgency faced isolation and retirement. In 1965 General Ruiz Novoa, the minister of war, was sent to early retirement after he publicly blamed political leaders for the continuation of the insurgency because of their failure to implement agrarian and social reforms, even calling for a "social-economic revolution." He was accused of "splitting the armed forces" and was replaced with General Gabriel Rebeiz Pizarro, an officer less inclined to support a social component and committed to a repressive strategy (Pearce 1990, p. 202; Ruhl 1981, pp. 135–6; Kirk 2003, p. 55; *Time* 1965). The former military dictator, General Rojas Pinilla, sought the presidency in 1970, seeking to represent the Conservative party on an anti-imperialist platform that heavily criticized the National Front, demanding "socialism on Christian bases in the Colombian manner" (as quoted in Safford and Palacios 2002, p. 330). His popular movement, the Acción Nacional Popular (National Popular Action, ANAPO) would ultimately be defeated through electoral fraud, and ANAPO would begin to decline with Rojas's weakening due to illness (Ibid, p. 331).

In 1974 the commander of the army, General Álvaro Valencia Tovar, openly embraced what Robin Kirk refers to as a "sociological" focus to counterinsurgency, publicly expressing criticisms of party leaders. Valencia Tovar was forced to retire and was replaced by General Luis Camacho Leyva, who maintained a hardline position that Robin Kirk describes as viewing the enemy as ". . . dissent in all its forms, only the most extreme of which was communism" (Kirk 2003, pp. 59–60). By the end of the 1970s serious ideological divisions within the armed forces were few as the military enjoyed its autonomy to pursue a militarized approach against the insurgency with the support of the civilian political and economic establishment. As former defense minister Rafael Pardo argued "... the counter-insurgency has been a factor of cohesion and generator of a sense of mission in the Colombian Armed Forces" (e-mail communication, 10/27/08).

This mission was advanced by the administration of Julio Cesár Turbay Ayala (1978–82). His government granted the military greater powers to detain and arrest civilians, and the military was granted jurisdiction to try suspects of subversive activities. Finally, these increased prerogatives complemented the military's continued control over the defense ministry, its supervision over its budgetary expenses, and general impunity over human rights violations (Premo 1989, p. 108). In 1980, more than 8,000 Colombians were detained for "political reasons," with the vast majority tried in military courts. During this same period a noticeable increase of forced disappearances and allegations of torture at the hands of military officials were documented by human rights organizations, as the state continued to meet its political and social challenges with repression (Giraldo Gustavo 1991, pp. 13–5). The result was the "limited militarization" of a civilian regime (Rouquié 1987, p. 216).

Public and international condemnation of human rights violations in the Turbay-Ayala administration led to the curtailing of many of these prerogatives in the Betancur administration (1982–86). During the 1980s and 1990s important divisions emerged between the military and civilian authorities over efforts by different administrations to negotiate with the armed insurgency, the military's relationship with paramilitary groups, and/or U.S human rights concerns. For example, governmental investigations during the Betancur administration into the links between paramilitary groups, which had assassinated political activists, and officers within the army, found fifty-nine officers with links to paramilitary groups, specifically Muerte a Secuestradores (MAS) (Human Rights Watch 1996). An attempt by Betancur's attorney general to criminally prosecute these individuals failed, with the charges ultimately being dismissed by a military court.[4] In addition, attempts to negotiate with the major guerrilla groups in the Betancur administration were scuttled in part by violations of the cease fire by the Colombian armed forces, which viewed the negotiations as a capitulation to their internal enemies. While different civilian administrations would continue to attempt a negotiated solution to an escalating internal war in the 1980s and 1990s, their commitment to such a solution varied in emphasis (similarly with the guerrillas). The military's autonomy in repressing the guerrilla threat, either through their indirect support of right-wing militias allied with sectors of the government and army (paramilitary groups) or their continuing impunity for human rights violations, were generally protected by different civilian administrations.

Throughout Colombia's history of counterinsurgent war, paramilitary groups and the armed forces have been effective at weakening potentially anticapitalist globalization sectors in civil society (leftist political parties, trade unionists, and indigenous activists) through political violence and displacement, viewing with suspicion all actors perceived as supporting the guerrilla insurgency (Angel Urrego 2001). The contemporary incarnation of these groups emerged in the early 1980s through the financing of the Medellín cartel, cattle ranchers, and members of the political elite in the Magdalena Medio region of Colombia, a sector of the establishment that organized to repel guerrilla kidnapping and extortion. The armed groups that were developed worked with elements of the Colombian military, primarily targeting the civilian population viewed as sympathetic with the guerrilla insurgency (peasant organizers, trade unionists, and human rights activists) in an effort to undermine whatever political support these guerrillas received. For example, between 1986 and 2002 more than 3,000 trade unionists were killed in Colombia, the vast majority by paramilitary actors (Solidarity Center 2006, p. 11). The leftist political party, the *Union Patriótica*, was decimated in the 1980s and 1990s, with thousands of its members assassinated, primarily by paramilitary groups (Angel Urrego 2001; United States Institute for Peace 2004). The level of state and parastate repression in Colombia during this period and into the 2000s far exceeded the level of political killings that took place in many military regimes that governed Latin America during the 1960s and 1970s (Giraldo 1996).

Finally, paramilitary groups have long been associated with the drug trade and in the displacement of millions of Colombians, facilitating land concentration as well as transnational/national direct investment (Richani 2005). In 1997 paramilitary groups organized a nationwide force, the Self-Defense Forces of Colombia (AUC) and operated on a nationwide basis. Many of their activities were aided by the armed forces, with civilian authorities regularly failing to prosecute military personnel implicated in supporting paramilitary groups (Avilés

2006b). Furthermore, they have been directly involved in securing the investments of transnational corporations such as Chiquita Bananas, Drummond Coal, and Coca-Cola through the defense of coal or banana shipments, to the execution of trade union activists seeking to improve the working conditions within their operations (Richani 2005). In fact, Chiquita Bananas paid paramilitary groups almost $2 million between 1997 and 2004 to help safeguard their operations (Gibbs and Leech 2009, p. 61). Not only has the legal left been debilitated by paramilitary repression over the last three decades, but the armed guerrilla insurgency also has privileged militarist solutions over political ones throughout the 1990s, with some members of the legal left being directly victimized by guerrilla units (Ambrus 2007). This armed conflict worked to fragment much of Colombia's social movements, which were pressured to support their armed struggle and/or were often displaced by their political activities (Pizarro 1996, p. 222).

By the end of the 1980s the Colombian state was not only confronting a guerrilla insurgency, but also increasingly had to address corrupting and destabilizing narcotrafficking cartels. Through bribery and murder, narcotraffickers steadily embedded themselves within Colombian society and government while profiting wildly in the export of cocaine to the United States. Their resources were not only used to influence the state, but they also helped to subsidize death squads/paramilitary groups to attack their enemies, as well as sectors of the left that undermined their influence. Colombia would become the principal source of cocaine for the U.S. market, thus making Colombia the prime target for U.S. counternarcotics policies.

The U.S. "war on drugs" since the late 1980s has consistently been tied to democratic politics and civilian control over the military. The emphasis upon "civilian authority" complemented the various human rights provisions included in antinarcotics agreements (Youngers 2004, p. 135). In 1990 the U.S. Congress passed the International Narcotics Control Act which required the President to issue a determination that "the government of [the recipient] country has effective control over policy and military operations related to counternarcotics and counterinsurgency activities" (as quoted in Call 1991, p. 120–1). The promotion of market competition was also important. In announcing the $2.2 billion Andean Initiative to reduce the production of drugs in the Andes, President George H. W. Bush declared that the assistance would "encourage and support fundamental economic reform in the countries of the region on the basis of market-driven policies" (as quoted in Gibbs and Leech 2009, p. 50). By 1990 the Colombian state was dealing with an ongoing counterinsurgency war, narcotrafficking violence, and increasing pressure from the United States for greater results against powerful cocaine cartels.

Neoliberalism and Plan Colombia, 1990–2002

Between the late 1980s and early 1990s a set of political elites came to power in Colombia committed to neoliberalism and economic globalization. Along with their ideological commitment to economic reform, they also pursued policies to subordinate their respective armed forces to civilian control. This was most clearly represented in the administration of César Gaviria (1990–4). As the Colombian weekly *Semana* described Gaviria's cabinet, "they are the defenders of democracy first and foremost, with a civilian conception of society and a rejection of the use of violence to solve social problems....[they are]....anti-communist, anti-populist, anti-third worldism and anti-statist" (August 7, 1990, p. 28). These intellectuals worked to cement the links between the political and economic direction being established globally to the policymaking of the Colombian state.

In part, their success in obtaining power reflected the public's willingness to give these reformers an opportunity to address a political and social crisis of insurgent and narcotrafficking violence that many felt was leading the country into chaos (Leal Buitrago and Zamosc 1990). These domestic factors were reinforced by international pressures. Economically, the government received pressures from the World Bank and the Office of the U.S. Trade Representative for greater economic openness and liberalization in Colombia (Urrutia 1994, p. 303; Juárez 1994). Politically, the Gaviria administration's democratic vision was, according to Gaviria's defense minister Rafael Pardo "...derived from the hemispheric priority in the promotion of democracy and in the disqualification of military coups initiated by the United States, which had validated this conduct during the Cold War" (e-mail communication, 10/27/08, translation mine and hereafter).

These modernizing technocrats were central to the development of political plans to reform the country's economy and politics. During the Barco (1986–90) and Gaviria administrations, economic policies

included reducing import tariffs, weakening labor regulations, promoting privatizations, and strengthening the autonomy of the central
bank (Juárez 1994; 1996). These political actors were also central in
reforming the country's civil–military relations.

The need to expand civilian authority over the armed forces was
promoted by a Presidential Commission for the Reform of Public
Administration that was established in 1989 through Decree 1150
during the Barco administration. A majority of the commission represented members of Colombia's neoliberal policy coalition (Avilés
2006a, p. 63; *Semana*, Oct. 15, 1991; *Semana*, Aug. 7, 1990). This
majority included Rudolph Hommes, Gaviria's minister of finance
and an economist; Fernando Botero, Samper's first defense minister
and an advocate of neoliberalism; and Alfonso Esguerra, a corporate
attorney for foreign investors, among others. The commission called
for the centralization of analysis, design, and the direction of national
security strategies in a civilian-led office (Leal-Buitrago 1994, pp.
130–1). The election of César Gaviria in 1990 would bring about
changes consistent with this agenda. Gaviria selected a civilian to
head the defense ministry in 1991, the first civilian defense minister
in forty years. In September 1991 a civilian replaced the military
head of the country's domestic intelligence agency, the Department
of Administrative Security (DAS) (*El Tiempo*, Sept. 6, 1991: p. 11A).
Also, a special unit was established within the civilian-led National
Department of Planning[5] with the sole responsibility of oversee-
ing military spending during his government (Avilés 2006a, p. 64;
Pizarro 1995). Neoliberal governments that followed Gaviria in the
1990s and 2000s maintained a civilian official in the defense ministry
and at the head of domestic intelligence and continued the government's expanded oversight of military budgets.

Throughout the 1990s and 2000s different national governments
have publicly pressured the military for results, as greater supervision
is being exerted over how efficiently the military is fighting the internal war (Gutiérrez 2003, p. 89). The military leadership publicly com-
plained about budgetary shortfalls in the Gaviria (1990–4) and Samper
(1994–8) administrations (FBIS February 17, 1993, p. 46; *Star Tribune*,
September 5, 1996, p. 7A; Dávila 1999, p. 309), while the military was
being funded during the 1990s at a percentage of GDP below the level
in other Latin American countries (The Military Balance of 1995/1996;
Concha Sanz 2003, p. 194). These budgetary shortfalls were consistent with a historical trend in which the military was funded enough
to "contain" the guerrilla threat (Richani 2001, pp. 37–58). Finally,

the military high command had to deal with increasing criticisms of its performance from the Colombian congress and mass media after a series of successful attacks by the FARC against military bases and specialized guerrilla units, with the major newspaper daily *El Espectador* arguing in March 1998 that "...the armed forces requires a profound rectification" (as quoted in Villamizar 2003, p. 27).

The problems with military budgets and tactics changed in a substantive way during both the Pastrana (1998–2002) and Uribe (2002–10) governments where civilian-initiated progress has been made to increase the number of professional soldiers and modernize the military to ensure greater military results and efficiency. Pastrana's first civilian defense minister, Rodrigo Lloreda, went beyond military proposals for reform, purging officers deemed too close to former General Harold Bedoya[6] as well as working to improve the military and intelligence capabilities. The administration promoted General Fernando Tapias to the head of the armed forces, someone who Lloreda believed represented a "global vision" and "cultured" view, rather than the militarist, authoritarian views of General Bedoya and his allies within the army (Leal Buitrago 2002, p. 167; Leal Buitrago 2006, p. 203). Both of these administrations have substantially increased military budgets; however, the need to ensure that these resources are efficiently spent continues to guide budget policy. According to Colombia's Controller, between 1991 and 2006 spending on security and defense increased from 9.8 percent to 19.2 percent of the national budget and from 1.8 percent to 4.5 percent of GDP, though the Controller noted that the military must "design much more efficient mechanisms in the use of its resources" (El Economista.es 2007). In addition, these governments initiated the improvement of military technology and capabilities in intelligence gathering, aerial military operations, and nocturnal combat, as well as increasing the number of professional soldiers to 30,000 between 1999 and 2001 (Villamizar 2003, pp. 48–56, 61).

With regard to the behavior of the military in the conduction of the internal war, progress has been made in reducing its level of autonomy, though it still remains high. Both President Samper and President Pastrana successfully demilitarized regions of the countries to obtain the release of hostages and engage in peace negotiations with the FARC, respectively, over the resistance/criticism of the military in both instances. The two governments also forced the retirement of army generals because of their involvement with human rights abuses and/or because of their resistance to the human rights conditions of U.S. aid (Samper 2000, pp. 184–5; Center for International Policy 1999).

Those conditions were related to the 1997 Leahy Law, which conditioned U.S. aid upon a set of human rights requirements. Though there have been problems with its implementation (Center for International Policy 2003), the amendment did hold important symbolic value for the Colombian military, with Colombia's military leaders regularly complaining about the human rights demands of the United States (Tate 2007, pp. 270–5). In fact, Laurienti argues that the yearly process of vetting the Colombian military for human rights violators "... provides the greatest angst for the Colombian armed forces" (2007, p. 75).

Political interventions by U.S. ambassadors played a role in promoting human rights and continued civilian political control over the military. For example, in 1995 U.S. ambassador Myles Frechette was approached by officers within the Colombian military interested in removing President Samper from power on account of his alleged linkages within the Cali Cartel, a step that Frechette immediately opposed, demanding that constitutional measures be sought to remove Samper (*Semana* August 20, 1996; *Semana* Nov.10, 1997, pp. 38–42; Samper 2000, p. 210; *The New York Times*, August 22, 1996, p. A1). In the summer of 1997 Frechette was instrumental in obtaining the agreement of the Colombian armed forces to U.S. human rights conditions after resistance from the commander of the armed forces, General Harold Bedoya. Bedoya would be retired by Samper, in part due to the involvement of Frechette, who maintained that U.S. military assistance would continue to be withheld without the human rights conditions (*El Tiempo*, July 15, 1997, p. 8A; Salinas 1997–8, p. 33).

The Andres Pastrana administration, like other administrations in the 1990s, continued to rely upon a group of technocrats similar in their ideological orientation to the group that advised the Gaviria administration (interview with Colombian Ambassador Luis Alberto Moreno, July 13, 2004). Structural adjustment policies implemented in December 1999 met stiff resistance among sectors of civil society. State workers launched some of the biggest strikes of the 1990s to protest these policies (Ahumada 2002, pp. 224–6). Also, like previous governments, Pastrana symbolically promised a struggle against paramilitarism while tolerating/facilitating its activities. This struggle included the dismissal from service of Generals Fernando Millán and Rito Alejo del Río for their alleged connections with paramilitary groups and a proposed military penal reform bill that threatened military impunity over certain human rights violations (*Cambio*, May 31, 1999, p. 20; Leal Buitrago 2002, pp. 169–71). The military's penal code in August 1999 (the penal code would only come into force in August 2000) specifically prohibited the military justice system from investigating the crimes of disappearance, genocide, and torture, which could only be investigated by civilian courts (Leal Buitrago 2002, pp. 170–2; Lemus, Stanton, and Walsh 2005, p. 127). Extrajudicial executions or displacement could still be considered by the military justice system.

In addition, a new National Defense and Security Law was established in August 2001, which according to the administration, "empowers the state to protect its citizens from violent groups. The bill sets the stage for smoother more efficient military operations..." (Colombian government 2001). The bill was criticized because it granted greater authority to the armed forces in defining national security policies and in establishing internal security, as well as allowing greater military powers in specific areas of operation (International Crisis Group 2002, pp. 7–8; International Crisis Group 2003, p. 15). Paramilitary groups continued to increase in their size and military activities, with the government seemingly unable to combat them. The U.S. State Department's Andean desk officer found in January 1999 that "all indications are that paramilitarism has continued to grow...and the government has done little to confront them," and that "security forces did not intervene during 19 separate attacks in which 143 civilians were killed over four days in January" (Evans 2005). In September 1999 the CIA's daily *Senior Executive Intelligence Brief* found that local Colombian military commanders "do not challenge paramilitary groups operating in their areas because they see the insurgents as the common foe" (CIA, *Senior Executive Intelligence Brief* 1999).

Pastrana's progress in reducing military prerogatives is even more impressive in that it took place during the worst economic downturn in seventy years and a popularity rating of 20 percent in October 2000 (BBC Summary of World Broadcasts 2000a; Rohter 1999). However, his administration would be bolstered by the military and political support from the Clinton administration through the U.S. aid package, Plan Colombia.

Despite the state's continuing relationship between the Colombian military and paramilitarism in July 2000, President Bill Clinton signed into law the aid package popularly known as Plan Colombia, the U.S. government's contribution to a Colombian counternarcotics and development plan. The policy would commit approximately $1.3 billion dollars in U.S. financial and military assistance to the Colombian government (with a small part for its Andean neighbors) primarily to strengthen Colombia's military capabilities and effectiveness against guerrilla insurgents over a three-year period. The United

States contributed to a strategy that prioritized the militarization of the counternarcotics struggle in an effort to establish the rule of law in those regions of Colombia deemed crucial to success in the U.S. "drug war," specifically areas of heavy coca cultivation with a long-established FARC presence. The plan emphasized the importance of strengthening Colombia's armed forces and the rule of law as key to successful economic development and resolving Colombia's political crisis.

The economic strategy employed was one focused upon balancing the national fiscal budget, expanding exports, and creating incentives for greater private investment. The first two of ten strategies in Plan Colombia emphasized "the expansion of international commerce, accompanied by better access to foreign markets" and a fiscal and financial strategy based on "severe austerity and adjustment measures in order to stimulate economic activity" (as quoted in Bergquist, Peñaranda, and Sánchez 2001, p. 234).[7] This was in contrast to the earlier drafts of Plan Colombia developed by the Pastrana administration that had maintained a greater social development and antipoverty focus as opposed to facilitating international investments. Furthermore, the defense of energy investments by U.S.-based transnational corporations played a role, as did securing potential future sites of investment. In 1999 the secretary of energy in the Clinton administration, Bill Richardson, stated that "[t]he United States and its allies will invest millions of dollars in two areas of the Colombian economy, in the areas of mining and energy, and to secure these investments we [are] tripling military aid to Colombia" (as quoted in Gibbs and Leech 2009, p. 53). Occidental Petroleum in particular spent millions lobbying the U.S. Congress between 1995 and 2000 on Latin American, and mostly Colombian, policy, with the aim of obtaining greater security for its investments (Forero 2002). In oil-producing regions such as Arauca and Putumayo, the Colombian army has directly benefitted from U.S. support and is aware of its role relative to oil companies. In 2004 army Lieutenant Colonel Francisco Javier Cruz, who operated in Putumayo, stated that "security is the most important thing to me. Oil companies need to work without worrying and international investors need to feel calm" (Gibbs and Leech 2009, p. 58). Plan Colombia continued the trend in which the security of the investments of transnational corporations would be secured through the expansion of military, and indirectly paramilitary, repression. Foreign direct investment (FDI) increased at an annual average of 55 percent during the 1990s, and by 2005 400 transnational corporations produced an annual income of approximately $15 billion representing 15 percent of the country's GDP (Richani 2005, p. 115).

Plan Colombia was renewed in the Bush administration, and by 2008 Colombia had received more than $7 billion in military and development aid since 1999. This aid created important incentives for the Colombian military to defer to the continued political control of civilian authorities, as this aid was increasingly being dedicated to the war against the FARC (USAID 2008). In fact, in both the Peruvian and Colombian cases, U.S. "drug war" assistance was intricately tied to these countries' counterinsurgency struggles, as the drug industry helped to finance the armed activities of both the Shining Path and the FARC. This was especially the case in Colombia after 9/11, when the United States allowed Plan Colombia aid to be used against "domestic terrorists" such as the FARC or paramilitary groups throughout the country, and not just in areas of heavy coca cultivation.[8] In addition, the U.S. government applied political pressure for greater increases in military spending by the Colombian government. Different U.S. governmental officials publicly argued in multiple meetings with Colombian governmental representatives between the end of 2001 and the middle of 2002 that more resources should be committed by the Colombian government to its armed forces (Ahumada 2002, pp. 296–7). In fact, continued U.S. military aid was made contingent upon a greater budgetary commitment from the Colombian government to its military (Tickner 2003, p. 85).

Plan Colombia was passed with a set of human rights conditions that the Colombian government had to meet in order to receive approximately 25 percent of the aid (Amnesty International and Fellowship of Reconciliation 2008, p. 7). The conditions required that the U.S. secretary of state certify to Congress that those Colombian military officers who allegedly had committed human rights violations and/or worked with paramilitary groups were suspended, that the government was pursuing human rights investigations, and that progress was being made to cut linkages with paramilitary groups (Ramírez Lemus, Stanton, and Walsh 2005, 128–9). While these conditions have often been unevenly met (see Amnesty International and the Fellowship of Reconciliation 2008), they represent a continuing and potential threat to much-needed U.S. military assistance, assistance that has been instrumental in militarily weakening the FARC in the 2000s (DeShazo, Primiani, and McLean 2007, pp. viii–xi).

Plan Colombia was presented to the Colombian public as one part of Pastrana's strategy to bring the war to an end. The other part consisted of the demilitarization of a large swath of territory in order to engage in negotiations with the guerrilla leadership of the FARC. This concession of territory to the FARC was maintained despite military opposition. Almost half of the army's generals, as well as more than 100 army colonels, majors, and subofficers publicly expressed their support for the minister of defense, who resigned in protest of Pastrana's negotiating strategies with the FARC (Leal Buitrago 2002, p. 167). Ultimately, the negotiations with the FARC failed. The FARC refused to stop its attacks upon the state or its kidnapping, while the Pastrana administration failed to prevent an explosion of paramilitary violence against alleged FARC supporters in civil society.

In the end, the disagreements over human rights policies or peace negotiations between the military and civilian authorities during the 1980s and 1990s did not address economic policy or social development policies. Neither did Colombia witness divisions within the armed forces over Colombia's neoliberal direction, as intramilitary solidarity increased throughout the 1990s, with the military viewing itself as defending "*la patria*" against Communist subversion, a struggle that it has continued into 2010 (Pizarro 1996, p. 213). The failure of the peace talks would lay the basis for the conservative, militarist presidency of Álvaro Uribe (2002–10) and the expansion of the formal war against the insurgency.

Álvaro Uribe, 2002–10

The failure of Pastrana's peace process in February 2002 and U.S. pressure for an expansion of coercive strategies of social control in its "war on terrorism" were key domestic and international variables underlying a shift to an overt military strategy against the guerrilla insurgency with little attention to negotiated solutions. Álvaro Uribe, elected in 2002, promoted this overt military strategy while maintaining a neoliberal agenda that had already contributed to exacerbating social and economic inequality in Colombia (Hagen 2002, pp. 24–29). International Monetary Fund (IMF) agreements during his administration have committed the government to reducing its fiscal deficits and have facilitated continuing privatizations as well as the completion of a free trade agreement with the United States (though the U.S. government has not ratified this agreement as of June 2009) (Rochlin 2007, p. 73; Murillo 2008b). Uribe's defense ministers have also represented this ideological perspective, as they uniformly have been neoliberal technocrats and/ or economic elites tied to finance, insurance, or export capital, such as the first female defense minister Marta Lucia Ramirez de Rincon (2002–3), who was the former president of the National Association of Financial Institutions, or Juan Manuel Santos (2006–09), former minister of foreign trade and the chief executive of Colombia's delegation to the International Coffee Organization.

Between 2002 and 2009 defense and security spending increased by approximately 80 percent, with overall spending nearing 5.2 percent of GDP, as Uribe continued the trend begun by Pastrana to increase efforts to strengthen and modernize the armed forces (International Crisis Group 2004, p. 4; Quiroga 2010). However, the FARC continued to survive and even escalate its military actions relative to 2008 (Valencia 2009, p. 1). Uribe's democratic security plan, which called for increased state resources by the armed forces, provided the framework that guided the development of the military's counterinsurgency plans, as civilian authorities continued to maintain overall direction of the military and the armed forces were allowed the autonomy to prepare their own counterinsurgency plans in line with Uribe's strategic framework (Marks 2007, p. 6). The plan laid out the security responsibilities of different governmental ministries and the strategic objectives of the public security forces, as well as prioritizing the nation's enemies (Leal Buitrago 2006, pp. 240–1).[9] In 2004, following a recommendation from the U.S. Southern Command, Uribe created the Coordinating Center for Integrated Action (CCAI), which was dedicated to establishing governance in regions that had previously been under the control of armed groups. The program is dedicated to ensuring that state institutions such as public health and education, as well as justice and infrastructure projects are established soon after the military displacement of the FARC, the ELN, or the AUC from specific regions (Isacson 2009a). While the application of the program has thus far been limited to only a few communities, as of 2009 it represents another example of civilian initiative, aided by the U.S. military, guiding Colombian security strategies. Of course, Uribe's administration is not the first example of this, as the Gaviria administration created the Presidential Council on National Security to increase the role of civilian authorities in directing/developing national security strategies. Also, in March 1999 President Pastrana initiated plans to modernize the armed forces, including its intelligence system, increasing the number of professional soldiers, and strengthening respect for human rights, a process that contributed to the military's success in the Uribe administration (BBC Summary of World Broadcasts 1999a).

U.S. assistance continued in the Uribe government. In 2005 Colombia was receiving two-thirds of all U.S. security assistance in the Western Hemisphere, eight times higher than the second largest recipient Peru, while the U.S. armed forces trained more than 28,000 Colombians, almost half of all the military personnel trained in the region by the United States (Laureinti 2007, p. 74). In fact, Colombian military analyst Alfredo Rangel cautions that without continued high levels of U.S military assistance, "Uribe without Plan Colombia (or continued support under the Andean Defense Initiative) cannot do great things" (as quoted in Porch 2008, p. 146). During the Obama administration (2008–present) the United States signed a Defense Cooperation Agreement in 2009 allowing U.S. military personnel long-term access to seven Colombian military bases located throughout the country. The Uribe administration justified the agreement as necessary in their struggle against narcotrafficking and the guerrilla insurgency. However, a U.S. Air Force document revealed that the United States also viewed access to Colombian bases as a "a unique opportunity for full spectrum operations in a critical sub region of our hemisphere where security and stability is under constant threat from narcotics funded terrorist insurgencies, anti-U.S. governments, endemic poverty and recurring natural disasters" as well as "...improving the U.S. ability to respond rapidly to crisis, and assure regional access and presence at minimum cost" while "...providing access to the entire South American continent with the exception of the Cape Horn region if fuel is available, and over half of the continent unrefueled" (Department of the Air Force 2009).

U.S. military involvement, assistance, and training continue to be tied to various human rights conditions and objectives. Partly in response to these conditions, in 2003 the Colombian military established the Colombian Armed Forces School of Human Rights, International Law, and Military Penal Justice, a school presented as the central designer of human rights policies for the military (Ibid, p. 76). After the 2007 U.S. State Department certification, Colombian army commander General Mario Montoya Uribe argued that "the [U.S.] Department of State report motivates us to continue with these policies, to incline in all moments for the Defense of the Human Rights. The Army has increased the Human Rights culture, especially in the last two years" (Ejército Nacional de Colombia 2007). The army's Human Rights office trained nearly 60,000 men in human rights and humanitarian international law between 2004 and 2007 (Ejército Nacional de Colombia 2007). In 2008 the civilian-led Defense Ministry presented its "Integral Policy for Human Rights and International Human Rights" integrating the practice of human rights in actual military operations (Ministerio de Defensa Nacional de Colombia 2008, October). By the early 2000s Colombian military scholar Francisco Leal-Buitrago had concluded that "the pressure of the international community, in particular of the United States, for the government to adequately address the problem of human rights violations committed by the public forces produced improvements with the diminishment of violations" (2006, p. 210).

Consistent with these public measures toward improving human rights, the Uribe administration was instrumental in the demobilization of thousands of paramilitary members. Divisions within paramilitary groups over their role in drug trafficking, as well as the U.S. classification of the groups as terrorists in 2001, were contributing factors to their interest in a demobilization process with the Colombian government. This negotiated demobilization of paramilitary groups contributed to declines in the number of massacres, as well as of political assassinations of leftist leaders and unionists by 2008 from their peaks at the end of the 1990s (Amnesty International 2008, p. 7). However the demobilization law, which established a process to legally structure the appropriate punishments and expectations upon those who demobilize, was fraught with problems. The new law, according to Human Rights Watch, "...does not ensure that paramilitaries confess their crimes, disclose information about how their groups operate, or turn over their illegally acquired wealth. Nothing in the law effectively disbands these mafia-like groups. Disarmed troops can be easily replaced through new recruitment and promises of high pay. Commanders convicted of atrocities or other serious crimes, such as drug trafficking, will get away with sentences little longer than two years, probably in agricultural colonies. When they reenter society, their wealth, political power, and criminal networks will be intact" (Human Rights Watch 2005, p. 2). According to one demobilized paramilitary fighter, "The demobilization...is a farce. It's a way of quieting down the system and returning again, starting over from the other side" (Human Rights Watch 2005, p. 1).

The fears of Human Rights Watch have been partly confirmed, as antiglobalization movements within Colombia continue to face narrow political channels for participation and state/parastate repression (Zibechi 2005b). Colombia continues to be considered "one of the most difficult settings to wage resistance for social justice" (Webber 2007a, p. 2). In fact, Colombia continues to be the most dangerous place for a trade unionist to operate. In 2008 forty-nine trade unionists were killed , 60 percent of the worldwide total, adding to the hundreds that have been killed between 2000 and 2008 (Justice for Colombia 2009; Rochlin 2007, p. 75). Between 2003 and 2004 there was a 57 percent increase in the arbitrary arrests of trade unionists, while in 2004 the Ministry of Social Protection declared the majority of strikes illegal given their effect upon "public order" (Hristov 2009, p. 31). Unionists, such as the Oil Workers Union (USO), continue to fight against the privatization of the state-run oil industry and against privatizations in health, education, and telecommunications (Rochlin 2007, pp. 76–7).

In 2008 reorganized paramilitary groups (such as the "Black Eagles"), sometimes with the support of the Colombian armed forces and members of Colombia's political class, threatened unionists, community and student leaders, and perceived leftist politicians (Haugaard 2008, p. 16; Valencia 2010, p. 4).[10] In addition, these groups have been associated with the control of narcotrafficking distribution networks as well as internally displacing populations to facilitate investments in Colombia's mineral and palm oil resources (Avila Martínez 2009, p. 8; Gibbs and Leech 2009). According to the Organization of American States and the National Reparation and Reconciliation Commission, approximately 3,000 to 5,000 paramilitary combatants continued to operate throughout the country in 2007 (Amnesty International 2008, p. 14). A February 2010 Human Rights Watch report concluded that these new paramilitary groups "...have repeatedly targeted human rights defenders, trade unionists, displaced persons including Afro-Colombians who seek to recover their land, victims of the AUC [the coalition of paramilitary groups that had ostensibly been demobilized] who are seeking justice, and community members who do not follow their orders" (Human Rights Watch 2010). At the same time, a "para-politics" scandal rocked the Uribe administration, with approximately sixty of his congressional supporters implicated in working with paramilitary groups, and even the head of domestic intelligence (the DAS) was accused of providing "hit lists" containing human rights and union activists to paramilitary organizations. This complemented the illegal surveillance conducted by DAS against leftist politicians, members of the Colombian Supreme Court, and journalists (Noticias Uno 2010; Comisión Intereclesial de Justicia y Paz 2009; Darío Restrepo 2009).

Despite this continuing repression, Colombia's popular sector continues to struggle within the political space that it is allowed. In October 2008 more than 12,000 indigenous activists marched and blocked highways to protest against a U.S-Colombia free trade agreement, the militarization of their communities, and the failure of the Uribe administration to provide the land, education, and health that the government had promised (Murillo 2008a). Government security forces responded violently to the protesters, wounding over 120 and killing one. The government's direct repression took place days after unidentified gunmen had killed two other activists, bringing the total to eleven indigenous activists killed throughout Colombia in the three weeks prior to the protests (Murillo 2008a). In November 2008, a leading indigenous rights organization, the Association of Indigenous Councils of Northern Cauca (ACIN), sent a letter to President-elect Obama arguing that "large transnational corporations have profited from oil and gas contracts, mining concessions, privatizations, and low wages, and are now after the biodiversity of our territories" (Zibechi 2008).

Activists representing the Campesino Association of the Cimitarry River Valley (ACVC) have also been targeted by the government and paramilitary groups. The ACVC is one of the most successful campesino groups in the nation, effectively providing legal alternatives for small farmers while resisting the encroachment of national and transnational agribusinesses seeking land for export production or the crop eradication programs of the government (Willis Garcés 2009). Since 1996 six of its leaders have been killed, while eleven of its members have been killed in the department of Antioquia during the Uribe administration, and two central leaders were being prosecuted in 2009 for the crime of rebellion on the basis of little evidence (Ibid).

Since 2002 there has been an increase in the extrajudicial executions of civilians by Colombia's armed forces, with many of these civilians dressed up to look as if they were guerrilla combatants, while the military continues to enjoy relative impunity for many of these crimes (Haugaard, et al. 2008). These deaths, or "false positives," were often used by military personnel as a way to improve their combat statistics, which could lead to salary bonuses or vacation time. In June 2009 the UN Rapporteur on Extrajudicial Executions, Philip Alston, examined this scandal as well as the overall situation of human rights in Colombia. He found that the "false positives" scandal implicated approximately 1,000 members of the armed forces in the killing of more than 1,700 civilians (Colombia Reports 2009). According to Alston's press statement on the issue, "The sheer number of cases, their geographic spread, and the diversity of military units implicated, indicate that these killings were carried out in a more or less systematic fashion by significant elements within the military" (as quoted in Isacson 2009b).[11]

Despite continuing human rights violations, a new left political opposition has emerged within Colombia's political system, the Polo

Democrático. The Polo Democrático represents a central part of Uribe's political opposition and emerged during the 2000s to, according to the party website, "support the resistance to the neoliberal model and to secure effective vigilance of social rights of the population" (Sandoval 2009). The party presents a legitimate challenge to Uribe's political coalition, but has been dismissed by Uribe as a group of "disguised communists" and faces real limits to its influence (Haste 2007). According to former Colombian senator and Polo Democrático leader, Gustavo Petro, neoliberalism will not be substantially challenged anytime soon in Colombia "...because here in Colombia the popular movement that represents the root of those peaceful proposals on the left is itself being destroyed through assassinations" (Leech 2007).

By 2010 the armed forces continue to retain a level of autonomy over internal security and the FARC has been militarily weakened into a "strategic retreat." However, previously held military prerogatives over counterinsurgency strategies, military budgets, control over the defense ministry, and oversight of human rights policy were eroded in a context of global promotion of democracy and internal security threats that interacted/reinforced the initiatives of neoliberal policy coalitions that governed during the 1990s and 2000s in Colombia. Publicly, and often symbolically, the Colombian state was making the various institutional reforms indicating progress in democratic civil-military relations, but the state and parastate retained the operating space to silence, displace, and intimidate members of the popular sector seeking alternatives to capitalist globalization and low-intensity democracies.

Peru

Military Government and State Capitalism, 1968–80

The institutional history of the Peruvian military differs in several respects from the military in Colombia. Unlike Colombia, Peru's military has played a central role in Peruvian politics for much of its history, with fifty of its seventy-six executives between 1821 and 1968 being military men (Vásquez 1996, p. 338). In the most recent period of military rule (1962–3; 1968–80) the military pursued a nationalist/populist agenda while in power. Despite this important historical difference with Colombia, the evolution of civil-military relations in Peru moved in a similar direction.

Peru, like many nations in Latin America in the decades following World War II, was grappling with various state-oriented strategies of economic development, increasing urbanization, and social mobilization in the countryside for greater reforms. The leading mass-based political party, the American Popular Revolutionary Alliance (APRA) had been the party representing a nationalistic populism seeking to co-opt this mobilizing public since 1930. However, the business and landed elite, in alliance with dominant factions within the military, effectively prevented APRA from directly taking or maintaining power in the decades that followed, despite its general popularity throughout much of this time (Palmer 1996, pp. 206–7).[12] APRA also tended to be quite opportunistic in its alliances, at times sacrificing ideological objectives in its quest for political power (Palmer 1996, p. 207). The civilian government of Fernando Belaunde (1963–8) of the Popular Action party (AP), a more leftist and reformist party than APRA, was able to implement some social reforms in the 1960s, but these were often limited and underfinanced due to the obstructionism of a conservative congress dominated by APRA and its conservative allies. A declining economy, the emergence of peasant protests in response to the lack of agrarian reform, and the possibility that APRA might obtain power in the next presidential election led to the military's intervention in October 1968 and the establishment of institutionalized military rule (Schneider 2007, pp. 342–3).

The leader of this coup, General Juan Velasco Alvarado, helped to establish a military junta referred to as a "Revolutionary Government of the Armed Forces" that placed Velasco as president, with the heads of the different service branches and other officers directly taking positions within the cabinet and bureaucracy (Schneider 2007, pp. 343–4). These officers had been part of a generation of officers that increasingly questioned the military's traditionally conservative role, while developing a new doctrine of national security that linked defense to development (Schneider 2007, p. 344). Their educational studies at the Center for Higher Military Studies (CAEM), experiences in a short counterinsurgency struggle in 1965, the fact that many of these officers came from lower-middle-class backgrounds, and an extensive army-led civic action program all played a role in developing a revolutionary and nationalist perspective on national security (Schneider 2007, p. 344; Palmer 1996, p. 208).[13] CAEM promoted a military ideology in which "...Peruvian society was in need of restructuring and modernizing" while much of the military leadership that went through this program grew concerned with Peru's increasing economic dependence upon the

United States and the "ruling oligarchy" (Vásquez 1996, pp. 346, 349). Agrarian reform, nationalist energy policies, and state planning were promoted as the tools necessary to weaken the emergence of guerrilla insurgencies, undermine the power of a landed oligarchy, and develop Peru. Their first manifesto stated "The time has come to dedicate our national energies to the transformation of the economic, social, and cultural structures of Peru" (as quoted in Palmer 1996, p. 208). These economic changes were supplemented with efforts to organize the public in military-dominated institutions as well as neighborhood organizations, worker communities, and cooperatives while directly disbanding or weakening interest groups representing the business community (Palmer 1996, p .209; Conaghan and Malloy 1994, pp. 77–8). Import-substitution industrialization policies were promoted, an ambitious land reform program was implemented, foreign firms[14] were expropriated, and the state sector entered into direct ownership of certain industries while the U.S. military mission was expelled in 1969 (Schneider 2007, p. 344; Clayton 1999, p. 254).

However, this nationalist and developmentalist focus was not supported by all in the armed forces, as other sectors existed that were sympathetic with market-based solutions and the demobilization of civil society, as well as maintaining good relations with the United States (Schneider 2007, p. 344). While the economy was growing, the nationalist/state developmentalist policies of Velasco maintained popular support, but with oil price hikes in 1973 and increasing foreign debt, as well as the failure by Velasco to consolidate his control over the state and maintain military unity (in part because of his own illness), greater opposition within the military and civil society emerged. In 1975 the Velasco government would ultimately be removed from power by a more conservative faction, led by General Francisco Morales Bermúdez, who directed the transition to democracy through an alliance with traditional elite groups who felt their interests were better served in a democracy (Mauceri 1996; Burt 2006, p. 232). Many of the reforms of the Velasco government would be abandoned, while many military radicals would be expelled from the armed forces (Cleaves and Pease García 1986, p. 336).

1980–90, Democratic Transition and Insurgency

The second administration of Fernando Belaunde (1980–5) and Alan García's first administration (1985–90) were buffeted by unprecedented levels of economic and political instability. The region-wide debt crisis and declines in the price of Peru's central exports led to increasing levels of foreign debt and inflation. These economic problems required the government to turn to the IMF for financing and accept neoliberal conditions for these funds. Belaúnde would only implement some of these reforms, ending the loan agreement with the IMF. In addition, on May 18, 1980, the Shining Path began its "people's war" against the Peruvian state in its goal of establishing a peasant revolutionary state (Palmer 1996, pp. 210–11). By 1985 the guerrilla group Tupac Amaru Revolutionary Movement (MRTA) had also emerged. The failure of the military's reformist project as well as the belief that a "proletarian revolution" was imminent contributed to the emergence of these armed actors. By 1985 more than 6,000 people had been killed in the political violence and over $1 billion in property damage had occurred (Schneider 2007, p. 465; Palmer 1996, p. 211).

The state's internal war with these guerrilla groups in the 1980s and 1990s influenced civil–military relations in significant ways. The military commander of Ayacucho, General Adrián Huamán, was dismissed from the armed forces in August of 1984 because he publicly expressed his concern that the government was not doing enough to address the developmentalist sources of the insurgency and relying too heavily upon military repression (Burt 2007, 60). Enrique Obando posits that the internal war had the effect of pushing the military ideologically to the right and weakening those nationalist/state developmentalist sectors within the military. Obando concludes that "by the end of the Belaúnde administration [1980–5], the surviving *velasquistas* clearly constituted a minority within the increasingly conservative Armed Forces" (1998a, p. 387). For example, during the Belaunde administration when General Adrián Huamán proposed greater economic and social support to complement military repression in the war against the Shining Path he was replaced by a general "...supportive of a purely military solution" (Obando 1994, p. 109). While the Belaúnde government did establish the constitutional requirement that Congress needed to ratify the promotions of generals and admirals, as well as weakened the military's intelligence gathering system, it allowed the military extensive autonomy over its military budgets and the counterinsurgency war (Obando 1994, pp. 108–9). The military created special zones where it effectively governed on a regional level and, as in Ayacucho, carried out a "dirty war" against its inhabitants (Obando 1994, p. 110).

The military's autonomy in the counterinsurgency war, in part, contributed to the weakening of Peru's civil society, which was also weakened by the actions of the Shining Path. The Shining Path regularly and deliberately targeted social movements that potentially could act as alternatives to their armed struggle and potentially undermine their justification for insurrection, engaging in a campaign of terror to displace competing popular peasant and union movements (Oxhorn 2006, p. 71; Instituto de defensa legal 1990, p. 173). According to Peru's "Truth and Reconciliation Commission" the Shining Path was responsible for 54 percent of the approximately 69,000 people (mainly civilians) who died or disappeared between 1980 and 2000, while state and para-state agents were responsible for 37 percent of the total people who died or disappeared (BBC 2003; Amnesty International 2004). Furthermore, the weakness of civil society in Peru was exacerbated by the absolute economic crisis that the country faced in the late 1980s during the Alan García administration (1985–90).

Alan García, representing APRA, promoted a nationalistic message to pull Peru out of its economic problems. He limited repayments on the international debt in an effort to restart the economy, which did grow in the first two years of his government, but the failure of his bank nationalization drive as well as the suspension of all foreign debt repayments brought disaster to the economy. García's policies led to the collapse of foreign investment/loans and runaway hyperinflation of over 7,000 percent in 1990. At the same time the internal war continued, with casualties exceeding 20,000 and damages of $14 billion by the end of his administration.

This economic crisis also affected the armed forces. Adequate budgets for military operations increasingly became difficult in this economic environment, undermining military morale and support for García. The armed forces would increasingly lose the ability to pressure for military budgets that they supported. On average, military spending represented 2.4 percent of GDP during his government, down from 4.19 percent in the previous government. This erosion of budgetary prerogatives would continue in the neoliberal regime of Alberto Fujimori (Hunter 1997b, p. 469; Obando 1994, pp. 111, 119). In addition, García worked to co-opt the military leadership during his tenure, promoting and financially supporting those officers who were personally loyal him (Obando 1998b, p. 193). García also created a new Ministry of Defense, combining the different service ministries with the National Secretariat of Defense and the Joint Chiefs of Staff in order to more effectively ensure the political loyalty of the armed forces to García, not as "a technical measure to rationalize the defense structure" (Obando 1994, p. 112). However, the change to the establishment of the defense ministry was only a small step in furthering civilian control.[15] His government also expanded the number of special military zones in the country, thus granting the military greater autonomy on a regional/ local level, especially in areas where the Shining Path had killed or driven off previously existing civilian authorities (Obando 1994, p. 112). The military utilized its autonomy to establish and expand rural peasant patrols (*rondas campesinas*) that were established in these zones of military control to supplement the armed forces in providing security and obtaining intelligence. They would increase from 200 in 1984 to more than 4,000 in 1993 as increasingly peasants turned to these organizations in rejecting the terror of the Shining Path (Masterson 1996, p. 421). The continuing insurgent war, the economic crisis, and García's personal politicization of the military contributed to greater dissension within the ranks, which was concretely represented in a series of coup rumors and plans that emerged in García's last year (1989) among junior officers and officers in the high command (Obando 1998a, p. 393). One plot, initiated by sectors of the high command, involved the development of an elaborate governing strategy that called for an authoritarian order to bring stability to Peru and a series of economic/ political reforms aimed at transforming the state in a neoliberal direction (Obando 1998a, p. 394; Rospigliosi 1999, pp. 440–5).

The plan referred to as *El Libro Verde* or *Plan Verde*, represented the "adaptation of military thinking to the liberalized market economy" by promoting the privatization of state-owned assets and a reduction of state regulation over the economy (Obando 1998b, p. 197). Rospigliosi concludes that the military planners enjoyed connections with the business community, arguing that the business community ". . . probably provided the economic ideas which they agreed with, the necessity of a liberal economic program as well as the installment of an authoritarian government which would impose order" (2000, p. 82). However, these coup plots and plans never materialized into actual coup attempts, in part because of the opposition of the U.S. ambassador *and* the expectation that a neoliberal candidate would win the 1990 election (Mauceri 1996, p. 70; Rospigliosi 2000, p. 83). In 1990 U.S. Ambassador Alexander Watson advised members of Peru's high command not to implement coup plans against President García, warning of U.S. sanctions and international isolation (Rospigliosi 1999, p. 438). In addition, the neoliberal candidate Mario Vargas Llosa was expected to win the 1990 presidential election, but he lost to Alberto Fujimori, who was also supportive of the market direction proposed in *Plan Verde*.

The Government of Alberto Fujimori, 1990–2000

Alberto Fujimori convincingly won the 1990 presidential election and would soon embrace neoliberal economic strategies early in his administration. Pre-inaugural meetings between Fujimori and the International Monetary Fund and the World Bank played a role, convincing Fujimori that neoliberal austerity measures were necessary (Dietz 1992, p. 252). Fujimori's central advisor, Vladimir Montesinos, a retired military officer, was sympathetic to the opening of Peru's economy and was made aware of the *Plan Verde* program in the early days of the government (Rospigliosi 2000, p. 84). Rospigliosi concludes that "itisn't clear if Montesinos made Fujimori immediately aware of this plan or not, but it seems that an understanding was established between Fujimori, Montesinos and some of the military officers that participated in the coup plan prior to July 28, 1990, the date that Fujimori assumed the presidency" (2000, p. 84). Within the first month of Fujimori's presidency he embarked upon a series of austerity measures to bring down inflation and reduce the fiscal deficit in the hopes of pleasing international financial institutions and improve Peru's access to international credit. Fujimori appointed neoliberal technocrats to key economic positions and enjoyed the support of much of Peru's domestic business elite that embraced Fujimori's privatization measures and deregulatory policies (Burt 2007, 163–164). Trade liberalization policies and reductions of labor rights would all be implemented in the following years.

Fujimori and Montesinos effectively "co-opted" the armed forces by rewarding those officers loyal to Fujimori and Montesinos through promotions, leading to a split between Fujimorista officers and "institutionalists" that resisted this co-optation. These differences were disconnected from the policy or economic strategies pursued by Fujimori and focused more upon the negative consequences to professionalism of such politicization (Obando 1998a, p. 398). However, Fujimori went further in extending civilian influence over the military with a series of decree laws in 1991 that eroded military prerogatives.

Decree law 752 ended the traditional promotion system, which required the changing of the senior leadership on a yearly basis, to a system in which the president had the power to nominate the commanders of the various branches of the armed forces, who would not have to retire after thirty-five years of active service, infringing upon the military's prerogative to manage the promotion process. Decree law 746 effectively unified the country's main intelligence services under the control of the National Intelligence Service (SIN), led by Montesinos, who was required to report directly to the president (Fujimori on Trial 2008; María Vidal 1993, pp. 64–6). These measures were developed by civilian presidential advisors working at SIN and not by the military (Obando 1994, p. 113). Montesinos effectively utilized his control over the state's intelligence service to monitor and oversee the armed forces to ensure that his control was maintained and that any efforts to challenge Fujimori would be squashed (Rospigliosi 2000). This included a November 1992 coup plot against Fujimori organized by officers angered by Fujimori and Montesinos's manipulation of promotions and resistance to increasing salaries for military officers (U.S. Department of Defense 1992). Finally, for the first time in the conflict, in June 1991, the civilian government designed a national counterinsurgency strategy, eroding the military's prerogative over determining such strategies (Obando 1994, p. 113). The reduction of military prerogatives on a national level was viewed as possibly helping "... to bring the armed forces under civilian control" (Obando 1994, p. 121).

Fujimori's Autogolpe and Global Democracy Promotion

In April 1992 Fujimori, with the support of the military and a majority of the public, closed the Peruvian congress and the judiciary and began to rule by decree. Frustrated with a more assertive congress and its opposition on human rights issues as well as economic reform, Fujimori felt this drastic action necessary. He passed a series of decrees that granted greater counterinsurgency powers to the military but under the tighter direction of Fujimori and his advisors, concentrating power in the executive and the armed forces. However, Fujimori and his supporters underestimated the extent of international reaction (Obando 1992, p. 99).

The United States suspended $30 million in economic aid and $15 million in military assistance that had not been allocated from the 1991 foreign aid budget, while an additional $275 million in aid requested for Peru for 1992 was placed under review (Goshko 1992a). Approximately thirty U.S. Green Berets who had been training Peruvian army units in antinarcotics field operations were withdrawn in order to express U.S. opposition to the "self-coup" (Goshko 1992b). Finally, the U.S. publicly opposed the approval of international credit for Peru until Fujimori re-established the democratic institutions that he had absolved (McClintock and Valles 2003). The decisions on loans from the World

Bank, the IMF, and USAID were postponed in part due to U.S. opposition to the self-coup (Graham 1994, p. 8).

After Fujimori's *autogolpe* the Organization of American States (OAS) passed a resolution demanding the restoration of democratic institutions in Peru, which supplemented U.S. pressures. Fujimori was given an ultimatum to begin the process of restoring Peru back toward a democratic direction by May 23, 1992, or face economic sanctions (*The New York Times* 1992). Ultimately international pressure from the United States and the OAS required Fujimori to attend an OAS meeting in Barbados in May 1992, where he agreed to take a set of specific steps to reinstate democracy. These steps included the electoral supervision of the Peruvian elections by the OAS (Santa Cruz 2007, p. 148). The international condemnation of Fujimori's decision was central to facilitating the relatively quick return to electoral competition and re-establishment of the Congress, however weak the level of competition or the power held by Peru's legislative branch.

Power remained concentrated in the executive branch after the re-institution of democratic institutions. While some progress was achieved in reducing certain military prerogatives the military's autonomy on a local and regional level was expanded. In both the García and Fujimori governments, the military was granted the autonomy and independence on a regional/local level to fight the government's internal war and re-establish public order while infringing upon constitutional rights/liberties. The military's "emergency zones" would ultimately cover most of Peru's territory and half the country's population (Treaster 1989). In addition, the Fujimori administration actively promoted the use of *Rondas Campesinas*, rural militias that worked with governmental security forces in disrupting the operations of the Shining Path in the countryside. These *Rondas* were placed under the direct control of the armed forces, expanding the ability of the government to monitor and control the civilian population. Finally, the military would be used by the Fujimori administration in its political campaigns, with members of the armed forces actively campaigning for Fujimori in 2000, including the spraying of pro-Fujimori graffiti and signaling to the country that Fujimori was the candidate of "stability." This included the dismissal of two regional commanders who were unable to prevent anti-Fujimori protests in their area of operations in April 2000 (U.S. Embassy in Peru 2000).

Civilian authorities also initiated other repressive institutions. For example, in 1991 the Fujimori administration (1990–2000) created a specialized squad of military and intelligence officers, the Colina

Group, which was created to "eliminate" suspected terrorists (Human Rights Watch 2006).[16] The group was headed by Montesinos and participated in various massacres against the civilian population between 1991 and 1994. According to Burt and Youngers "Fujimori *redefined* the national counter-insurgency strategy...a formal public strategy that claimed to respect human rights was put in place, together with a parallel, clandestine strategy designed to violently eliminate suspected subversives" (2010, 7, *emphasis mine*). In 1995 Fujimori successfully promoted and implemented an amnesty law, which ended all judicial proceedings against military and police officials accused of human rights violations (Rochabrun 1996). This was coupled by the state's extensive use of "anti-terrorism" legislation against a variety of organizations that were critical of the political and economic direction of the Fujimori administration (Burt 2004, pp. 262–8).[17] In the early 1990s Fujimori's administration maintained a "crackdown" against leftist dissidents and, according to the government, "terrorist sympathizers" and "apologists," including some community leaders who had opposed the Shining Path. Hundreds of Peruvians with no links to the guerrilla movements were arrested and sentenced to long prison terms (Constable 1992; Burt 2007, 177). The continuing violence of the internal war and Peru's economic crisis led social movements to increasingly focus upon self-help (such as communal soup kitchens) and self-defense efforts, as opposed to oppositional efforts against Fujimori's neoliberal project (Avritzer 2006, pp. 43–7).

U.S. influence upon Peru's human rights situation and in promoting democratic civil-military relations was a mixed one. Between 1990 and 2003 the National Endowment for Democracy (NED) committed almost $1 million to Peruvian organizations that were focused on developing "democratic" civil-military relations in the country (through conferences, meetings between the military high command and politicians, and academic studies), approximately 18 percent of total NED funding for this period (NED 2006). For example, the Peruvian Political and Strategic Studies Institute was granted $89,000 in 2002 to "conduct seminars to train civilian members of congress, the defense ministry, and political parties in military and strategic issues" (NED 2006). As early as 1992 Peruvian military officials sought the aid of the U.S. Southern Command in their effort to integrate human rights and the law of armed conflict training into their military, which ultimately led to the establishment of various human rights training handbooks that were integrated into the training of soldiers and police officers (Addicott and Warner 1994). This was more than likely a response to the delays in U.S. funding for the Peruvian military because of allegations of human rights abuses and corruption by the military (Isikoff 1992). Finally, Palmer finds a correlation between substantial declines in human rights violations (though not their elimination) by the Peruvian military in the early 1990s with attempts by the Peruvian government to obtain U.S. military assistance (Palmer 1994, p. 134).

In response to international pressures on human rights, the Fujimori administration even passed a law that criminalized torture by civil servants and public officials (including the military) (Amnesty International 1999). By 1999, with the decline in the intensity of the conflict, the government had reduced the extent of its emergency zones to only about 6 percent of the country in which 5 percent of the population lived, with security services under the "effective control" of civilian authorities (U.S. State Department 2000). However, despite the various international pressures for greater human rights protections, the CIA and the U.S. State Department provided funds throughout the 1990s to Montesinos and his intelligence agency (SIN), who were central to numerous human rights violations. (Youngers 2004, p. 138).[18] In fact, both Montesinos and Fujimori would be convicted for human rights crimes, with Fujimori receiving a twenty-five-year prison sentence in 2009 for his role in forming the military death squad the Colina Group (Romero 2009). Like in Colombia, U.S. commitment to upholding democracy and human rights was often inconsistent and symbolic. However, the maintenance of an internal security and repressive role for the military was, and is consistent with, the functioning of low-intensity democracies.

Low-Intensity Democracy and Civil-Military Reforms, 2000–10

The Fujimori and Montesinos alliance would ultimately be removed by domestic and international pressure in response to the publicized links between drug traffickers and Montesinos, Montesinos's direct bribing of congressional officials, and Fujimori's illegal attempt to maintain power through fraudulent elections in 2000. These and other corruption scandals motivated an increasingly assertive democratization movement that sought the removal of Fujimori from power. The weakening of the Shining Path and reduction of terrorist actions created greater space for opposition groups to organize and mobilize their supporters against Fujimori's regime, though not necessarily in opposition to neoliberalism (Burt 2007, 232–3). In November 2000 Fujimori was determined to be "unfit" to be president by the congress, which elected

Valentín Paniagua to be interim president. Paniagua, a supporter of neoliberalism, appointed a number of modernizing technocrats to his cabinet and continued Fujimori's neoliberal agenda (BBC Summary of World Broadcasts 2000b). By 1997 extensive neoliberal progress had been achieved, including in privatizations (more than 180 state holdings were privatized between 1990 and 1998), the elimination of capital controls on foreign investment, the expansion of tax collections, and the substantial reduction of tariff barriers (from 60 percent under the García government to 16 percent in 1996). According to the U.S. State Department the economic stabilization and liberalization programs of the 1990s led to Peru having "...the most open investment regime in the world," attracting $10 billion in foreign direct investment between 1992 and 2001 (U.S. State Department 2005). These economic policies also directly undermined military involvement in development and state companies, reducing their prerogative over economic concerns (phone interview with Captain Juan Carlos Llosa Pazzos, head of the office of information for the Peruvian Joint Command of the Armed Forces, 10/21/08).

Paniagua oversaw the transition to new elections in the spring of 2001, but in his short time he removed all of the generals from the same graduating class of Montesinos and sought greater financial transparency in military budgets, requiring that all income produced by the military be deposited directly into the Central Bank rather than into military accounts (Selmeski 2002, p. 8; *Latin American Weekly Report* 2000). The Alejandro Toledo administration (2001–6) maintained and built upon Fujimori's and Paniagua's progress in civil-military relations and economic reforms. Toledo, a former World Bank economist and a researcher in the field of international development at the Harvard Institute for International Development, was a strong advocate of free markets and the modernization of the state.

In 2001 Toledo appointed the first civilian minister of defense in Peru's history and retired more than 1,000 army, navy, and air force officials from the military and from the National Intelligence Service,[19] in part to remove those actors sympathetic with Fujimori (Lama 2001). Within the first year of his administration Toledo replaced the National Intelligence Service with the National Intelligence Council (CNI), though he would disband this agency in 2004 due to the continuing presence of Montesinos supporters within it (Notisur 2004). The agency was led by a series of civilians between 2001 and 2004 with several of them tied to the political use of intelligence or corruption (Ibid). In 2005 the Peruvian congress approved the creation of the National

Directorate of Intelligence (DINI) providing the congress and the Supreme Court with some oversight and potential control over intelligence, while leaving most responsibility in the hands of the armed forces (Weeks 2008, pp. 55–6).

In October 2001 Toledo created a new commission to draw up plans for restructuring the army and expanding greater civilian authority over the armed forces. The commission was presided over by Prime Minister Roberto Danino. Danino was a corporate attorney with the Washington law firm Wilmer, Cutler, and Pickering and a strong free-market advocate, someone who was "...close to many influential U.S. political and financial leaders" (Jaime Cisneros 2001). Toledo's first civilian defense ministers were David Waisman (2001–2) and Aurelio Loret de Mola (2002–3), businessmen and members of Danino's defense reform committee (Jaime Cisneros 2001; *Latin American Weekly Report* 2002). According to the vice-minister of administration and economics within the defense ministry in the Toledo administration, Luis Alberto Otárola Peñaranda, who was a special advisor to the reform commission, Peru's military reforms were influenced by the regional commitment to democracy as well as the conclusions of a conference of Latin American defense ministers, who agreed to the "indisoluble relación entre seguridad nacional y democracia" (Otárola Peñaranda 2003, p. 174).

The reforms that emerged from Danino's commission as well as from the political commitment of Toledo himself to reform the armed forces included the passage of the Defense Ministry Law (Ley #27860 on Nov. 12, 2002), which stipulated that the defense ministry be the body to formulate, execute, and supervise national defense policy (Otárola Peñaranda 2003, p. 175). In addition, Toledo's administration established mechanisms for the publication and transparent review of the military's budget, allowing the public full access to military expenditures, a first in Peru's history (Otárola Peñaranda 2003, p. 177). Toledo proceeded to cut the defense budget by 15 percent to pay for antipoverty programs and also cut the budget of the National Intelligence Service (*Washington Post*, June 13, 2002: p. A34; *The Economist* 2003). This was also in keeping with the letter of intent signed by the Peruvian government in 2002 pledging to the IMF that it would hold its budget deficit to 1.9 percent in 2002 and 1.4 percent in 2003 (Obando 2006, p. 193). Finally, as a part of Toledo's reform effort, the Center for International Human Rights was established in July 2002 within the Joint-Command of the Armed Forces to promote the formation, investigation, and diffusion of international human rights law throughout the armed forces (Obando 2006, p. 178).

The progress achieved in the Toledo administration in reducing military prerogatives was in line with the various programs and assistance promoted by the United States. Of the thirty-two countries that received U.S. international military education training (a program dedicated to advancing military professionalism) in the Western Hemisphere between 2000 and 2006, Colombia and Peru ranked #1 and #9, respectively (and #1 and #4 for South America) (Center for International Policy 2006a). The human rights conditions on this assistance were supplemented by the civil-military relations work of the USAID and the Office of Transition Initiatives (OTI). In 2000–1 the USAID provided training and technical assistance for the Peruvian congress to improve its decision making on defense issues as well as fund programs to increase communication between civilian and military groups. USAID also financed projects in Peru to increase the understanding of military policy by civil society groups in order to support a more effective voice for reform (USAID 2005).

This was related to the goals of the USAID "Transitions Initiatives" office, which was established in Peru in 2001 to support/facilitate the democratic opening that took place with the resignation of President Fujimori. One of the five key areas that this office is dedicated to is increasing civilian oversight of the military and improving overall civil-military relations. Between 2001 and 2003 the OTI dedicated $850,000 toward fifty specific civil military projects, which led to the training of more than 7,000 civilians in security matters, and a series of civil-military dialogues. Almost 1,000 active members of the military also participated in these civil-military dialogues. USAID found that these programs had a "major impact" upon civilian-military matters, particularly in increasing new civilian interlocutors on security affairs, as well as in contributing to congressional debates on defense-related laws and easing overall tension between civilian and military actors (USAID 2003, p. 9). The trend in USAID and NED assistance is consistent with the overall direction of U.S. economic and military assistance, as Peru was second only to Colombia in receiving U.S. economic and military aid in Latin America between 1995 and 2004 (USAID 2008). However, this U.S. focus upon democratic civil-military relations has not eliminated the emergence of "radical populists" from within the Peruvian armed forces.

With the Shining Path reduced to pockets of any type of military presence in the 2000s, space for civil society has clearly widened, with major demonstrations and strikes erupting in May and June of 2003, leading to President Toledo calling a state of emergency, banning strikes and protests for thirty days. The protests included teachers striking for raises, workers opposing the privatization of utility companies, and farmers seeking greater governmental protection from imports (Freedom House Report 2004; Schulte 2003). The 2006 presidential candidacy of Ollanta Humala, a former army officer at the head of a nationalist and antineoliberal political movement, illustrated the degree to which nationalist/populist factions continue to exist within or emerge from the Peruvian armed forces (Bigwood 2006). During the campaign Humala expressed admiration for Velascos's military regime and promised to expand state involvement in the economy, increase taxes on foreign investors, and prioritize Peruvian companies with governmental credit and assistance (Hayes 2006). In October 2000, he had engaged in a small and short military rebellion against Fujimori, made up of seventy soldiers and that lasted two weeks (Sánchez 2006a). This rebellion was centered upon corruption in the Fujimori administration, in particular the close ties between certain military officers and Montesinos. His brother, Antauro Humala, led 170 ultra-nationalist followers in his own military rebellion against President Toledo in January 2005, in which he demanded the resignation of Toledo and the defense minister. Humala accused Toledo of corruption, condemning the promotions of generals with ties to Fujimori and Montesinos as well as "selling out Peru to Chilean interests" and foreign capital in general (*Peruvian Times* 2008; Zelaya 2005; *Weekly News Update of the Americas* 2005). Prior to this rebellion Antauro Humala had been involved in political organizing around a nationalist/populist project (etnocacerismo), which enjoyed important support from military reservists and former soldiers. The movement viewed the revolutionary government of Velasco in the 1970s as a model, stressing its efforts at promoting Peru's economic and social development while maintaining an anti-U.S./anti-imperialist perspective (Humala 2001, pp. 330–5). Both rebellions by the Humala brothers failed, but they laid the basis for Ollanta Humala's presidential run in 2006 on a nationalist and anticorruption platform, which described his movement as "anti-imperialist, and [...does] not accept the notion and imposition of a unipolar world" (as quoted in Sánchez 2006a)

While Ollanta Humala's politics struck a chord with many Peruvians, his support from the military seemed minimal. In a 2005 speech by General Paul Da Silva, commander of the seventh infantry brigade in the northern city of Lambayeque, he declared that someone who led a rebellion against the government cannot be elected president, a sentiment that other military leaders shared. Institutional discipline and unity were considered important, and Ollanta Humala had clearly violated these norms. This focus upon institutional professionalism was illustrated by the opinions of Captain Juan Carlos Llosa Pazzos, head of the office of information for the Joint Command of the Armed Forces, who dismissed the extent to which Humala represented a faction within the military (phone interview, 10/21/08), though others argued that he did enjoy strong support within the military (see McClintock 2006, p. 100). Ultimately, Humala would narrowly lose the 2006 presidential election to Alan García.

The second government of Alan García (2006–11) has continued the trend set by Toledo, appointing civilian ministers of defense who have been tied to globalist/neoliberal agendas. This is in keeping with the government's commitment to following a free market model, claiming Chile as his country's model for success (Hearn 2006, p. A13). For example, Allan Wagner was appointed defense minister in 2007, an individual who had represented Peru in trade negotiations, on the Latin American Free Trade Association, and as secretary general of the Andean Community (International IDEA 2005). During his time as defense minister Wagner attempted to increase the level of transparency in military spending and budgeting (Vivas 2008). His successor, Ántero Flores Aráoz, considered himself to be nonideological, arguing that "I am a social Christian. Rightists, leftists have passed out of fashion. In a globalized world what is important is efficiency" (Rosales Ferreyros 2007). Efficiency and a less influential military were illustrated by the García government's willingness to pursue investigations or prosecutions of about 700 members of the armed forces for crimes committed during the internal war in the 1980s and 1990s (Reuters 2008).

While the government continued its modernizing direction, the armed forces continued to address an internal security threat and engage in repressive practices against the civilian population. The resurgence of remnants of the Shining Path in the Apurimac Valley and in the Valle del Río Mantaro have resulted in the displacement of peasant communities and accusations against the military for abuses against the population, including beatings and death threats (Navarro 2008). According to International Crisis Group, in November 2007, in response to an increase in coca cultivation and Shining Path activities, the president of the Council of Ministers Jorge del Castillo proposed an increase in the security forces budget and the re-opening of military bases in the Amazon "...to fight terrorism and insurgents" (2008, p. 22).

While the Shining Path continues to fight, it bears little resemblance to the internal security threat that it was, and social movements that had been targeted by this group in the past are re-emerging. For example, in 2008 Peru's indigenous organizations met to discuss a political model that would allow them to compete nationally for the 2011 presidential elections. With an indigenous population that makes up 45 percent of the country's population, the hope is that an indigenous leader like Evo Morales in Bolivia could be supported who would promote the recognition of the country's ethnic diversity as well as allow greater political/economic autonomy over indigenous territories (Salazar 2008). These groups have also been associated with antiglobalization struggles. In June 2009 the government was implicated in the deaths of more than forty individuals after García sent in the security forces to suppress a protest launched by indigenous communities resisting oil exploration by foreign companies in their Amazonian communities, protests that García associated with terrorist threats. The government ultimately rescinded the laws in the face of societal pressure as well as the political pressures of Humala's nationalist party, which demanded changes in the law and the end to governmental repression of the indigenous activists (*Peruvian Times* 2009). The use of repression in this case complemented governmental and corporate spying on nongovernmental organizations viewed as "anti-establishment," including groups that promote human rights or wage struggles against mining companies (Páez 2009). This included the use of private security firms to spy upon "ALBA Houses," which are social centers providing basic needs in poor areas and that receive some funding from the Venezuelan government (Ibid).

The continual survival of an internal security threat has allowed for the maintenance of a counterinsurgency mission, mitigating, but not eliminating, the emergence of developmentalist/populist orientation within the military, while civilian authorities utilize security forces to target groups resisting capitalist globalization (Navarro 2008). The maintenance of civilian political control and the erosion of military prerogatives in Peru were the result of an interaction between global democracy promotion initiatives, the existence of internal security threats, and the pursuit of market reform and political liberalization by different neoliberal governments that steadily eroded military prerogatives over the defense ministry, national intelligence, military budgets, oversight of human rights policy, and national security strategies.

Conclusion

Civilian authorities effectively maintained political control and eroded the military's powers and influence despite the existence of serious internal security threats to the state. The existence of internal security threats in Colombia and Peru contributed to creating a policy space for the erosion of military prerogatives. These internal wars provided (and continue to provide) the justification for the weakening of their respective civil societies while marginalizing those sectors of the military interested in state developmentalist/populist strategies of governance. The erosion of military prerogatives over budgets or national security strategies by neoliberal policy coalitions has been reinforced by the international legitimacy they enjoyed with the United States, intergovernmental organizations, and international financial institutions that seek the establishment of market or low-intensity democracies in the Western Hemisphere. The existence of internal security threats in the context of the global dissemination of market or low-intensity democracies and the ascendance to national power of neoliberal policy coalitions were instrumental to an overall decline in military prerogatives.

CHAPTER 3

"Radical Populists" and Military Prerogatives in Venezuela and Ecuador

That is not democracy, but corruption. If democracy leaves 90 percent of Ecuadorians in total poverty, then we are against democracy. But we believe in democracy ; we know that democracy was born as an ideal in opposition to absolutism, inequality, injustice and oppression.

—Ecuadorian colonel
Lucio Gutiérrez (Gutiérrez 2001, p. 164)

As Chapter 2 illustrated, civilian authorities in Colombia and Peru maintained political control over the military and even reduced military prerogatives (the appointment of civilian defense ministers and greater control over military budgets and domestic intelligence agencies) despite the existence of severe internal security threats, weak states, and party de-institutionalization. In contrast, Venezuela and Ecuador have regularly failed to meet the criteria of civilian control since 1990. During the 1990s and 2000s Ecuador has had seven presidents, with three removed either by direct military intervention through a coup (President Mahuad in 2000) or in part because of the withdrawal of military support for the president (Bucaram in 1997 and Gutiérrez in 2005). In addition, the military maintains control over various state companies (military and nonmilitary related) as well as a significant role in economic and national development (Selmeski 2002, p. 1). In the case of Venezuela there has been one briefly successful military coup (2002) and two coup attempts (both in 1992). The government is presently being led by one of the 1992 coup leaders, Hugo Chávez, who has gone far in militarizing Venezuelan politics through governmental appointments of military officers and the expansion of their social/ economic responsibilities since he was first elected president in 1998. Military coups and coup attempts, as well as the establishment or continuation of economic/social development roles for the military far outside traditional security missions, have been a part of civil-military relations in the two countries since the late 1980s. Military prerogatives in both countries have been maintained at high levels or substantially expanded. What has prevented Ecuador and Venezuela from reducing military prerogatives as other Andean nations have done? Can this failure be solely attributed to institutional/doctrinal factors within the military or even societal factors *within* these nation-states? Is there a relationship between the lack of civil-military reforms and the failure of neoliberal policy coalitions to establish or maintain their hegemony?

In these two cases, popular and military resistance to neoliberal/globalist policy coalitions and their economic agendas have not only forestalled economic reform, but have created the political opportunity for counterhegemonic projects. Nationalist and reformist factions within the military often allied or supported this resistance through attempted military coups, public critiques of neoliberal economic policies, and/or directly running for elected office. The lack of internal security threats have not only created greater political space for anticapitalist globalization movements in civil society, but also have given legitimacy to alternative developmentalist/nationalist missions within the armed forces. Finally, the resistance to neoliberal/globalist policy coalitions has also led to the disruption of international measures and strategies to create low-intensity democracies in Ecuador and Venezuela.

The following examines the emergence of nationalist/populist military factions and their influence in specific policy coalitions, international influences underlying the push for civilian control/democracy, and the conflict between nationalist/populist coalitions and neoliberal policy coalitions within the two countries. My analysis focuses primarily on the period in which neoliberal policy coalitions attempted to establish their political/economic models as well as the nationalist/populist response to this effort (1989–present in Venezuela and 1984–present in Ecuador).

Ecuador

Military Rule and Reform, 1972–9

For most of the twentieth century Ecuador's military has directly governed and/or arbitrated between competing political factions with ties to economic elites based in the coastal city of Guayaquil and the Andean city of Quito. The armed forces were historically led by officers allied with a landowning oligarchy in the Sierra, often intervening to prevent social or progressive change in Ecuador's economic relations or its political system (Pineo 2007, p. 140). However, there were exceptions in which the military played a reformist role, with the 1970s military regime being the most prominent. The United States largely supported a conservative role for the military in the decades following World War II, supporting the military regime that came to power in 1963 with intensive counterinsurgency training and military aid while actively working to undermine the development of influential Socialist or Communist parties and leftist unions within Ecuador (Pineo 2007, pp. 170–1).[1] According to Pineo, "in the cold war years Ecuador grew more dependent on the United States, making it Ecuador's sole supplier of weapons and military supplies—even the lubricants used by the Ecuadorian armed forces had to be purchased through the Pentagon" (2007, p. 170). Despite these close ties with the United States and conservative landowning interests, there did exist factions within the Ecuadorian military concerned about the corruption and inefficient behavior of Ecuador's political elite. They strongly believed that social reform was necessary for Ecuador's national security.

In the decades that followed World War II, efforts to promote economic development and social reform were often frustrated by the opposition of landed elites, exporters, and bankers (North 2004, pp. 187–188). The military reformists that came to power in February 1972 aimed to rectify this decades-long failure with a military coup that prevented the coming to power of political figures viewed as dishonest and corrupt. The military regime began its tenure in the midst of an oil boom and attempted to use these resources to promote land reform and modernize the economy along nationalist/statist lines. According to J. Samuel Fitch during the 1970s many officers[2] supported a broad view of national security, one that included the "...country's economic base, popular morale, international alliances, and the quality of national leadership" (1986, p. 156). The leader of the 1972 coup, General Guillermo Rodríguez Lara, referred to this process as "revolutionary nationalism" (Rivera Vélez and Ramírez Gallegos 2005, p. 124). This included the creation of state-run companies, often run directly by the armed forces, as part of an effort to replace foreign-produced goods and services with nationally produced goods and services. The state expanded its role in industries such as the telephone service, airlines, tourism, hotels, and steel (Pineo 2007, p. 181). In addition, the government joined the Organization of the Petroleum Exporting Countries (OPEC) in solidarity with other oil-exporting countries, leading to a suspension of U.S. military aid (Rouquié 1987, p. 328). The regime increased taxes and regulations on foreign oil companies while increasing state royalties on exports (Pineo 2007, p. 181). In 1973 the military government created a Directorate of Industries, which according to an army spokesman, required that the armed forces "...contributed to the socioeconomic development of the country, creating organisms which will promote, organize and administer basic industries,...through owned enterprises or through associations with the private sector" (as quoted in Martz 1987, p. 99). Between 1972 and 1976 the state sector's contribution to GDP increased from 16 to 23 percent (Pineo 2007, p. 183).

The military's role in development took place in a regional context of military governments and state-led industrialization projects (such as the economic strategies of Brazil's military regime). The military regime of Rodríguez Lara was most especially influenced by the Velasco Alvarado military government in Peru, with Ecuadorian military leaders regularly visiting the Peruvian regime for assistance and advice (Pineo 2007, p. 179). Within Ecuador the discovery of large deposits of oil in the Amazonian interior provided the state access to the resources necessary to carry out these proposals (Martz 1987, p. 100; Schneider 2007, p. 365). In addition, the corruption and instability generated by civilian political leaders, most especially the populist José María Velasco Ibarra, convinced the armed forces that they could outperform civilian authorities in the managing of the state.

The 1970s military regime built on earlier proposals of governments in the 1950s and 1960s that were often short-lived due to a lack of sufficient resources. The country's executive during the first years of the military regime, General Rodríguez Lara, faced increasing pressures for greater reform and social redistribution from below and pressures from above from transnational companies and the Ecuadorian business community, which demanded greater flexibility and accessibility to the Ecuadorian state (Martz 1987, pp. 131–53). Rodríguez Lara was forced to resign in 1976 and was replaced by a military junta. His resignation speech accused imperialism of undermining Ecuador's military and that his enemies were "...instruments of pressure groups, of opportunists and pseudo-democratic empresarios, who instead of utilizing the patriotic idealism that characterized the soldier, hesitate in placing burdens on their soldiers... [instead] accusing them of all errors" (as quoted in Martz 1987, p. 152). The failure of Rodríguez Lara to build popular support for a national/developmentalist project, as well as differences over policy within the armed forces, also contributed to the failure of his reformist project (Martz 1987, p. 154). Opposition to Rodriguez Lara primarily came from older, conservative, higher-ranking officers who no longer wanted him in power, while his regime enjoyed support from younger officers (Pineo 2007, p. 185). The military junta that came to power in 1976 was made up of three service ministers who agreed upon a series of economic austerity measures[3] and began negotiations for a staged military withdrawal from power, which took place in 1979. The ultimate winner of the 1979 presidential election, Jaime Roldós Aruilera, was opposed by the military due to Roldos's family relation to the hated populist Assad Bucarám; however, under heavy U.S. pressure the military handed power to Roldós in August 1979 (Schneider 2007, pp. 366–7). The end of military rule in 1979 reflected important (and continuing) ideological divisions among the elite, with globalist/neoliberal sectors within the chamber of commerce and industry being uneasy with the expansion of state regulation under military rule and ownership, as well as their relative exclusion from economic decision makers within the state (Martz 1987, p. 213; Conaghan, Malloy, and Abugattas 1990, pp. 7–9). Conaghan and Malloy find that given the business community's frustrations with trying to influence the military regime, this sector sought ". . . a political alternative to military authoritarianism and for an economic model that embodied their . . . vision of capitalism." The return to democracy in Ecuador in 1979 was the beginning of an effort to establish a low-intensity democracy, one in which civilian authorities could modernize the economy and the state. However, this effort would be continuously frustrated by societal opposition as well as resistance from elements within the Ecuadorian armed forces.

Democratic Rule and Neoliberalism, 1979–96

After Ecuador's 1979 democratic transition, different civilian governments have generally allowed the armed forces a great deal of autonomy to determine their national security mission and administer state corporations, while Ecuador's military spending led the region as a proportion of governmental expenditures during the 1980s (Bustamante 1989, pp. 24–5). The military's autonomy and influence within Ecuador would be partially safeguarded by the its role in 1979 democratic transition (Martz 1987, pp. 212–3). The 1978 constitution required that defense ministers must be senior general officers and reduced the role of presidents in military promotions while maintaining an economic/social development role for the military and control over a number of state corporations (Bustamante 1989, p. 29; Martz 1996, pp. 333–4; Selmeski 2002, pp. 2 and 4). This democratic period would also be punctuated by the demands of Ecuadorian creditors and the International Monetary Fund, which regularly required various austerity measures in exchange for new loans so that Ecuador could service its burgeoning foreign debt,[4] a significant legacy of the military regime. Thus, Ecuador's political system obtained the civil liberties and political institutions associated with representative democracy, but economic policy was increasingly determined by international financial institutions following the 1979 transition. Not all political or social actors objected to this arrangement.

The Ecuadorian academic Fredy Rivera argues that Ecuador's democratic period of instability and socioeconomic crisis has been accompanied by "a dynamic political conflict between an internally fractured and segmented reformist pole, composed of rightist parties, houses, economic technocracies, supporting the agenda of structural adjustment promoted by the so-called Washington consensus; and a more united coalition of anti-reformists led by the indigenous movement, supported by public unions, civil organizations and leftist parties" (Rivera 2004, p. 152). In this political conflict, neoliberal/globalist policy coalitions have often wielded control over the executive branch but have been frustrated by congressional opposition, societal protests, and/or military resistance to their economic/political objectives. Democracy during this period has been viewed by some as "artificial" and "merely formalistic at best" (Martz 1998, p. 469).

The 1970s military regime illustrated the extent to which the military was not unified behind a nationalistic perspective. Within the military, pro-business/market factions (allied with their civilian supporters), as well as institutionalists with no interest in developmental issues, have all vied for influence with more revolutionary/nationalist sectors, with nationalist/leftist factions representing a smaller proportion of the military in the 2000s (Bustamante 1989, p. 29; Fitch 2005, p. 51). However, through the post-1979 period, nationalist/populist sectors of the military have periodically expressed their misgivings about corruption and specific neoliberal economic strategies while defending the military's developmentalist role (Bustamante 1999). In Fitch's examination of the Ecuadorian military journal *Revista de las Fuerzas Armadas* between 1979 and 1991 he finds strong evidence of the military supporting the belief that development and social justice are directly tied to security (Fitch 2001, pp. 73–4). In one article a "democratic-pluralist form of government" is viewed as an important way to establish peace, one "...with the full exercise of the liberty, the law, and social justice...a government that fights with social measures the subversion that has in many cases not been defeated by arms" (as quoted in Fitch 2001, p. 74).

Military programs such as health clinics, public works, establishing technical assistance for communications, and even providing legal advice are examples of certain social measures viewed as helping to maintain internal order and prevent internal armed threats (Bustamante 1999, p. 346). These programs have also been aimed at establishing and/or strengthening the allegiance of the indigenous population to the state, with many of these programs emphasizing community participation, helping to establish close relationships between these communities and the army, convincing most indigenous organizations that the army is concerned about the well-being of society (Bustamante 1999, pp. 346–7; Rivera Vélez and Ramirez Gallegos 2005, p. 133; Selmeski 2007, p. 177). Fitch concludes that "for at least portions of [the] Ecuadorian population, the armed forces have become a major provider of social services" (Fitch 2003, p. 14).[5] Beginning in the early 1990s military recruiting and training increasingly recognized and accepted Ecuador's multiculturalism, respecting indigenous culture in order to attract and co-opt these communities (Selmeski 2007, pp. 158–9).

Approximately 40 percent of Ecuador's population is indigenous, and they have been economically/socially marginalized for generations; but increasingly throughout the 1980s and 1990s, they actively sought to obtain greater respect, autonomy, and social justice for their communities through national strikes and protests. The central umbrella organization for many indigenous groups *and* the overall popular resistance to capitalist globalization has been the National Confederation of Ecuadorian Indians (CONAIE), which was founded in 1986. By 1992 CONAIE represented 70 percent of the indigenous population, uniting different indigenous federations from each province under one banner (Selverston-Scher 2001, p. 6). CONAIE's demands to the government in a major 1990 uprising included land reform, debt forgiveness, long-term financing for bilingual education, and the provision of water for indigenous communities (Selverston-Scher 2001, p. 135). CONAIE's political stance often found sympathizers among Ecuador's urban poor (indigenous and nonindigenous) and labor unions, as well as from elements within the military.

As early as 1986, General Frank Vargas Pazzos partially justified leading a military rebellion against President Leon Febres Cordero (1984–8) on the need for greater social justice. The U.S.-educated

Febres Cordero was a close ally of Ronald Reagan and former head of the Guayaquil Chamber of Industry, who supported market-based models, the strengthening of the private sector, and U.S. foreign policy in the region.[6] After signing an agreement with the IMF in 1985, he proceeded to implement a number of austerity measures, though he was often frustrated in carrying out all that the IMF requested due to opposition within Ecuador's Congress. In addition, with a drastic decline in the price of oil and a 1987 earthquake that disrupted oil production, these policies did little to reduce inflation, unemployment, or deficits (Gerlach 2003, p. 44). These economic problems were coupled with direct military challenges to his authority. He was detained by military units for two hours in January 1987, who rebelled out of loyalty to General Frank Vargas Pazzos. Vargas Pazzos had been arrested after his failed attempt to spark a military uprising in March 1986, which was driven by Vargas Pazzos's disgust with the government's privatization initiatives, governmental corruption, the politicization of promotions, the increasing presence of U.S. military advisors on Ecuadorian soil, and Vargas Pazzos's desire for a "real social democracy" (BBC Summary of World Broadcasts 1987; González Casanova 1988, p. 55). According to the Uruguayan newspaper *Brecha*, Vargas Pazzos represented a political project that was "nationalist, democratic and popular" and anti-imperialist (as quoted in González Casanova 1988, p. 56). The military protests galvanized the public opposition to Febres Cordero and strengthened the antineoliberal coalition within the Congress (Conaghan and Malloy 1994, pp. 169–71). Febres Cordero was followed by Rodrigo Borja (1988–92), who maintained a critical perspective against neoliberalism, but was required to turn to the IMF for assistance in order to address the declining price of oil. Again, he was unable to implement the level of austerity the IMF expected and the IMF withheld much of the funds Ecuador required (Gerlach 2003, p. 45). Borja was also forced to concede millions of acres in concessions to foreign oil companies in the face of declining prices, leading to major CONAIE demonstrations (Gerlach 2003, pp. 73–4).

Sixto Duran-Ballen (1992–6) was an important instigator of serious neoliberal economic reforms, but was also frustrated by his opponents. Sixto Durán-Ballen not only faced nationwide protests in opposition to his economic policies, but the military itself vetoed a privatization project involving Ecuador's national oil pipeline (Bustamante 1999, p. 345; Gerlach 2003, p. 88). In 1993 the military controlled thirty state companies, ranging from munitions factories, a bank, a travel agency, a shipyard, and a commercial airline, and was unsupportive of their privatizations (*Latin American Weekly Report* 1993). The military viewed privatization efforts, in part, as a threat to their budgetary privileges and income, while indigenous groups and unions felt that privatization would lead to higher prices and greater inequality (Gerlach 2003, p. 88). In 1998 CONAIE's views on key concepts included supporting the state's control over "strategic resources" such as petroleum, electricity, and telecommunications (in line with the opinion of nationalist/ populist factions within the military). CONAIE claimed that Ecuador's government was formed and led by a "dominating class" (CONAIE 1998). During the period between 1992 and 1996 strategic pacts and agreements in opposition to Duran's privatization drive were established between public unions and elements of the military that enjoyed a strong presence in specific "strategic" state companies (Ramírez-Gallegos 2001, pp. 356–7). Durán-Ballen would only be able to privatize a handful of state companies, far short of the 80 percent he projected at the beginning of his administration (Gerlach 2003, p. 88).

U.S. foreign policy with Ecuador during the 1980s and 1990s, like with Colombia and Peru, was guided by the notion of promoting "market democracies" internationally, but with less attention to U.S. "drug war" aims in comparison to Colombia and Peru. Ecuador's level of assistance in terms of military grants, training, or weaponry paled in comparison to what countries such as Colombia, Peru, and Bolivia received in the 1990s and 2000s, or what Central America received in the 1980s. (This was consistent with a historical trend of Ecuador being granted a low-priority status with regard to U.S. military and economic aid, with Ecuador receiving only 2 percent of total U.S. governmental loans and grants given to Latin America between 1961 and 1987 (Fitch 1993, p. 5; Pineon 2007, p. 153).

In the context of the "drug war" Ecuador was considered to be a Tier II country, primarily a transit country, and not given the priority of countries that directly produced and trafficked illegal drugs (Call 1991, p. 89). In fact, between 1989 and 2003 Ecuador and Venezuela received the lowest yearly average of U.S. military aid in the Andes, averaging about $40 million a year (Just the Facts 2008a). In relative terms U.S. military aid, military training, or economic assistance has not been substantial, allowing Ecuador's military a greater level of ideological/institutional autonomy from U.S. pressures (Fitch 1993, pp. 15 and 18–9; Bonilla 2006, p. 110). U.S. direct leverage over the Ecuadorian military has not been substantial and its record in the 1990s and 2000s in maintaining in office Ecuador's neoliberal presidents has had mixed results.

Rebellions and Reaction to the Neoliberal Agenda, 1996–2006

President Abdalá Bucaram (1996–7) sought to continue some of Durán-Ballen's policies, including the cutting of fiscal subsidies and a program of privatizations, but corruption allegations, his erratic behavior, and growing opposition from different sectors of civil society shortened his term.[7] He received little respect from the military, as he was viewed as someone with little interest or knowledge of national security, as well as extremely corrupt (Lopez Molina 2005, p. 54). In fact, the military's own reputation was being undermined, as it was indirectly involved in various kickback schemes as officers provided security for customs offices and government-sponsored charities, which were used by Bucaram to personally enrich himself and/or his allies (Pineo 2007, p. 207). On February 5, 1997, the United Workers Front scheduled nationwide strikes that were backed by CONAIE, the Coordinated Social Movements (CSM), and a variety of other groups in civil society (approximately 2 million people participated in the strike), which protested Bucaram's neoliberal economic policies and corruption (Gerlach 2003, pp. 92–4). CONAIE continued to be central to an effective anti-neoliberal coalition of public labor unions, church-based communities in popular *barrios*, and a coalition of thirty-four labor and social organizations in the *Coordinadora de Movimientos Sociales*, which joined together to resist privatization measures and promote land reform and social justice, as well as seek cultural/territorial autonomy for Ecuador's indigenous communities (Petras and Veltmeyer 2005, pp. 138–49).

The protests against Bucaram were supported by the Congress and the military high command. The military withdrew its backing of Bucaram and supported his removal by a simple majority vote in the Congress because of his alleged "mental unfitness" (International Crisis Group (ICG) 2007, p. 3; Gerlach 2003, pp. 94–106). The removal of President Abdala Bucaram by a wave of massive social protests and military opposition was not opposed by the United States, given the high level of corruption in his government, though the United States did express opposition to the succession process (Fitch 1998, p. 90; Toscano 2005, p. 118; Gerlach 2003, p. 99). In the case of Bucaram, despite U.S. opposition, the military high command endorsed the solution of Ecuadorian political elites and supported the appointment of Fabián Alarcón (the then-president of the Congress) as interim president (Gerlach 2003, pp. 102–4).

The inability of the United States to choose the successor of Bucaram reflected, in part, its continued weak leverage over the Ecuadorian military. Approximately 5 percent of Ecuador's military and police received some form of U.S. training between 1999 and 2006, in comparison to over 20 percent in both Bolivia and Colombia (Just the Facts 2008b). Ecuador received over $100 million in military aid between 1999 and 2003, which on average represented about 7 percent of Ecuador's yearly military budget (Bonilla 2006, p. 121). The average amount of military and police aid to Ecuador and Venezuela between 1997 and 1998, as well as between 2002 and 2003, was lower than what Colombia, Peru, or Bolivia received, as illustrated in Table 3.1.

The relatively distant relations with the United States and its military would partially change with the Mahuad (1998–2000) and Gutiérrez (2003–5) administrations, which sought to adapt to U.S. national security interests in exchange for U.S. economic assistance and support in Ecuador's relations with the IMF and the World Bank. Mahuad's signing of an agreement in 1999 leasing the Ecuadorian military base in Manta to the United States for a ten-year period and Gutiérrez publicly supporting the militarized "drug war" strategies of the United States were examples of these shifts (Bonilla 2006, pp. 106–7, 121). The Ecuadorian military did receive some benefits in increased training and assistance from the United States from this commitment, but there was resistance to a counternarcotics role, as well as complaints that U.S. resources were insufficient (Rivera 2004, p. 242). In the end, these closer relations with the United States would be disrupted with the removal of Mahuad and Gutiérrez from government (Bonilla 2006, pp. 104, 111).

The Jamil Mahuad administration (1998–2000) was an example of a government committed to the idea of economic reform, but Mahuad was eventually removed due to an escalating economic crisis caused by a drop in oil prices, the Asian financial crisis, and extreme weather conditions that undermined the agroexport economy.[8] The failure of the

Table 3.1   U.S. Military and Police Aid to the Andes (in millions of U.S. dollars)

	Average for 1997–8	*Average for 2002–3*
Colombia	100	488.2
Peru	37	70
Bolivia	25	50
Ecuador	7	30
Venezuela	8	5

Source: Isacson 2004, p. 47.

banking sector and the eventual governmental bailout of certain banks would be viewed by much of the population as personally enriching Mahuad and his allies (Rivera and Ramírez Gallegos 2005, p. 131). Mahuad's policies to address this crisis included attacks upon military prerogatives over budgets and training, specifically with a four-year freeze on new arms purchases; the assignment of 25 percent of the armed forces to the fight against organized crime rather than hiring more police; and training conscripts only during the weekends rather than through the week (BBC Summary of World Broadcasts 1999b). The peace agreement signed with Peru in 1998 contributed to this push for cuts in military budgets (Ramírez 2001, p. 357).

Mahuad went on to remove subsidies on domestic fuels and electricity, and placed restraints on wages—all policies implemented in the hopes of obtaining a stand-by loan of $308 million from the International Monetary Fund and ultimately attract almost $2 billion in additional foreign credit (Gerlach 2003, p. 124; *New York Times* 1999). In response to this economic crisis and austerity measures, massive strikes supported by CONAIE and labor unions were launched for ten days and twelve days in March and July of 1999, respectively, undermining Mahuad's ability to govern (International Crisis Group 2007, p. 4). Ultimately, Ecuador's economic crisis would continue throughout 1999, with an inflation rate of 60 percent and unemployment at 30 percent, and the economy would contract by 7.5 percent (*The New York Times* 2000a; Rohter 2000a). Early in January 2000 Mahuad declared that he would replace Ecuador's inflated currency with the U.S. dollar, sparking nationwide anger in response and bringing his popularity rating to 9 percent while the armed forces enjoyed a level of popularity higher than the Catholic Church (*The New York Times* 2000b; Rohter 2000b).

The military also raised concerns about Mahuad's administration. The commanding general of the armed forces, General Carlos Mendoza, feared that the government was considering the "Fujimori" option, meaning closing the Ecuadorian congress, centralizing political power in Mahuad's hands, and implementing the neoliberal project that he was committed to. Mendoza claimed that Mahuad's minister of defense José Gallardo and foreign minister Benjamin Ortiz proposed on two occasions to establish a Fujimori-style dictatorship. Mendoza believed that Mahuad "...was the prisoner of an economic oligarchy and of corrupt bankers" (Gerlach 2003, pp. 133, 135). In December 1999 the high command proposed that Mahuad reverse some of the austerity measures and negotiate with social movements or resign

(Gerlach 2003, p. 148). These concerns complemented the anger felt by some nationalists that Ecuador had been betrayed in a peace agreement Mahuad signed with Peru's president Alberto Fujimori, which settled a decades-long border conflict that had led to military clashes in 1995 (Pineo 2007, p. 211).

In the months leading up to January 2000 (the month that Mahuad would be removed by a military-civil society coup) junior army officers, such as Colonel Lucio Gutiérrez, met with other military officers and indigenous representatives discussing how they could remove Mahuad from power. In the year prior to the coup Gutiérrez repeatedly informed members of the high command of his disagreement with Mahuad's neoliberal banking policies in the context of an impoverished population (Gutiérrez 2001, pp. 153, 158–9). The military faction led by Gutiérrez admired Chávez's government in Venezuela and sought a reversal of Ecuador's neoliberal economic agenda, larger military budgets, and tougher controls on corruption (Gerlach 2003, p. 174). This perspective was in line with at least some of CONAIE's politics and policy agenda. In 2000 CONAIE described the armed forces as "... the only institution that had demonstrated preoccupation with the situation of the poor" (as quoted in Gerlach 2003, p. 169). On January 21, 2000, nationalist/populist factions within the military joined CONAIE and other social movements in the occupation of the Congress, establishing a "people's parliament" and a "Junta of National Salvation" that removed Mahuad from office. The removal of Mahuad from power followed a week of protests in which thousands of indigenous rights and other social movement activists filled the capital streets demanding a "popular government." In the face of this mass protest and the storming of government buildings, Mahuad fled the palace after he rejected a request by the military high command to leave office. The military high command feared a "social explosion" in the face of the mass protests and hoped Mahuad's removal would placate the situation (*The New York Times* 2000a). The 2000 coup illustrated the influence of nationalist/populist factions within the army, with approximately 120 officers participating (*The New York Times* 2000a). One of the leaders of the military-civilian junta, Lt. Col. Guillermo Pacheco Perez, identified with "the cause of Bolivarian liberation" and the "ultrafree Bolivarian Republic of Venezuela" (as quoted in Rohter 2000b). However, most of the army, the other services, and the high command opposed this nationalist/populist junta (Fitch 2005, p. 51; *The New York Times* 2000a). In addition, economic elites from Guayaquil and Quito united in opposition to the coup (North 2004, p. 191). The military high command, with closer ties to the political and economic establishment and concerned about the disruption to institutional hierarchy, would ultimately remove the junta from power (Barracca 2007, p. 147).

The reaction by the high command also reflected the influence of international pressures. The high command was made aware that the continuation of a military government would face U.S. economic and political isolation (BBC 2000). In addition, senior military officers not tied directly to the coup were made aware of the potential for economic isolation (Fitch 2005, p. 50). The head of the Junta of National Salvation, General Carlos Mendoza Poveda, received several calls from Washington, D.C., specifically from Peter Romero, U.S. Assistant Secretary of State for Latin American Affairs, that threatened an economic blockade against Ecuador if the civil-military regime that replaced Mahuad were to stay in power (Molina Flores 2005, p. 116). The Organization of American States (OAS) was also active in its attempt to safeguard Mahuad. For example, the OAS gave its "full and determined backing" to neoliberal President Mahuad and "firmly" condemned efforts to oust him" (BBC 2000). Weeks after the coup the secretary general of the OAS, César Gaviria, stated that "...the level of isolation and economic harm to the country would be so great as to make the Junta [which replaced Mahuad] unsustainable" (as quoted in Gerlach 2003, p. 189). Though these international actors were unable to prevent Mahuad's removal, they contributed to the replacement of Mahuad with the conservative and neoliberal Noboa, who pledged to continue with IMF-promoted reforms (Gerlach 2003, pp. 212–5). From hiding, Mahuad recognized the coming to power of Noboa and wished him luck in taking over the presidency (Rohter 2000a).

Gustavo Noboa (2000–2) continued the IMF's economic agenda and Mahuad's dollarization plan in the hopes of obtaining the much-needed credit to assist Ecuador with its inflationary problems and budget deficits. Noboa enjoyed friendly relations with Guayaquil's business community as well as the main private-sector groups that publicly backed his government, viewing him as the "right man" for economic reform (*The Economist* 2000). The OAS, with the United States, made proposals on the necessary financial reforms to obtain foreign loans as well as the changes needed to keep the military from launching another coup. Not only did Noboa pursue a globalist economic agenda, but he also took some of the first substantive steps to reform civil-military relations (Gerlach 2003, p. 212). Lopez Molina 2005, p. 75). His national security proposal, the "Strategic Plan-Ministerial Vision 2010," aimed to modernize the laws, training, armaments, operating, and technical capacity in the three branches of the armed forces (Lopez Molina 2005, p. 75). As a part of his plan a "White Book" on national defense, an idea initiated in Latin America by a U.S.-sponsored conference of defense ministers in 1995, was written that outlined Ecuador's strategic goals and security interests in a public and transparent manner, and for the first time civilians would be involved in the development of these policies (Lopez Molina 2005, p. 168; Comisión Andina de Juristas 2002a). His administration also witnessed greater rationalization of military budgets. This was in keeping with a public commitment made by Noboa to streamline and reduce military spending at a 2002 conference of foreign ministers and defense ministers of the Andean Community of Nations (CAN) held in Lima (Comisión Andina de Juristas 2002b; BBC Summary of World Broadcasts 2002).

Noboa's effort to implement neoliberal economic policies would, like Mahuad, have to adapt to continued societal resistance. In February 2001 Noboa had to reverse initiatives to reduce subsidies on fuel and transport mandated by the IMF after nationwide protests by unionists and indigenous groups protested against the rising prices. After meeting with representatives of CONAIE, the government agreed to increase resources toward social development and to freeze fuel prices. Noboa would also release all protesters arrested by security forces during the state of emergency that he called in the face of the unrest in which four protesters were killed (Healy 2001). Noboa's privatization initiatives would be stalled by complications in privatization procedures and a burgeoning corruption scandal involving Noboa and members of his family. Although progress was made in democratizing civil-military relations, Noboa had to scale down the significance of his austerity measures and other neoliberal policies in the face of social protests (Gerlach 2003, pp. 216–8; International Crisis Group 2007, p. 5). By the end of 2003 the armed forces still retained ownership or co-ownership of a hotel, a major domestic airline, two shipping companies, shrimp export farms, and cement plants, among other entities (Fitch 2003, p. 15).

In 2002 the former coup leader Lucio Gutiérrez was elected president and spent much of his first three years violating his antineoliberal campaign promises by supporting an IMF-sanctioned austerity plan, supporting dollarization, and agreeing with a free trade agreement with the United States, as well as backing U.S. drug policy in the region (Rivera Vélez and Ramírez Gallegos 2005, p. 138; Fertyl 2005). Gutiérrez's violation of his promises, his questionable packing of the Supreme Court, and his support of the disgraced former president

Bucaram would drop his popularity rating to 15 percent by the end of 2003. The military increasingly opposed him due to his politicization of military promotions and appointments, as well as his promotion of U.S. drug war policies without obtaining the necessary U.S. assistance for basic supplies and armaments (Global Security 2005; Molina Flores 2005, pp. 79–85). His attempt to bring the disgraced former president Abdala Bucaram back from exile in order to obtain greater support from Bucaram's party in the Congress intensified societal opposition to his presidency. Between April 14 and April 20, 2005, mass protests by students and pensioners, as well as sectors of CONAIE, confronted the Gutiérrez administration demanding his resignation. At one point more than 100,000 people descended upon the capital and violently faced off with Ecuadorian security forces as well as governmental supporters. In the face of this social disorder the Ecuadorian congress voted to remove Gutiérrez for "abandoning his post," alleging that his steps to replace the justices on the Supreme Court were unconstitutional, and replaced him with his vice-president Alfredo Palacio (Fertyl 2005). Gutiérrez refused to resign, but given the military's refusal to support his continuation in power and the police chief of Quito resigning rather than repress the protesters, Gutiérrez fled for the Brazilian embassy. The command general of the armed forces, Gen. Víctor Hugo Rosero, argued that the military could not "remain indifferent before the pronouncements of the Ecuadorean people" (Forero 2005). Even with the removal of the president, some protesters worked to occupy the congressional building, demanding that the government end its support of Plan Colombia, remove the U.S. military from the Manta air base, and place a moratorium on the foreign debt (Fertyl 2005).

The U.S. government attempted to prevent the removal of President Lucio Gutiérrez in the face of massive societal protests and the withdrawal of military support. On April 20, the U.S. ambassador, Kristie Kenney, met with the Ecuadorian high command, lobbying in support of Gutiérrez and requesting that the military give Gutiérrez more time to resolve the political conflicts in the country . The high command refused, and Gutiérrez was forced to flee. With the removal of Gutiérrez, the OAS, as well as other foreign governments, urged members of the military not to organize a civilian-military junta Gutiérrez(an idea that they were considering) and allow the vice-president, Alfredo Palacio, to take power (Molina Flores 2005, pp. 85–6; Bruneau 2006, p. 4). Palacio replaced Gutiérrez in April 2005 and completed his term. Though little was accomplished with regard to civil-military reforms during Gutiérrez's tenure, the government of Alfredo Palacio (2005–6),

Gutiérrez's vice-president and a member of Durán Ballen's cabinet, did make progress in moving Ecuadorian civil-military relations closer to the model of market democracies.

Palacio's one year in office witnessed a continued effort to integrate Ecuador's economy globally through the pursuit of a free trade agreement with the United States as well as successfully negotiating a new loan agreement with the World Bank, despite widespread opposition to both propositions. In addition, the president's popular economic minister, Rafael Correa, resigned on August 5, 2005, over a disagreement with Palacio over Correa's effort to increase economic ties with Venezuela, as well as Correa's public critiques of international financial institutions. STRATFOR's (Strategic Forecasting, inc.) analysis of the resignation found that "Correa's forced departure confirms that some political and business groups in Ecuador are pushing for Palacio to keep the country aligned with the United States. Correa said Aug. 8 that Palacio is being pressured by the U.S. government. Separately, Latin American diplomatic sources in Quito said Aug. 8 that Palacio also is being lobbied quietly by several Latin American countries— including Colombia, Peru, Bolivia, Brazil, and Chile—to avoid falling into the oil-funded embrace of Chávez's Bolivarian revolution" (EUROMONEY 2005; STRATFOR 2005; BBC Monitoring Latin America 2006a).

Palacio's sympathies toward the United States over Venezuela were also reflected in his appointment of retired General Oswaldo Jarrín at the head of the defense ministry, illustrating the modernizing and liberal direction promoted by the U.S. Defense Department. Jarrín was the principal thinker behind the Ley Orgánica de Las Defensa Nacional (no.74, December 2006). The law continued the Noboa government's agenda established in the 2002 "White Book," which Jarrín played a role in crafting, that had been disrupted by the disorder of the Gutiérrez government (Molina Flores 2005, pp. 175–6; phone interview with Jarrín, 10/22/08). It required the military's disinvestment from non-military-oriented industries, the possibility that the military could be judged by civilian judges, and the creation of the Vice-Minister of Defense, which would be occupied by a civilian. The new law included a provision that would remove civilians working in the defense ministry from the direct supervision of the armed forces and require that they register under the Civil Service and Administrative Career Law. In addition, it created the post of deputy defense minister that would be occupied by a civilian (*El Comercio* 2006; BBC Monitoring Latin America 2006b). Finally, the law required that military personnel be tried in civilian courts for nonmilitary-related crimes and that the role of the minister of defense should shift from an advisor to the president to someone who *executes* the president's decisions and strategies (*El Universo* 2006). This was in keeping with Jarrín's objective to depoliticize the armed forces and emphasize professional/military doctrine, seeking "... to bring order to professional values so as to reinforce vocation, the spirit of service and all the military attributes: discipline, hierarchy, command and democratic culture" as well as have the armed forces "return to our barracks and dedicate ourselves exclusively to our specific missions" (BBC Monitoring Latin America 2005).

Jarrín, who was also Gutiérrez's first chief of the Joint Command, maintained close ties with U.S. institutions and neoliberal policy-planning organizations both prior to and following his position in the Palacio government. Jarrín was a graduate of the Curriculum Design and Instructional Methodologies Course of the Center for Hemispheric Defense Studies (CHDS) in 2004 and received a PhD in educational sciences from the OAS-affiliated Inter-American Defense College (CHDS 2008b). The Center for Hemispheric Defense Studies is based at the National Defense University in the United States and represents a U.S. effort to convey the values/principles of "democratic" civil-military relations in Latin America (CHDS 2008a).

Ultimately, Jarrín would be dismissed from his position in August 2006. According to Jarrín, his dismissal was the result of pressure from "petty sectors" who were opposed to Ecuador's involvement in the "war on drugs," arguing that "It seems that those who engage in illicit trades have more allies in this country than those who worry about state security" (BBC Monitoring Latin America 2006c). Jarrín would go on to participate in the Andean Working Group of the Interamerican Dialogue, a transnational policymaking organization based in Washington, D.C., that is dedicated to the spread of market democracies and economic integration in the Western Hemisphere. The Andean Group represented a working group of advisors on the state of the Andean region and U.S. policy toward the region (January 2007; Andean Working Paper). Jarrín later joined the faculty of the Center for Hemispheric Defense Studies as the new "Minister of Defense" chair in the department (CHDS 2008b). His connections and attitudes regarding a professional armed forces and its mission were in line with the model promoted by the United States. Jarrín's perspective was shared by others in the high command during the Palacio administration. The former director of planning for CONAIE, Nelson Nuñez, described this sector as "pro–north American," one that opposed efforts to reduce training linkages with the United States and distrusted the popular rise of Rafael Correa, a leftist political leader who would be elected to the presidency in November 2006 (Nuñez 2006).

Rafael Correa, Radical Populism, and the Armed Forces, 2006–10

On November 26, 2006, Rafael Correa, a vocal critic of neoliberalism, was elected president of Ecuador at the head of his *Alianza País* electoral coalition that included support from various leftist parties and elements of the social opposition to the Gutiérrez presidency (Conaghan 2008, 49). Correa promoted twenty-first–century socialism, claiming that market deficiencies could be overcome by state action, and that labor should be prioritized over capital while maintaining respect for market processes. Correa also campaigned on a critical stance against the United States, rejecting any free trade agreement with the United States and pledging not to renew a U.S. military base in Manta, Ecuador.

His reformist impulses immediately influenced civil-military relations with the appointment of Guadalupe Larriva, the first female and the first nonmilitary-serving person to be appointed as defense minister (Valdivieso 2006). Larriva's objective, before she died in a helicopter crash only nine days after being officially appointed minister, was to expand the military's social and developmentalist role, arguing that "... the role of the Armed Forces will be decisive in the [country's] social and economic reactivation" (BBC Monitoring Latin America 2007). During the appointment ceremonies of a new military high command in February 2007, Correa declared that "The political decision of this government is that the Armed Forces in times of peace should integrate in helping social and economic development" (Mercopress 2007). For example, early in Correa's administration, the army's corps of engineers was granted central responsibility in emergency road repairs throughout the country, which provided much needed resources to the military and tightened its links to Correa (Conaghan 2008, 55). The military's prerogatives over economic policy are being retained and expanded in the case of Ecuador. This is in conflict with neoliberal precepts of market liberalization or commonly viewed prerequisites for civilian control.

Oswaldo Jarrín has viewed such a direction as the unnecessary and improper politicization of the military that is consistent with a regional trend in which political leaders "... want to use the military to break the political balance of forces in society ... they want to use the military to advance the government's economic agenda" (phone interview, 10/22/08). The "subjective control" of the military by the dominant party in power is in contrast to the "objective control" that Jarrín sought to establish within Ecuador through his work on the Ecuadorian "White Book" and national security laws (phone interview, 10/22/08), a type of control that is being disrupted in the Correa administration.

The social service component for the military was also exemplified in Correa's *Plan Ecuador* that was introduced in April 2007. The plan was designed to better secure and develop Ecuador's northern region bordering Colombia. This region has long been economically neglected and was increasingly suffering the negative consequences of Colombia's internal war (increased refugee flows, the presence of narcotrafficking organizations, and armed groups). The military presence in the region was to be strengthened in order to protect cultural and governmental institutions, which would create the conditions for greater economic development. Also, the military is expected to play a role in safeguarding the environment (Pardini and Rivero 2008). Correa stressed that though the military's presence would be increased, the focus would be upon extending the regulatory power of the state and development, and not a militarized response. This was in line with nationalist sectors within the armed forces that were critical of the military's involvement in counternarcotics operations, which were viewed as an imposition by the United States, and sought to develop a militarized strategy appropriate for Ecuador (Nuñez 2006).

Correa's government also sought to reduce U.S. influence by proposing a new national intelligence law to obtain greater autonomy for the nation's intelligence agencies from international influences, committing to the closure of the U.S. military base at Manta as well as decreasing U.S. training/assistance (BBC Monitoring Latin America 2008a). The proposal for intelligence reform took place in the wake of the alleged failure of Ecuador's military intelligence to alert other sectors of the government to an impending bombing of Ecuadorian territory by the Colombian military on a FARC camp in 2008. The Correa administration demanded a series of forced resignations. Wellington Sandoval resigned as defense minister, and the head of the Joint Chiefs of Staff resigned, as did the army commander and the chief of police (Lucas 2008). Correa alleged that Ecuador's intelligence services had been infiltrated by the CIA and that reform was needed. In the wake of the scandal, one high-level Ecuadorian military officer argued that "... either the military as an institution returns to its nationalist orientation or it submits itself once and for all to impositions from the U.S."

(as quoted in Lucas 2008). He added that it was necessary for "…independent and progressive sectors to regain control over the institution" (as quoted in Lucas 2008). The Correa administration's defense minister Javier Ponce stated in April 2008 that "the specter of (U.S.) training, financial support and technical support inevitably has permeated the structure and behavior" of Ecuador's security forces, creating "a national security problem," and that all U.S. military programs with Ecuador would be under review (Associated Press 2008a).

Finally, in 2008 Correa led the formation of a constituent assembly dominated by his supporters, who produced a constitution that was approved by Ecuadorian voters on September 28, 2008 (BBC 2008). The constitution eliminated mandatory military service, prohibited foreign military bases on Ecuadorian soil, and continued an economic role for the armed forces while giving the president the power to select the officers for the high command in the armed forces and the police (Articles 63, 147, 163, and 164). The maintenance of this economic role also continued with the military's control over several state companies, with Correa even appointing military personnel to manage Petroecuador, the state oil company (Romero 2008). While the appointments of civilians reflects the type of civil-military progress in line with U.S. objectives and traditional conceptions of liberal democracies, the continued maintenance of a social/developmentalist role for the armed forces illustrates a strategy that continues to utilize the military in a manner outside of traditional security roles.

Venezuela

Civil-Military Relations, Internal Factions, and Civil Society

The Venezuelan case shares some important similarities and differences with the Ecuadorian case. In contrast to Ecuador, Venezuela has had elected civilian authorities governing the national state since 1958. Prior to this democratic period, the armed forces had a long history of political intervention, with the last military regime ruling between 1948 and 1958. This conservative military regime was a response to the reformist alliance between social democratic/mass-based political party Democratic Action (AD) and progressive military officers that governed between 1945 and 1948. The military supporters of the 1945–8 government came from the Unión Patriótica Militar (UPM) who committed to a leading role for the military in national development

(Coronil 1997, 128). This brief three-year government (the *Trienio*) sought a series of labor and social reforms, including the beginnings of a welfare state as well as increasing the state's share from petroleum profits (Peeler 1992, p. 91).

The regime that replaced the *Trienio* was led by General Marcos Pérez Jiménez (1948–58), a former supporter of the short-term reformist government,[9] but who shifted to an alliance with Venezuelan economic elites and foreign oil companies fearful of the policy changes being promoted (Peeler 1992, p. 91). His government was committed to the national development of Venezuela through the import-substitution-industrialization strategies prominent throughout the region at this time. State-controlled industries and the development of the oil industry, increased openness to foreign capital, and the repression of labor were all a part of his development agenda (Coronil 1997, p. 180). The regime pursued a series of major infrastructural projects in alliance with national businessmen and ruled through widespread corruption as well as the torture and murder of political opponents.

Opposition to Pérez Jiménez came from the *Patriotic Junta* (a coalition of civilian parties), business leaders alienated from the government's corrupting practices, as well as sectors of the military concerned about the consequences for the institution of such authoritarian/corrupt practices. In January 1958 Pérez Jiménez fled the country in the face of a national general strike and the refusal of the army to repress protesters after increasing casualties among the civilian population. By the end of 1958 the leading opposition political parties, AD, COPEI, and the URD, agreed to a power-sharing pact that divided power between the major political parties, Democratic Action party (AD), and the Christian Democratic Party (COPEI), as well as some smaller parties. The pact, which was supported by the military and business elites, resulted in the appointment of partisans of the different parties to the bureaucracy and in the leadership positions of key interest groups. The agreement excluded the Communist party, while maintaining a commitment to use petroleum revenues toward national development and the clientelistic control of core social groups, such as labor and peasants, in civil society (Hellinger 2006, p. 477; Schneider 2007, pp. 346–7). The pact also called for the "…modernization of the armed forces, which were to be considered apolitical, obedient, and noninterventionist" (Peeler 1992, p. 97).

The Punto Fijo pact allowed enclaves of institutional power for the armed forces, including autonomy over military/security affairs, while the military agreed to avoid direct involvement in political affairs. The military's focus in the 1960s was mainly upon the defeat of Castroite guerrilla armies that had developed in response to the Communist party's exclusion and the limits upon reform promoted by the dominant parties. The Venezuelan government received the full backing of the United States, which helped to train and arm the military in its fight against insurgents. According to some, this counterinsurgency struggle established a "...basis for military loyalty to the [democratic] regime" (see Bigler 1982, p. 176). Venezuela was viewed as a model for Latin America with its competitive elections complementing its anti-Communism. By 1969 most guerrillas accepted a negotiated reintegration into civil society, as they were unable to make much progress against the Venezuelan armed forces or to obtain much legitimacy among the Venezuelan people (Hellinger 2006, pp. 477–8). In the decades that followed the military's triumph against guerrilla forces, its security priorities have included securing the nation's borders and territorial waters to potential, but relatively insignificant, threats from Colombia, Guyana, and Brazil. Finally, the military was increasingly utilized in episodic internal repression/control missions in the 1980s and 1990s.

The division of authority between the military and politicians or the commitment to an "apolitical" armed forces did not prevent the establishment of partisan and clientelistic interventions into the armed forces in the decades following 1958. The 1961 constitution granted the Senate the power to approve the promotions of top military commanders. Generally, the Congress deferred to the wishes of the president, but as time passed the Congress increasingly used this power as an instrument to influence the military, with members of the armed forces seeking out the support of one of the parties or specific politicians (Manrique 2001, p. 321). According to retired general Alberto Muller Rojas, "the political elite of this consensual system co-opted military units and developed real networks of action... that dominated the military leadership for their own benefit and to the benefit of their patrons" (as quoted in Jacome 1999, p. 408). The strong base of support for the AD in the military worked to strengthen the military's support for the democratic regime in its early years (Rouquié 1987, p. 377). Party influence and a consensual elite arrangement contributed to maintaining stable civil-military relations, but Venezuela's immense oil wealth has also played a role. It allowed the country a degree of economic stability and growth, and also allowed the government to provide generous benefits/equipment to the military. Finally, during the first *Punto Fijo* government, political leaders replaced a joint command structure and allowed administrative and operational autonomy for each military branch, thus creating competition within the armed forces over budgetary distributions as well as undermining potential antidemocratic unity across services (Trinkunas 2002, p. 44; Trinkunas 2005).

The collapse in oil prices in the 1980s, rising interest rates, and a ballooning foreign debt plunged the country into an economic crisis in the 1980s and 1990s. Between 1980 and 1992 the average Venezuelan lost over half of their real purchasing power, daily caloric intake declined, and at the start of 1992 80 percent of Venezuelans were living at or below the poverty line (Burggraaf and Millett 1995, pp. 59 and 69). This economic crisis would not only play a role in delegitimizing the two dominant political parties, but in also disrupting Venezuela's history of relatively stable civil-military relations. The inability of the government to maintain high levels of military spending during a decline in oil prices, combined with the economic crisis, created high levels of discontent among certain sectors of the military. It also created an opportunity for Venezuela's neoliberal/globalist elite to pursue a series of market reforms in order to integrate Venezuela into the global economy.

Market Reform and Reaction, 1989–98

In the 1980s attempts were made to re-orient Venezuela away from inward-oriented industrialization to the market-oriented, free trade strategies of neoliberalism. The most serious effort to change Venezuela's state-developmentalist strategy was undertaken by the government of Carlos Andrés Pérez (1989–93). Andrés Pérez, who ran on an antineoliberal program, proceeded to implement the "great turnaround," a series of neoliberal measures in response to IMF pressures and a burgeoning foreign debt. His policies represented the most comprehensive and consistent effort to shift the Venezuelan economy in a free market direction. The president's cabinet consisted of largely foreign-trained technocrats, in contrast to the traditional patronage system of the past (Naim 1993, pp. 49–50). The neoliberal policies implemented by Andrés Pérez included the "...elimination of exchange controls, liberalization of virtually all prices, increased rates for electricity, water, telephone, gasoline, public transportation, and most other public services" (Roberts 2003, p. 258). Along with these economic changes were a number of political reforms, including eliminating the state's discretionary power; making provincial posts, state governorships, and mayors open to popular elections; and the decentralization of the country's administration. The defense ministry was also required to develop strategies to reduce costs, and the Congress and the executive branch increasingly involved themselves directly in the military budget process, eroding certain military prerogatives (Burggraaff and Millett 1995, p. 70; Naim 1993, pp. 46–7).

The economic changes led to a massive social and political backlash, which included the February 1989 *Caracazo*. The *Caracazo* of 1989 consisted of mass rioting in Caracas and other major Venezuelan cities in response to Andrés Pérez's economic policies. A state of siege was called, hundreds were killed, and thousands were arrested without charge. The national police was unable to handle the nationwide civil unrest, and the armed forces were sent to repress and reinstitute order in the country, with soldiers firing on crowds and individuals in order to make this happen. The traumatic effect of the *Caracazo* and Andres Pérez's economic reform measures were important in generating the sympathy of populist and radical factions within the Venezuelan armed forces for military coup attempts in 1992.

Since the early 1980s one military faction, the Bolivarian Revolutionary Movement (MBR-200), led by Hugo Chávez and Francisco Arias, had been planning, with their military colleagues and radical political groups in society, a rebellion against what they viewed as a corrupt political system. In fact, the MBR was one of several military groups that were conspiring to overthrow the government and/or promote some type of radical reform in the political system (Jones 2007). Civilian political groups that MBR-200 worked with before and after the coup included the Partido de la Revolución Venezolana, Causa R, Bandera Roja, the Liga Socialista, and former leaders of Venezuela's defeated guerrilla movement (López Maya 2004, p. 75). In fact, civilian actors such as the Revolutionary Party of Venezuela (PRV) had been studying the military since the 1970s in a concerted strategy to influence and ally with sympathetic elements within the military (Jones 2007, p. 75). Factors that influenced the emergence of this military faction included the more political and sophisticated university education that officers received in the 1970s and the fact that many military officers came from lower-class and working-class backgrounds. Leaders of this military movement, such as Chávez, had also been heavily influenced by the work of Peru's nationalist regime under Velasco Alvarado, viewing it as a potential model of what the armed forces can accomplish politically (Gott 2000, p. 38). Chávez recalled that in response to the Peruvian regime that "One began to see then that the military men weren't meant to massacre people, to wage bloody coup d'etats, to sever the rights of the people, but that rather they could serve the people" (as quoted in Jones 2007, p. 53). In the 1970s Venezuelan military educational institutions increasingly taught a conception of national security that stressed the centrality of economic development and the role of the military in that development. The cadets in Chávez's class did relatively little training at the U.S. School of the Americas, in contrast to their predecessors, while the military regularly promoted dark-skinned individuals from working to poor backgrounds to senior officer positions, creating the possibility of a more empathetic officer corps with those suffering economic difficulties (Jones 2007, p. 39).

The Bolivarian Revolutionary Movement within the military sought a "... civil-military alliance in order to stimulate revolutionary change" (López Maya 2004, pp. 75, 76). The 1989 repression during the *Caracazo* simply strengthened this military movement's resolve and belief that the political regime had to change and that neoliberal economic policies had to be ended. Chávez and Arias promoted a state developmentalist strategy and resented the agreements between President Carlos Andrés Pérez (1989–93) and the IMF. They also supported the development of a constituent assembly to reconstruct Venezuela's democracy while opposing an internally repressive role for the armed forces (Jacome 1999, p. 408, 412; Burggraaff and Millett 1995, p. 67). The movement led by Chávez and Arias attempted to overthrow the Andrés Pérez government in February 1992, while sympathizers of their cause attempted again to remove the government in November 1992. Both coups failed, as they were supported by a small segment of officers within the armed forces and as the high command and a majority of the armed forces continued to support the elected government. Jacome (1999, p. 411) estimates that 10 percent of the armed forces were involved in the February 4, 1992, coup attempt, while Burggraaf and Millett (1995, p. 65) estimate that less than 10 percent of army units took part, with literally no involvement by the air force or navy.

While the proportion of the military involved in the coup was relatively small, Moisés Naím, former minister of industry under Pérez, believes that the fatal blow to the continuation of economic reform came from the February coup attempt. The coup attempt, and Chávez's short speech to the public after he was arrested, mobilized the opposition to neoliberalism in a way that previous opponents of neoliberal policies had been unable to do in Venezuela. The coup attempt was fundamental to the convergence of the various groups in civil society (such as labor unions, farmers, and students), political parties, or sectors of the armed forces in focusing opposition against the government.

Ultimately, this resistance to this neoliberal government prevented the Andres Peréz administration from developing a "...stable coalition that could act as an effective anchor for the country's political system and allow the government to continue its program" (Naím 1993, p. 167). One of the February coup leaders remarking on his transfer to jail stated, "When we left military intelligence for the San Carlos jail was when we realized we had produced a true impact, that we had shaken up the bases of the system itself...when we were transferred in a caravan and we saw all the people in the streets...well, we said, we are like stars. The thing didn't fail like we thought" (as quoted in Jones 2007, p. 162).

The United States condemned the 1992 coup attempts, issuing a declaration that "the basis of U.S. policy in the region is the support of democracy, and even if we understand that Venezuela, among other nations, is going through a difficult period, authoritarianism is not the solution" (as quoted in Teresa Romero 2002, p. 110). Albert Coll, a subsecretary from the U.S. Defense Department, visited Caracas in 1993 to discuss low-intensity conflict, stressing that the "...United States would not support in any form, a Venezuelan government imposed or created by the military against constitutional authorities" (as quoted in Romero 1998, pp. 146–7). While civilian political control was being backed, the United States continued to press Venezuela on economic reforms between 1993 and 1998, demanding greater progress on privatizations, free trade, and exchange controls (Romero 1998, pp. 156–8).

The United States and Venezuela had enjoyed close political and trade relations throughout the Punto Fijo period, with Venezuela long representing a major source of oil for the United States and one of the top five sources of imported oil for the United States.[10] During the Cold War period, the United States and Venezuela maintained close military ties, with a U.S. military assistance group in Venezuela advising on strategy and tactics and Venezuelan officers regularly training at U.S.-run institutions (Myers 1996, p. 262). Venezuela and the United States were allied in their opposition to the spread of Communism in the region as well as in defending democracy in the post-Cold War period. Few Venezuelan leaders during this period challenged U.S. supremacy in the Western Hemisphere (Romero 2004, p. 133).

The relationship between civil society and the Venezuelan military has varied during Venezuela's market reform period. The public was generally sympathetic with the February 1992 coup plotters, with massive demonstrations in support after the coup as well as public opinion polls showing support for a "moderating" coup to replace Andrés Pérez

(Aguero 1995, p. 215; Norden 2001, p. 124). This clearly illustrated the increasing loss of legitimacy wielded by the dominant political parties and the popular rejection of the neoliberal project. Naím argues that opposition to neoliberal economic reforms emerged from a variety of actors who had benefited from the state developmentalist models, or who perceived market-oriented models as worsening their situation. Labor unions in specific state-run industries, conglomerates that benefited from state protections/subsidies, and party and military officials with ideological sympathies toward state-regulated/protected economies were part of this opposition (Naím 1993).

The February and November 1992 coups were not the only examples of military political intervention during this period. In December 1993 there were allegations of a planned right-wing coup by "constitutionalist" factions within the military concerned about the growing influence of leftist parties. The lack of U.S. support undermined these plans (Buxton 2001, pp. 162–3; Romero 2004, p. 135). The Venezuelan social scientist Jacome concludes that between 1992 and 1997 the Venezuelan military was divided between three sectors: those military officials with close ties to the traditional parties (the AD or COPEI), a sector focused upon the "Bolivarian movement" of Chávez and Arias, and finally an institutionalist sector made up of professionals committed to the defense of Venezuela's democracy and not interested in politics (Jacome 1999, p. 419).

Though the Caldera government (1994–8) that followed implemented some policies consistent with the neoliberal direction of Andrés Pérez, it would not approach the radical and orthodox nature of his administration. Caldera's relative shift away from the market orthodoxy of Carlos Andrés Pérez placated nationalists/populists in the military that sought a return to the import substitution industrialization policies of the past. In addition, Caldera successfully oriented the military toward traditional security concerns, specifically in addressing challenges from Colombian guerrillas on Venezuela's border, but also utilized the military to operate public services in order to confront increasing strikes by public-sector unions (Trinkunas 2005, p. 200 and 201). Finally, in 1994 his government pardoned the 1992 coup leaders in an effort toward reconciliation as well as to take advantage of their increasing popularity. These coup leaders began to establish the organizational structure of a political party, with specific small groups or cells at the local level ("Bolivarian Circles") as well as department, regional levels of organization, with a national directorate made up of civilians and retired members of the military (including Chávez). Parties such as Partido Comunista de Venezuela, Movimiento al Socialismo, and Patria Para Todos supported and worked within an electoral coalition that competed in the 1998 presidential elections. On the basis of this structure and the declining legitimacy of the dominant political parties, as well as the anti-establishment/antineoliberal rhetoric and charisma of Chávez, the movement was able to claim victory in the 1998 presidential election.

The Chávez Administration, 1998–2009

The election of Hugo Chávez in 1998 and his Bolivarian revolution would represent a significant break from progress toward neoliberal economic strategies. His success was, in part, built upon his consistent opposition to neoliberalism and the political parties associated with its policies, as well as the overall decline in the economy. The ultimate collapse of the traditional party system would be filled by the Chávez movement, which continues to seek the establishment of a counter-neoliberal/globalist model of development and democracy. From the beginning of military organizing in the early 1980s to Chávez's presidential election, the focus has been upon the elimination of the prior political system and the parties that dominated it as well as greater "economic democracy" to replace the market-driven model (Norden 2001, pp. 131–2).

In 1999 his movement wrote and passed a new constitution that recognized a number of social rights, promoted participatory democracy, and concentrated greater power in the national executive. In November 2001 Chávez passed forty-nine laws developed to reverse the country's neoliberal direction. These laws included the Organic Hydrocarbons Law, which gave the government a majority ownership of mixed companies; and under the Lands Law, idle land could be expropriated, while another law ensured governmental control over social security (Ellner 2008, p. 113). Venezuela's neoliberal policy coalition found themselves out of power with relatively few connections to state behavior. Civil-military relations in the country would also be changed and military responsibilities would be expanded in a manner wholly inconsistent with low-intensity democracies.

Early in his administration military officers were placed in key positions throughout the governmental bureaucracy, three officers in the cabinet, thirteen retired officers were elected as governors, and 50 percent of state companies and institutes were led by military officials (Manrique 2001, pp. 325–6). Critics have pointed to the dangers of the military's expanded role within the state, with Manrique stating that the military had become a political organization (*partido militar*) under Chávez (2001, pp. 328–9). However, during the 1970s the military had also been committed to a broader conception of national security that included national development. In 1974 a special commission was established by the Instituto de Altos Estudios de la Defensa Nacional (IAEDEN) to develop strategies to increase the participation of the armed forces in development, including military industries, the development of agriculture, health education, and general infrastructure (Alberto Buttó 2005, pp. 155–6; Bigler 1982, pp. 184–5).

In addition, the armed forces have consistently implemented the policies and institutional changes promoted through referendums and civilian authorities (Harnecker 2003a, p. 1). The Chávez administration appointed Jose Vicente Rangel to head the Ministry of Defense (from 2001–2), the first civilian to hold that position in Venezuela's history (Wilpert 2007, p. 41). Within the National Assembly, the Commission on Defense and Security enjoys the power to determine military budgets and spending (Manrique 2001, p. 333). However, the assembly's powers were limited with the 1999 constitution, which gives the president power to promote officers above the rank of colonel or naval captain without the involvement of Congress, ensuring that Chávez can promote individuals that share his belief in this expanded social/political role for the armed forces, thus establishing a form of subjective civilian control. In fact, in the spring of 2009 the Chávez administration pushed for the early retirement of senior officers and redeployed military units at reduced numbers in an effort to reduce defense expenditures during a global economic crisis (Sanchez 2009). The constitution also grants the military the right to vote (Article 330) and requires that the military play an active role in national development (Article 328).

The administration is clearly committed to the establishment of a new form of civil-military relations, one that utilizes the resources, training, and professionalism of the military to attack social problems. The first central example of this expanded military role in the Chávez administration was the president's *Plan Bolivar* of 2000. This was a civil-military plan that included more than 40,000 soldiers and was involved in the cleaning up of streets and schools, fighting endemic diseases, and rebuilding social infrastructure in urban and rural areas (Harnecker 2003a, p. 1; Harnecker 2003b, p. 2). Millions of dollars in governmental assistance were distributed to local military garrisons throughout the country to be spent on the various social projects that military commanders prioritized (Pion-Berlin and Trinkunas 2005, p. 17). In describing the justification for military programs like *Plan Bolívar* the first director of the Centro de Estudios Militares Avanzados (CEMA), Brigadier General Carlos Martinez Mendoza, stated "la pobreza constituye un elemento importante que atenta contra la seguridad, para defenderse de ella hay que actuar" (as quoted in Alberto Buttó 2005, p. 156). The turn to the military was also in response to the significant opposition Chávez faced from the Congress, the national bureaucracy, and the Supreme Court, as well as the rising expectations of the public (Jones 2007, p. 233).

By 2005 over $50 million of the defense ministry's budget was being spent on social work projects (Nunez 2006). *Plan Bolívar* would represent a precedent for other connections between civil society and the military. For example, the military would become involved in supporting the work of communal councils, small neighborhood councils that have been provided billions in government funds to directly address social and infrastructural projects in their communities outside of formal political institutions. The armed forces have representatives on the Presidential Committee for Communal Power, which was given the power to set guidelines for the administration of resources within the communal council system (Bradley 2007). Venezuelan social activist Roland Denis has found, "The popular movement does not consist of only social movements, there are also military movements....soldiers and young military officers who go to workshops and participate in the dynamic of the popular movements" (as quoted in Gindin 2005, p. 29). Harnecker finds that the military's experiences of working with the poor made them "more socially aware and engaged," arguing that "junior officers now belong to the more radical sectors of the process" (Harnecker 2003a).

The April 2002 Coup

Civil society and the military also contained (and contain) sectors in opposition to the Chávez administration's civil-military alliances and nationalist/statist program. Members of this opposition have accused the Chávez regime of seeking to turn Venezuela into a Communist republic led by a totalitarian leader. Though many objections were raised by the traditional parties and other groups to the 1999 constitution, the largest expression of societal opposition to Chávez occurred in April 2002, specifically in the actions of the Coordinadora Democrática (Democratic Coordinator; CD), a coalition of parties, business groups, and labor unions. The two largest member groups were Federación de Cámaras y Asociaciones de Comercio y Producción de Venezuela (FEDECAMARAS—the Federation of Business and Producer Chambers and Associations of Venezuela) and the Confederación de Trabajadores de Venezuela (CTV—Confederation of Venezuelan Workers), a conservative federation of unions. This alliance of groups was instrumental in organizing mass protests, marches, and general strikes that ended violently on April 11, 2002, allowing sectors of the military high command to publicly justify a momentarily successful coup against Chávez. Pedro Carmona, the president of FEDECAMARAS, was placed as interim president.

The divisions within the military reflected in the coup are illustrated in a study by the *Dirección de Inteligencia Militar* (DIM), which found that sixty officers and admirals identified themselves as "revolutionaries," eighty-five as institutionalists, and thirty-three as dissidents (2001, p. 330).[11] In regard to the 2002 coup, the decision to remove Chávez was made six months before April among a group of dissident officers in the Venezuelan navy and air force, which spread to other dissidents in the army and national guard angry with Chávez's social development projects with the military and the government's alleged close relations with Colombia's leftist guerrillas (Wilson 2002a).

Carmona's first decisions reflected much of this political perspective. They included the closing down of public broadcasting stations sympathetic to Chávez, dissolving the legislature (which contained a majority of elected Chávez supporters), and rescinding the Chávez government's land reform and oil reform policies as well as the other laws that Chávez had passed in December 2001. Carmona also decreed the end of oil deliveries to Cuba, withdrew Venezuela's support for OPEC, and reappointed the state oil company managers who had long supported the market-opening and privatization policy in the oil industry of previous administrations (Lander and López-Maya 2002, 23).

The objectives of the failed April 2002 coup against Chávez were reminiscent of the important objectives accomplished by the "self-coup" achieved by Alberto Fujimori in 1992 in Peru. In both cases, an effort was made to centralize political power in the presidency through an alliance between right-wing sectors of civil society and the armed forces. Furthermore, the stated economic goals of the 2002 coup were to reorient Venezuela on a neoliberal track, with the support of the U.S. government and international financial institutions. Carmona's cabinet appointments privileged elite, conservative parties while ignoring moderates within the opposition that were not as committed to the neoliberal project. This was in keeping with the goals of FEDECAMARAS (Ellner 2008, pp. 114–7).

In response to this coup and the refusal to accept the claim that Chávez had resigned, there were massive protests involving tens of thousands of people throughout the country in opposition, many surrounding military bases demanding that the armed forces resist the coup. Middle-level officers and several generals refused to recognize Carmona's authority and demanded that Chávez be released and returned to power. As Ellner points out, "the concept of a 'civilian-military alliance,' developed by Chávez in the 1980s, played itself out on April 12 and 13" (2008, p. 115). Within two days of the coup Chávez was returned to power. Scores of officers were detained and/or cashiered after the 2002 coup, with many of them joining the opposition in retirement, while Chávez effectively promoted and shifted officers in a manner to secure greater loyalty from the military for his government.

The United States and the 2002 Coup

The Chávez's administration was greeted with a "wait and see" attitude from the Clinton administration, which stressed analyzing Venezuelan governmental actions rather than the rhetoric of Chávez. However, there were concerns as early as 1999 about the role of nationalist/populist members of the military holding key policy positions in the state. According to Romero "... Washington was uneasy with the leftist orientation of this [military] faction and feared that its leaders lacked a firm commitment to democracy and free enterprise" (2004, p. 139). Early in the Chávez administration, its opposition to U.S. "drug war" policies was reflected in the banning of mixed-crew drug interdiction flights over Venezuelan territory (in 1999 and again in 2005) after years of close cooperation over drug war policy (International Crisis Group 2008, p. 23). Throughout the 2000s Venezuela has received the most funds, relative to other Andean nations, from the National Endowment for Democracy (NED). Between 2000 and 2002 the amount of aid provided to NED and USAID for Venezuela increased from $200,000 to almost $4 million in 2002 (James 2006, p. 4). In August 2002 the USAID established an Office of Transition Initiatives in Caracas, which is designed to promote democracy and peace in countries in crisis (Jones 2007, p. 368). Though support for oppositional groups in Venezuela has marked a substantial part of NED funds, overall the level of direct U.S. economic and military assistance to Ecuador and Venezuela pales in comparison to the support received by other countries (Colombia,

Peru, and Bolivia) in the Andean region since 1990. Between 1990 and 2006 U.S. economic and military assistance combined to Ecuador and Venezuela governments never surpassed 100 million dollars in any single year (in Venezuela, it never surpassed $50 million), while in Colombia, Peru, and Bolivia, U.S. economic and military assistance often surpassed $100 to $200 million (with Colombia receiving more than $1 billion in 2000) (USAID 2008). The relatively small levels of assistance to Venezuela and Ecuador reduced the degree of leverage that the United States possessed to influence policy outcomes within these countries, blunting the extent that the United States could influence civil-military relations during a period of increasing social conflict.

However, the assistance that was given to various anti-Chávez groups/organizations in the year preceding April 2002 was not insignificant. An investigation by the State Department's inspector general into the role of the U.S. government in the coup concluded that the NED, the Pentagon, and other assistance programs had "provided training, institution-building, and support to individuals and organizations understood to be actively involved in the brief ouster of the Chávez government" (quoted in Jones 2004). U.S. officials met with Carmona and leaders of his coup coalition as well as with Gen. Lucas Rincon Romero, chief of Venezuela's military command and a supporter of the coup, in December 2001 (Cooper 2002). Central military leaders of the coup, Efráin Vásquez Velasco (the army commander in chief) and General Ramírez Poveda, were trained at the U.S. School of the Americas (School of the Americas Watch 2004). Rear Admiral Carlos Molina, another leader of the coup, argued that "We felt we were acting with U.S. support...we agree that we can't permit a communist government here. The U.S. has not let us down yet" (Wilson 2002b).

According to the former Mexican foreign minister Jorge Casteñeda, after the coup Mexico and Chile successfully opposed attempts by the United States, Spain, Colombia, and El Salvador to construct diplomatic support for the Carmona government (Forero 2004). U.S. State Department spokesperson Phillip Reeker announced only hours after the unconstitutional arrest of Chávez, "We wish to express our solidarity with the Venezuelan people and look forward to working with all democratic forces in Venezuela to ensure the full expression of democratic rights" (Hallinan 2002). Otto Reich, the assistant secretary for Western Hemisphere Affairs, contacted Carmona after he had taken over, allegedly asking him not to dissolve the National Assembly, as the United States sought to maintain the regime's legitimacy (Cooper 2002). This support was complemented by Thomas Dawson, the IMF's director of external relations, who committed the IMF to helping the new government meet its "immediate needs" (Kozloff 2006, p. 69).

Continued Divisions and the Consolidation of

a Counterhegemonic Model: 2002–10

The failure of the 2002 coup strengthened Chávez's hand, but did not prevent the opposition within the military or civil society from attempting to remove him from power by other means. Between October 2002 and February 2003, some officers (retired and enlisted) began a "sit-down strike" in a public plaza, denouncing Chávez's leftist policies and "politicization" of the armed forces and demanding his resignation (Trinkunas, p. 222). CTV, FEDECAMARAS, and the executives of the state oil company as well as upper-level employees engaged in a national general strike between December 2002 and February 2003 in the hopes of forcing Chávez to resign. Although oil production and the overall economy severely contracted, the government was able to rely upon a majority of oil workers, the military, and foreign contractors to continue oil production and survive the strike (Wilpert 2007, p. 25). In addition, the Venezuelan armed forces directly oversaw the distribution of food throughout the country in response to the economic consequences of the strike. In early 2004 the opposition sought to push the military to remove Chávez from power through widespread street confrontations and chaos (the Guarimba Plan), but the placement of *Chavistas* in key positions within the military undermined this plan (Ellner 2008, p. 140). Finally, the opposition sought to remove Chávez through the legal means of a recall referendum in the summer of 2004, which also failed. With each failure Chávez became stronger electorally and politically, while the opposition weakened.

In the years after the recall election, Chávez went on to win reelection in 2006 and continue the process of establishing "Bolivarian Socialism for the 21st century." Through a series of extensive "missions" dedicated to expanding health care, literacy, housing, high school and college educations, a series of nationalizations (such as a major telephone and steel company, a national bank, and the cement industry), worker cooperatives, and the creation of hundreds of Socialist factories,[12] the Chávez government sought to radicalize his movement. This radicalization also affected the armed forces. In April 2007 soldiers were required to shout the slogan "Fatherland, Socialism, or Death" to their superior officers, which led to the resignation of forty-nine officers in

May 2007, while hundreds of others were without formal duties and approximately 1,000 officers[13] sought early retirement because of their disagreements with the ideological direction of the military (Latin American Regional Reports, Andean Group Report 2007; Sanchez 2008). Constitutional reform proposals made by Chávez in August 2007 called for the unification of the three branches of the armed forces (army, navy, and air force) into the *Bolivarian* Armed Forces, rather than the National Armed Forces, to emphasize the institution's connections to the government's "revolutionary" process. The reform would also allow the president to promote all military officers, not simply high-ranking ones. This armed force would also be described as an "anti-imperialist body" (LARR Andean Group Report, 2007). According to retired general Alberto Müller Rojas, a majority of the military objected to these changes, concerned about the threat to an apolitical professionalism (Müller Rojas 2007).

In November 2007 retired defense minister General Raúl Isaias Baduel, who had supported Chávez, openly criticized these changes, calling on the military to analyze the proposals and demanding that they be stopped (Janicke 2007). In September 2008 several people were detained in an alleged coup plot that included four retired military officers as well as several active military officers. Recordings between the alleged conspirators indicated that they planned on capturing the president's residence and television stations with the support of specific units in the army and air force as well as in the police (Pearson 2008). Military intelligence effectively disrupted the plot. In June 2009 the government required officers and soldiers to report to their superiors any criticisms or offensive remarks they received about the government in an attempt by the Chávez administration to reduce dissension within the ranks and undermine efforts by the opposition in civil society in influencing the armed forces (Ocando 2009).

Finally, the military relationship with civil society continued to be advanced. In 2005 the *Ley Orgánica de la Fuerza Armada Nacional* (2005) was passed requiring that civilians must have input and co-responsibility for national defense (Wilpert 2007, p. 51; Ellner 2008, p. 167). This was in keeping with the 1999 constitution (Article 326), which states that:

> "National security is based on shared responsibility between the State and civil society to implement the principles of independence, democracy, equality, peace, freedom, justice, solidarity, promotion and conservation of the environment and affirmation of human rights, as well as on that of progressively meeting the

individual and collective needs of Venezuelans, based on a sustainable and productive development policy providing full coverage for the national community."

Civilians have been recruited to support the military through the conception of co-responsibility that Venezuelan vice-president Nicolas Maduro described as a "fusion of army and people in one being, to construct new realities" (Nunez 2006). In February 2006 Chávez proposed the training and arming of one million civilian volunteers to fight in the national reserve (Nunez 2006), and in June 2008 more than 40,000 Venezuelans, including the military, the military reserves, community council members, and civilians, participated in military exercises of resistance against a foreign invasion (Suggett 2008a). According to the 2005 law, the national reserve would answer directly to the president and operate outside of the defense ministry; however, Chávez has appointed an active-duty general to direct the reserve (Ellner 2008, p. 167). In February 2010 Chávez announced the creation of a new peasant militia, which is to become part of the national armed forces. The militia was charged with protecting poor farmers who had for years been targeted by rural paramilitary militias hired by larger landowners and cattle ranchers seeking to resist the land reform agenda promoted by Chávez (Janicke 2010). The model of co-responsibility represents not only an effort to integrate the population into security affairs, but also a strategic decision to address what the government perceives as its greatest threat, an invasion from the United States or some other foreign power (Nunez 2006). Major General and Defense Minister Carlos Mata Figueroa described the peasant militias as a "strategic arm for the defense of our republic" (Janicke 2010), while in regard to the June 2008 military exercises, Colonel Francisco Salcedo, a chief coordinator of the exercises, stated "A People united will never be defeated, and the People and the reserves together defend our sovereignty against an enemy invader" (Suggett 2008a). This type of irregular or asymmetric warfare involves the mixing together of soldiers, civilians and militias into a single fighting unit, one utilizing a lower level of technology in order to confront a technologically superior foe such as the U.S. (Shiefer and Dieterich 2006).

U.S.-Venezuelan Relations since 2002

Since the 2002 coup the U.S. government continues to employ strategies to assist and support Chávez's opposition. Central organizers of the

2004 recall drive and organizations, Leonardo Carvajal and Leopoldo Martínez (who had been selected by Carmona to be his education minister and finance minister, respectively), received NED funds (Jones 2004). In the years following the April 2002 coup, the NED distributed more than US $800,000 to various anti-Chávez organizations involved not only in the 2004 recall drive, but also in destabilizing strikes at the end of 2002 and early 2003 (Golinger, 2004a). During the same period USAID committed more than US$5 million annually to different groups in Venezuela, many a part of Chávez's political opposition and/or who had participated in the 2002 coup, including FEDECAMARAS (Golinger, 2004b; James 2006, p. 6).

Given the difficult relations with the United States and Chávez's objective of promoting greater Latin American autonomy and independence from the United States, military-to-military relations have been substantially reduced. For example, in the Andes, Venezuela received the lowest level of U.S. funding for international military education training (IMET) between 1996 and 2008, with Venezuela receiving zero funding between 2004 and 2008 (Just the Facts 2008c). Also, in 2004 the Chávez administration announced that Venezuela would no longer send troops to train at the Western Hemisphere Institute for Security Cooperation in Fort Benning, Georgia, with Chávez arguing that "this school deformed the minds of many Latin American soldiers, who from there went on to become dictators" (School of the Americas Watch 2004). In April 2004, a thirty-five-year old military cooperation agreement with the United States was terminated, bringing to an end the practice of U.S. military personnel being stationed in Venezuela (James 2006, p. 20). In 2006, the Venezuelan government removed John Correa, a U.S. military attaché, from the country, accusing him of collecting classified information from approximately two dozen Venezuelan naval officers, while on August 19, 2006, the U.S. Director of National Intelligence established a special CIA mission to administer intelligence activities in Venezuela and Cuba (*The Economist* 2006; Gollinger 2006). In the summer of 2007 a U.S. embassy official in Caracas commented that the United States had little to no access or knowledge of the Venezuelan military, a dramatic reversal from the period prior to 1998 (interview August 30, 2007, Caracas).

This independence has also been reflected in Venezuelan foreign policy. Chávez has increasingly spoken about the establishment of a multipolar world in which U.S. hegemony is undermined by multiple power centers. He has sought a range of military and economic relations with U.S. rivals such as China, Russia, and Iran while seeking ways to reduce Venezuelan dependence on the U.S. market for Venezuelan petroleum. Chávez has also sought greater integration of Latin American nations with regional initiatives such as the Bolivarian Alternative of the Americas (ALBA), which aims to promote trade and development on an equitable footing, or the South American Defense Council, which is a forum to reduce regional conflicts and facilitate military cooperation to address regional security issues. The defense council also seeks a type of academic integration, proposing a South American Center of Strategic Studies, a center for military studies outside of the U.S. orbit (Suggett 2009).

The declining role of military-to-military contacts between the United States and Venezuela, as well as Venezuela's relative economic independence (via its energy exports), weakens potential levers that the United States can use against Venezuela, and specifically the military, to ensure a model of politics and civil-military relations consistent with the interests of global capitalism. The indications of military opposition to Chávez illustrate that the military is not completely unified behind the Chávez project; however, the lack of any serious coup attempts since 2002, the effective use of military intelligence, and the control of key command and control positions by officers sympathetic with the Bolivarian project suggest that the military will continue to maintain and protect Chávez's constitutional right to power for the immediate future. According to Rocío San Miguel, director of the Caracas-based NGO Citizen's Civilian Control Association for Security, Defense and the National Armed Forces, Chávez has placed 200 strongly committed *Chavistas* to the armed forces' most important positions. Chávez's support for the army with new equipment (such as Sukhoi bombers and Mi helicopters) has also strengthened his hold over the central service within the armed forces (Sanchez 2009). The establishment of "co-responsibility" illustrates another potential mechanism of mitigating societal and military opposition to the Chávez government.

Conclusion

In Ecuador and Venezuela, the continued role and influence of the armed forces has been, and is, centrally related to the inability of neoliberal policy coalitions to obtain a hegemonic position within the state. Governments have come to power in Ecuador committed to this agenda, but have been frustrated by societal and/or military opposition. The administrations of Noboa and Palacios were able to make progress during relatively stable periods "modernizing" civil-military relations, but the disorder of the Gutiérrez government and the nationalist/populist administration of Correa have undermined continuing progress. In the case of Venezuela, the success and continuity of Chávez's nationalist/populist movement has established the foundations for a civil-military state directly challenging liberal conceptions of civil-military relations.

New movements have emerged attempting to replace (or that have replaced) the traditional parties (such as the Partido Socialista Unida de Venezuela in Venezuela and CONAIE with its Patchauck Party, or Alianza País in Ecuador) often working with sectors of the armed forces in order to advance their goals. In addition, these movements have sought to redefine traditional ideas about the meaning of democracy, one in which a broader role for the military is accepted, a type inconsistent with low-intensity democracies.

Though the United States has been successful in preventing a military regime from being established in Ecuador, it has failed to ensure the continuation of a specific neoliberal policy coalition. In Venezuela, though the U.S. government supported the coup of 2002, it has thus far failed in its efforts to destabilize the antineoliberal administration of Hugo Chávez. The struggle between neoliberal and nationalist/populist sectors continues in both countries; however, neoliberal actors have thus far been unable to maintain a leadership position within either state. The political and military reforms associated with their control in other countries in the region have been weakened as a result.

of these movements culminated with the successful presidential election of Evo Morales, a coca grower activist and vocal critic of capitalist globalization.

The failure to successfully repress and marginalize anticapitalist globalization movements is, in part, a reflection of the narrow nature of the military's internal security role. The involvement of the armed forces with coca eradication only involved specific units, while the majority of the military was generally disconnected from this struggle. Thus, the potential effect of a unifying internal mission in the face of clear domestic security threats was blunted in Bolivia, as the various social movements that emerged during the 1980s and 1990s were never viewed consistently or uniformly as national security threats. This is in contrast to the substantive threats faced by Colombian and Peruvian militaries during the same period.

Bolivia's relationship with the United States continuously stressed the establishment of a market democracy and the promotion of U.S. conceptions of Bolivia's security threats with its attempts to directly involve the Bolivian military in the "drug war." The U.S. "drug war" efforts contributed to enhancing the financial/training ties with specific units of the Bolivian military, but this did not prevent the emergence of nationalist critiques against the U.S.-imposed counternarcotics mission. The presidential election of the nationalist/populist Evo Morales has steadily disrupted this relationship with the United States while politically weakening conservative political leaders that have enjoyed close ties with sectors of the armed forces in the past. However, the Bolivian case remains in flux, with regional elites that enjoy close economic and ideological ties to capitalist globalization and U.S. interests continuing to prevent the establishment of a counterhegemonic project in Bolivia. In this effort, these elites have sought to influence factions within the military to support their agenda.

The following examines the interaction between domestic and international factors leading to the erosion of military prerogatives and the maintenance of political control in the post-1982 period as well as the factors that have begun to reverse this agenda. My analysis focuses primarily on the period in which neoliberal policy coalitions came to power and implemented a series of policies to reform the economy and state (1982–2000) as well as the societal and political efforts to establish a counterhegemonic project (2000–present). Again, as with the other cases, global and domestic factors interacted to strengthen and weaken specific policy coalitions and their respective policy agendas. Although neoliberal policy coalitions were able to maintain control over the state

CHAPTER 4

Low-Intensity Democracy, Popular Resistance, and Military Power in Bolivia

Although the armed forces have participated in helping us attend to social demands, the recuperation of our natural resources, I feel something is missing... unfortunately, in some military institutes, they continue to teach that the enemy is socialism. We have to change that. The real enemy is capitalism, not socialism.

—Bolivian President Evo Morales speaking during his inauguration for his second term, January 21, 2010.[1]

The case of Bolivia is examined separately from the other cases given its parallels with the four other countries examined thus far. Bolivia, like Peru and Colombia, was governed for well over a decade by different neoliberal/globalist governments that involved its military in an internal security mission, specifically suppressing coca growers and various anticapitalist globalization movements. They also made progress in reducing military prerogatives over the defense ministry and defense budgets, as well as in the development of security strategies. However, like Ecuador and Venezuela, Bolivia's military contained important nationalist/populist factions within its ranks as well as powerful anticapitalist globalization social movements resisting the policy dictates and influence of neoliberal policy coalitions. The Bolivian military has for decades been internally divided over governmental policies and civil-military reforms, with factions orienting around specific rightist/conservative parties promoting neoliberalism or others developing alliances with *campesino* movements and indigenous struggles. The struggle for almost two decades, they were unsuccessful in establishing their hegemony. Competing social blocs emerged to regularly challenge their agenda and as of this writing have partially displaced their control over the state.

Civil-Military Relations Before 1982

Throughout most of Bolivia's history, the military has played an instrumental role in its politics. Between 1825 and 1996 there were more than 190 coup attempts, with the military directly governing in the twentieth century in the late 1930s and early 1940s, and again between 1964 and 1982 (Gammara and Malloy 1996, p. 308). The military governments of the twentieth century have generally been tied to specific groups or organizations in civil society, with factions of the armed forces joining specific policy coalitions in opposition or in support of populist/nationalist projects that have regularly emerged in Bolivian politics.

For example, the military governments that came to power in the late 1930s represented a period of "military socialism" in which the army worked with leftist parties and movements to implement a series of progressive and socially redistributive measures.[2] In partial contrast, Bolivia's 1952 revolution was one in which the military became a target. The revolutionary government of the *Movimiento Nacionalista Revolucionario* (MNR) that came to power in 1952 successfully implemented agrarian reform policies, temporarily disbanded and reorganized the military, nationalized Bolivia's tin resources, established universal suffrage, and ended some of the racist policies/customs that had long been practiced against the indigenous population.[3] This revolutionary government was never able to fully consolidate its power and was buffeted by pressures from the left and right as well as from the United States. The armed forces, though disbanded early in the revolutionary government, would later be re-organized in part due to U.S. demands, enjoying greater power to repress radicalized labor groups unhappy with the direction and speed of governmental programs (Ledebur 2005, p. 148; Gamarra and Malloy 1996, **p.** 312; Mitchell 1977, p. 52).

The military regime that came to power in 1964 was strongly influenced by the United States, adopting the national security doctrine of defeating internal enemies. In fact, agents of the U.S. army and the CIA played a supportive role in the actual coup against the MNR regime (Hylton and Thomson 2007, p. 82). The objective of the United States had been to help re-create Bolivia's military with the expectation that the armed forces would step in if the MNR government went too far in its policies and/or leftists attained too great a level of influence over the government. As a State Department memo in early 1956 stated, the United States was seeking "insurance" in supporting the Bolivian army that "... might act as a balance and having the right capacity and orientation, be able to step into the breach in extreme circumstances" (as quoted in Lehman 1999, p. 149). Increasing U.S. aid provided the military a sense of greater legitimacy and influence (Lehman 1999, p. 149). In 1963 the entire senior class of the Bolivian military academy had been schooled in jungle warfare by the United States, while Bolivia had more graduates from the U.S. Army Special Warfare School than any other nation in Latin America. By 1964 the Pentagon was equal to the State Department in its role in Bolivia (Lehman 1999, p. 151).[4] Given this increasing power, it is not surprising that the MNR government would come to an end in 1964 via a military coup that was motivated by concerns about the weight of Communist and radical unions that sought to push the MNR agenda further to the left.

· However, this conservative orientation failed to fully consolidate itself within the armed forces, with military reformers coming to power in 1969. The military faction that held power between 1969 and 1971 was motivated by the nationalist/leftist politics of the Bolivian labor movement as well as the nationalist examples set by the Peruvian military at the time. Bolivia's military reformers, led by General Juan José Torres, supervised a governing congress in 1971 dominated by radical unions and peasants who proceeded to implement a number of policies in an effort to establish radical change, a "populist, nationalist and revolutionary" alternative (Mitchell 1977, p. 109). Torres's regime had followed the nationalist military government of General Alfredo Ovando, who governed from 1969 to 1970 and who nationalized the properties of U.S.-based oil interests and improved connections with the Soviet Union while reducing U.S. influence (Lehman 1999, p. 159). However, this military reformist period would also be cut short by a military coup in 1971. General Hugo Banzer led this military coup. Banzer had been trained in the United States and was supported by the conservative business elite in Santa Cruz. He promoted a less reformist set of policies and focused upon improving agroexport industries and assisting large estate owners (Hylton and Thomson 2007, pp. 84–6). Ultimately, his conservative policies would undermine the corporatist relations the military had developed with the peasantry since 1964, with the "military-*campesino*" pact coming to an end in 1974 after the implementation of a series of austerity measures that directly harmed peasant interests. After 1974 the regime had to become increasingly more repressive in order to maintain power, given the loss of this key social ally, while the business community strongly supported Banzer's strategies to marginalize trade union and leftist movements (Quintana 2005, p. 405; Conaghan and Malloy 1994, p. 58).

For most of this period (1964–78) military governments pursued a variety of state developmentalist or state capitalist projects in order to promote economic growth, stability, and modernization. Foreign investors and the Bolivian private sector benefited greatly from military rule, becoming a political pillar for military governments (Mitchell 1977, p. 101). The military also engaged directly in industrial development through the creation of the state-military enterprise COFADENA (Corporación de las Fuerzas Armadas para el Desarrollo Nacional). COFADENA became a highly diversified industrial corporation with investments in military munitions, leather goods, and even bricks (Gamarra and Malloy 1988, p. 100). While Bolivia's business community was largely supportive of Banzer, concerns were raised about the potential role of COFADENA as well as the increasing expansion of statist development in driving out private actors and investment (Conaghan and Malloy 1994, pp. 63–4).

The military generally was not motivated, especially after the 1971 Banzer coup, by a desire to redistribute wealth or promote social justice. They were focused upon stamping out Communism and weakening the political power of labor in line with the national security doctrine prominent in military regimes throughout the region, while advancing development (. In part, they were guided by the belief that only their institution could develop the Bolivian economy, given the failures of civilian regimes, as well as the various corporate benefits that such development could provide to the armed forces and its allies among the Bolivian elite based in Santa Cruz. Finally, the military high command was motivated by the need to maintain institutional integrity and greatly feared that the military would "split into rival camps over class-based political issues" as it had in the past (Mitchell 1977, p. 124; see also Hylton and Thomson 2007, pp. 84–9). The Banzer government pursued a variety of economic and political policies that facilitated expanded international trade and increased Bolivia's economic ties with Brazil's bureaucratic authoritarian regime while administering nationwide repression against Communists and other political dissidents (Encyclopedia of World Biographies 2005–6; Estellano 1994, pp. 36–7).

The military's unity in mission and economic policy would be undermined in the late 1970s and early 1980s by the region-wide debt crisis, major declines in the prices of key exports, the infiltration of narcotrafficking elements within the military, international pressures for democratization, and major social mobilizations against their continuity in power. The organized business community, in particular the *Confederación de Empresarios Privados de Bolivia* (CEPB), increasingly demanded progress toward a democratic transition, citing its inability to directly influence the military regime, as well as frustration with the expansion of the state's intervention in the economy (Conaghan and Malloy 1994, pp. 64, 85, 89). The holding of national presidential elections during this period was repeatedly interrupted by conservative business and landed elites as well as narcotrafficking organizations allied directly with factions of the military that sought to prevent the election of a leftist political coalition and to hold out for a more conservative government in the United States (Rouquié 1987, p. 464). Between 1978 and 1982 five different military juntas would come to power, while leftist trade unionist and Socialist parties actively pursued a more radical agenda (Conaghan and Malloy 1994, p. 89). Business elites, such as CEPB, were active during this period in demanding military coups. However, this would change in the face of the international isolation and elimination of international credit that confronted the narcotrafficking military regime of General García Meza and the weakening of the military within Bolivia. One CEPB leader concluded that

> "You see, we always looked at the military as an important means of saving us from the extreme left in this country. And the less prestige they had the less we could count on them... and we knew that this meant that the longer [the military] stayed, the greater the chances that the extreme left would take over the country in a coup....We could not allow the prestige of the military to suffer, so we started a campaign to begin a true democratic process" (as quoted in Conaghan and Malloy 1994, p. 90).

Ultimately, this conflict and disorder would be resolved and a democratic transition in 1982 would successfully be accomplished with the assistance of military factions that rejected the corruption and repression associated with narcotrafficking elements within its ranks.

Civil–Military Relations, 1982–2000

Civil–military relations during the democratic period after 1982 have been described as a form of "hybrid" relations in which the military has been conditionally subordinated to civilian authorities, with the military conceding certain prerogatives while maintaining others. Bolivia's first democratic government did propose an ambitious plan for reforming civil–military relations, but had to reverse course in the face of military opposition (for example, the president had to replace his first civilian defense minister with one that was retired from the military). However, the high command did purge the military of a number of corrupt officers/soldiers tied to narcotrafficking. In fact, trials were conducted against members of the drug-trafficking regime of García Meza, but were not conducted for the human rights violators that preceded him, especially since prominent political parties had supported and worked with these past military regimes (Quintana 2005, p. 410-1). Another example of this conditional subordination took place in July 1984 when a sector of right-wing officers, conservative politicians, and cocaine traffickers kidnapped the leftist president Hernan Siles Zuazo for ten hours in an attempted coup. Institutionalist officers, labor protests, and international pressures (including a threat by the United States to end all diplomatic relations) brought the coup attempt to an end with approximately 100 conservative military and police officers and politicians arrested in the aftermath (*New York Times* 1984). Finally, while the military would ultimately allow a series of civilian ministers of defense, it retained the power to directly negotiate with the president through the chief commander of the armed forces, as opposed to a line of command that would go through the defense minister (Quintana 2005, pp. 412–3). Between 1982 and 1997 nine of the twelve defense ministers were civilians, with four of these civilians coming from the business community (Quintana and Barrios 1999, p. 247). However, the military's maintenance of influence within the executive branch was insufficient to prevent substantial reductions to its budgets throughout the 1980s and 1990s. International pressures for economic reform and the political project of Bolivia's neoliberal policy coalition dedicated to a shift away from state capitalism over-rode most military resistance to budget cuts.

Dominant parties such as the MNR and the National Democratic Action Party (ADN) agreed through a series of "party pacts" to a neoliberal direction of the country following a period of severe economic instability and disorder that characterized the leftist government that ruled between 1982 and 1985. Major labor strikes, over 11,000 percent inflation, and declining export revenues, coupled with a burgeoning foreign debt, had brought the country into economic crisis and created the policy space for a radical shift from state capitalist policies. The 1985 election brought to power Victor Paz Estenssoro, head of the MNR, who had finished second to General Hugo Banzer representing the ADN, but with neither winning a majority, a compromise was worked within the Congress to allow Paz to come to power. A "Pact for Democracy" was established between the two parties, with an explicit commitment to economic reform, a new economic policy that included free markets, trade liberalization, and the reduction of state influence/control in the economy (Orias Arredondo 2005, p. 47). The economics associated with the pact were strongly supported by Bolivia's capitalist class, which welcomed the shift to a market orientation and the rejection of the statist policies of the past (Conaghan and Malloy 1994, pp. 121–2). The economic crisis of the early 1980s and the fragmentation of the Bolivian left contributed to the political support for these neoliberal party coalitions, while a large informal sector (50 to 60 percent of the laboring population) further undermined the ability of the radical left to organize an effective left response (Quintana and Barrios 1999, p. 225). In addition, the various episodes of resistance, such as the general strike of September 4, 1984, was heavily repressed by the police and army, which detained more than 200 hundred leaders, while a mass march on the capital in March 1986 was stopped by the army (Conaghan and Malloy 1994, pp. 149–50).

Bolivia's neoliberal direction was reinforced by international financial institutions. At different times in the 1980s and 1990s Bolivian governments had to sign loan agreements with these institutions that regularly required cuts in government spending, in particular, military spending. By the mid-1990s Bolivia had become a regional model of neoliberalism, inflation was low, and moderate economic growth was established with increasing levels of foreign direct investment and ownership of the economy (Lehman 2006, p. 131). According to Jeffrey Sachs, a key World Bank advisor to different Bolivian governments, the first ten years of Bolivia's market democracy, Bolivia "made a fundamental turn toward macroeconomic stability" while remaining a "very poor place" (Sachs 2000).

Bolivia is the poorest country in South America with two-thirds of its population living in poverty and 30 percent of the population surviving on less than $1 a day, while it has the second highest infant mortality rate in Latin America (Ledebur 2005, p. 146). Given this economic situation, the country has been dependent upon foreign aid, relying upon the United States, the World Bank, and the Inter-American Development Bank to mitigate the country's extreme poverty. Of course, this aid has been contingent upon Bolivia pursuing neoliberal economic reforms and U.S. "drug war" strategies, which it did throughout the 1980s and 1990s. President Sánchez de Lozada (1993–7, 2001–3) stated "the dependency is terrible; the International Monetary Fund comes, the United States Embassy comes, the World Bank comes, and they all tell us what to do" (as quoted in Ledebur 2005, p. 146).

The military resistance to this process was near nonexistent, in part, due to its substantial loss of legitimacy from the repressive/narcotrafficking military governments of the late 1970s and early 1980s. In addition, leading military factions were co-opted to this agenda through clientelism and U.S. intervention/influence in the country. According to the Bolivian political scientist and presidential advisor to Evo Morales, Juan Ramon Quintana, "the civilian authorities ensured that the military's obedience would be effective only during their time in government with little importance to the future. For that, they employed different strategies of co-optation and patronage that allows, on the one hand, to cancel institutional demands for modernization, and on the other hand, to exercise political control over the military elite through unconstitutional incentives that promote corruption" (2005, p. 396). Throughout most of the post-1982 period the promotion process was politicized, with promotions to the high command that responded more to specific partisan or personalist loyalties as opposed to meritocracy. The military was most closely aligned with the ADN political party that was led by former military dictator Hugo Banzer, who retained a number of close ties with the active armed forces (Quintana and Barrios 1999, p. 256).

Bolivia's neoliberal policy coalition successfully used its political intervention to appoint civilians to head the Ministry of Defense throughout the 1980s and 1990s, with few exceptions and cut military budgets. In 1980 defense received $390 million, while in 1990 it only received $120 million (Quintana and Barrios 1999, p. 247, p. 238). These cuts led to the suspension of subsidies for state corporations operated by the armed forces through COFADENA, even undermining civic action programs leading to "...the most traumatic blows that the military institution suffered during this period" (Quintana and Barrios 1999, p. 238). By the mid-1990s Gamarra and Malloy concluded that "the Bolivian military had become impoverished" (1996, p. 324).

By the end of 1991 the neoliberal government of Jaime Paz Zamora (1989–93) passed a Ley Orgánica de las FFAA (N°1405), which reaffirmed with more clarity the subordination of the armed forces to civilian authority, clearly specifying its subordination to the president and its mission to defend the country's democratic institutions (Quintana and Barrios 1999, p. 233; Red de Seguridad y Defensa de América Latina 2008). In addition, new laws on the control and administration of state spending associated with the neoliberal reforms in the 1980s reduced the discretion the military had enjoyed in the use of military budgets (Quintana and Barrios 1999, p. 250; see also Barrios Morón and Antonio Mayorga 1994, p. 80). This took place after years in which the military enjoyed the prerogative of control over the purpose and size of military budgets under previous governments.

The cuts in military spending were mitigated by the support of the United States, which backed the military's increasing role in internal security and coca eradication. Beginning slowly in the 1980s and escalating dramatically in the 1990s, the Bolivian military was brought into the U.S.-imposed "war on drugs." During this period Bolivia became one of the central sources of coca, the central ingredient for cocaine, and the United States pressured the nation to promote its supply reduction strategy against the crop. The first Bush administration explicitly tied the U.S. "war on drugs" with free trade, signing into law the Andean Trade Preference Act (ATPA) in late 1991, which provided tariff-free access to the U.S. market for selective Bolivian products (Gamarra and Malloy 1996, p. 320) in order to support the Bolivian economy and provide economic alternatives for coca growers.

The national police was the central unit involved in this process, but in the face of growing dissent and protest by coca growers in the Chapare region, the Bolivian government was pressured to increase the involvement of the army. This led to an increasing level of influence by the United States upon Bolivia's army. U.S. troops were actually involved in counterdrug operations on Bolivian territory in 1986, and U.S. Special Forces trained specialized Bolivian police forces while funding the creation of special counterdrug units within the armed forces. In 1990 President Paz Zamora (1989–93) signed an agreement with the United States formalizing the role of the military in counterdrug missions and strategies (Ledebur 2005, p. 150). The Paz Zamora government embraced the U.S. drug war strategy in order to improve relations, committing to greater levels of coca eradication in exchange for continued U.S. military/economic assistance, as well as support in Bolivian-IFI negotiations. In fact, during the early 1990s the United States made millions of dollars in aid *contingent* upon the involvement of the Bolivian military in the U.S. "war on drugs" (Lehman 1999, pp. 206–7).

For example, in the first administration of Sánchez de Lozada (1993–7), an attempt by him to subordinate coca eradication to other developmental priorities led to the threatened U.S. cut-off of economic assistance. This forced Sánchez to send the army into Chapare to eradicate more coca, which only intensified political opposition against him (Lehman 2006, p. 134). A retired military officer argued that the U.S. embassy's role in counterdrug operations had "reached a grotesque level" and that "many Bolivian officials are beginning to question the U.S. occupation of the Bolivian armed forces" (as quoted in Ledebur 2005, p. 157). However, another soldier stressed the importance of U.S. aid, "Where else are we going to get training and equipment? We'll never get out from under the gringos; we might as well take advantage of it" (as quoted in Ledebur 2005, p. 157).

While it was clear that the Bolivian armed forces were receiving some advantages from this relationship, the benefits were not uniformly shared. Access to better training and equipment to fight drugs was disproportionately focused upon three elite antinarcotics units, with the rest of the military receiving relatively little (Gamarra and Malloy 1996, p. 324). In fact, when asked in a 1998 survey, 73 percent of the military admitted that their involvement in coca eradication was due to the imposition of the United States, while more than one-third believed that the military was neglecting its "traditional duties," including external defense (Ledebur 2005, p. 157). These concerns had been preceded by the organization of various political factions within the armed forces arguing that the government had become a tool of the United States. These factions included the "Army of Bolivar," which attacked IMF economic policies, and the "Vivo Rojo," which described their faction as "trotskist" (Nash 1992). Gamarra and Malloy argued in the mid-1990s that "sympathies for the rebellious officers in Venezuela [that launched a nationalist/populist rebellion against a neoliberal regime in 1992] are rather well known" (1996, p. 324). For example, the neoliberal government of Sánchez-Lozada (1993–7) faced open criticisms of his privatization policies from the armed forces. Sánchez viewed the armed forces as a "hindrance" and even believed that Bolivia's national development might require the disappearance of the armed forces altogether (Quintana 2005, p. 424). This dissension within the military regarding its role speaks to the extent that the armed forces were not unified behind a specific mission and objected to the domestic role being pressed upon them by the United States.

Sánchez de Lozada had been a central figure in Bolivia's neoliberal transition. An individual with substantial stakes in Bolivia's mining industry and a U.S. education in economics, he had been a central economic advisor to Paz Estenssoro and was crucial to the successful implementation of neoliberal economic policies. As Conaghan and Malloy remark, "he was a pivotal character in the making of the neoliberal coalition—rallying business elites of the CEPB, technocrats and the international financial community to support the experiment" (1994, p. 127). Sánchez de Lozada would apply this modernizing attitude toward defense with the appointment of his first two defense ministers, who represented the modernizing wing of his government. In addition, he violated the promotional protocol by retiring the head of the army, General Balderrama, with General Aguilera, an individual more amenable to Sánchez's privatization plans (Guzmán 2003).

President Sánchez's maneuvers with the high command and the military's public criticisms of his privatization policies reflected the persistence of a national developmentalist idea in the armed forces. Barrios Morón and Antonio Mayorga argue that the Bolivian military "...has an accentuated antiliberal tradition born from its continued presence in the administration of governmental power...they shared the idea that the state should have a broad role in directing the economy of the country" (1994, p. 83). Well into the 2000s the military continued to be involved in investments in land and industrial enterprises, which worked to help finance the Bolivian armed forces (Fundación, Libertad, Democracia y Desarrollo 2004, p. 7). The market orientation of Bolivia's neoliberal policy coalition also conflicted with the belief of many in the military that its role in national development was a central part of its mission and legitimacy in the country. In fact, public work projects, job training, medical clinics and home construction have all been a part of its developmentalist role, a role that is enshrined in the country's constitution and the Ley Orgánica de las Fuerzas Armadas de la Nación. Article 13 of the Ley Orgánica states "The Armed Forces participate actively in national development..." while Article 14 states "...the Armed Forces can participate in the country's basic and strategic industries" (Red de Seguridad y Defensa de América Latina 2008). This role is viewed as necessary to cushion the consequences of capitalist globalization, which allowed the military to enjoy more confidence and support from Bolivian citizens than either political parties, the Congress, or labor unions received during the 1990s (Quintana 2005, p. 451). Finally, the military regularly disrupted economic integration plans that involved closer ties with their historical rival, Chile, a country that eliminated Bolivia's access to the sea in a late-nineteenth-century war and was still viewed as a potential threat in the 1990s (Quintana and Barrios 1999, p. 252).

By 2000 the Bolivian military had been subordinated to civilian authorities through the demands of international financial institutions, partisan corruption, and a U.S.-directed/funded internal mission. However, internal factions continued to persist and military subordination to civilian authorities did not prevent public objections to the neoliberal project and/or a desire to preserve a state developmentalist role.

Civil-Military Relations, 2000–10

The period between 2000 and 2006 is described as a "revolutionary epoch" by Alvaro García Linera, the sociologist and current vice-president of Bolivia, in which "social sectors, blocs or classes previously apathetic or tolerant of those in power openly challenge authority and claim rights or make collective petitions through direct mobilizations" (2006, p. 81). The failures of Bolivia's neoliberal experiment were instrumental to the emergence of this anticapitalist globalization bloc. In 2003 the quality of life in Bolivia had worsened from what it had been five years earlier, with 90 percent of the highlands population living in poverty, more than 3 million with no electricity, and the income of the poorest 10 percent of the population declined by 15 percent while the richest 10 percent watched their income increase 16 percent between 2000 and 2003 (Dangl 2007, p. 79). The continuation of prohibitionist strategies against coca growers simply exacerbated this situation.

Beginning with the fierce resistance of coca farmers in the Chapare in the mid-1990s, the massive demonstrations in 2000 and 2003 in which whole cities were occupied by popular protest against the privatization of water utilities (2000), and the failure to nationalize natural gas (2003), a growing nationalist/populist social bloc emerged with the desire to take state power and replace the neoliberal policy coalition that had governed since 1985. The economic neoliberalism and internal repression/eradication of coca growers and their crops, which were the central tenets of Bolivia's low-intensity democracy and were ideologically and financially backed by the United States and international financial institutions, began to unravel. Progress toward the institution of a counterhegemonic model came about with the presidential election of Evo Morales at the head of his Movement Toward Socialism (MAS) party in December 2005. Morales, the indigenous head of a coca-growers union who had for years struggled against U.S.-imposed drug control policies, led a popular movement on an antineoliberal/pro-indigenous rights platform that was directly tied to the social struggles that had taken place prior to 2005. The military's role in this process of social change, this "revolutionary epoch," has been a mixed one, given the internal divisions that have long existed within the institution.

The shift away from state capitalist strategies to neoliberal economic ones contributed to declines in formal employment, increases in economic inequality, and increasing urbanization with the corresponding decline of peasant agriculture. Relatedly, there was a substantial increase in the number of small farmers turning to the growing of coca to survive in this more competitive and open marketplace. As early as the mid-1980s, coca production was Bolivia's only growth industry that supported a livelihood for thousands of small farmers in the Chapare and Yungas regions (Lehman 2006, p. 133). The expansion of coca growers coupled with the demands of the U.S. state for increasing eradication brought the Bolivian military into the U.S. drug war.

In 1998 the government created a joint task force combining military and police eradication units that went on to heavily militarize the Chapare region. Between 1997 and 1998 the proportion of the military involved directly in the Chapare region increased from 1 percent to 10 percent of military personnel (Quintana 2005, p. 439). This sharp increase in the expansion in the role of the military took place during the Banzer government (1997–2001), which committed the Bolivian government to a "Zero Coca" policy referred to as "Plan Dignidad" in order to please the United States. Banzer continued the civil-military policies of previous governments by expanding the military's role in the "drug war," as well as through the promotion of personal loyalists, while regularly consulting with the military on policy matters (Quintana 2005, pp. 432–3). The military's increasing internal role, while inconsistent with traditional notions of civilian control, was in keeping with the role of the military within low-intensity democracies. The increasing levels of state repression that took place during the Banzer administration and later in the second Sánchez de Lozada administration are testament to this coercive response. As in the case of Colombia and Peru, domestic security is militarized not simply to address armed security threats, but also to repress popular opposition to capitalist globalization and/or security policies promoted by the United

States for the region—facilitating economic integration (such as suppressing organized worker movements).

In response to the government's more aggressive strategies, *cocalero* unions regularly marched, blocked highways, and worked to prevent the military and police from eradicating their fields, leading to intense confrontations, while the United States worked to undermine dialogue with the coca unions in order to maintain its militarized strategies. Throughout the 1990s the military and police forces were involved in the deaths of coca growers, illegal detentions, and the repression of peaceful demonstrations, with thirty-three coca growers and twenty-seven members of the security forces killed in Plan Dignidad operations between 1998 and the end of 2003. The Banzer government, as did previous governments, successfully resisted efforts to prosecute military or police personnel for human rights violations, allowing them the impunity to repress social protest. The military often refused to cooperate with investigations of their misconduct and insisted that *all* crimes that the military were accused of committing be tried in military courts (Ledebur 2005, 144-5, 169–70). U.S. efforts to limit human rights violations through the Leahy amendment were also ineffective, as the U.S. government consistently refused to withhold funds from military units accused of human rights violations (Ledebur 2005, p. 171). In April 2001 the George W. Bush administration promoted the Andean Regional Initiative, a counternarcotics plan that was an extension of Plan Colombia. The Andean Regional Initiative committed almost $4 billion to support "democracy, development and drug control" (Lehman 2006, p. 131). With the U.S. "war on terrorism" after 9/11, more efforts were being employed to tie coca growers with terrorism in order to provide further justification for a militarized approach.

U.S. influence was also central to Bolivia's 2002 presidential election of Gonzalo Sánchez de Lozada for his second term. His campaign was aided by a team of U.S. political consultants that supported him, in part, because, as the pollster Jeremy Rosner put it, "We believe in a particular brand of democracy, which is progressive, social democratic, market-based and modern" (as quoted in Forero 2006). Sánchez de Lozada's selection as president (2002–3) was decided by the Bolivian Congress when he only received 22 percent of the vote to Morales's 21 percent of the vote. Congressional support for Sánchez was brokered by U.S. ambassador Manuel Rocha, who convinced another elite party to support him over Morales (Lehman 2006, p. 147). This was after Rocha's comments during the campaign in which he warned Bolivians of the dangers to U.S. aid if they voted for Morales, which led to increased support for Morales's candidacy. This involvement of Rocha in the 2002 campaign only strengthened the existing perception that Sánchez de Lozada would defer to the interests and demands of the United States over Bolivian interests.

During his second administration, Sánchez de Lozada attempted to negotiate with coca grower unions in the first four months of his administration. However, the coca growers' proposal for the demilitarization of the Chapare region and a suspension of coca eradication was rejected by U.S. officials and thus was rejected by Sánchez de Lozada. The U.S. ambassador to Bolivia (Daniel Santos) argued that Bolivia risked losing access to trade benefits through the Andean Trade Preferences and Drug Eradication Act (ATPDEA), stating that "participation in the ATPDEA program is marked by certain requirements and conditions that dictate that the war on drugs must continue" (Ledebur 2003). In response to the breakdown of negotiations, coca growers and other social movements began protests throughout the country, which included road blockades. The military and police were utilized to demobilize these protests, leading to the deaths of eleven individuals (including two security members).

The demands of international financial institutions contributed to additional protests in February 2003. In an effort to reduce the government's budget deficit, as required by the IMF, the government issued a tax increase upon salaries greater than $110 a month. This increase heavily affected police salaries, leading to a police strike. The police, already believing they were underpaid before the tax increase, engaged in a work stoppage. In protest around the Presidential Palace, supporters of the police began to stone the building, while the military police and the presidential guard opened fire against the crowd, striking police officers and leading to fourteen deaths (ten policemen and four military men). This violence simply led to an escalating conflict as Sánchez de Lozada called upon the military to suppress the protesters and striking police, leading to the deaths of thirty-two people (including police and military personnel) (Ledebur 2005, p. 161; Hylton and Thomson 2007, pp. 108–9).

In September and October Sánchez de Lozada had to deal with further popular challenges to his power. This period of popular resistance encompassed the rights of coca growers, critiques of antidrug legislation, and demands that the country's national gas resources be nationalized and used to serve Bolivian needs, as well as an overall objection to the Free Trade Area of the Americas (Ledebur 2005, p. 163). Sánchez's government repeatedly turned to the military for support, not only in his confrontation with the police, but against social protest in general. Accountability for the human rights violations committed by the military in subduing the police in February 2003 was frustrated by the military's refusal to cooperate with prosecutors and their insistence that such investigations remain within the military justice system (Human Rights Watch 2004). During the "Gas Wars" in September and October 2003 the army again was utilized to bring order to the situation as indigenous protesters, miners, and unions from El Alto descended upon La Paz, as well as El Alto, successfully encircling and blockading these cities. The mass mobilization represented an effort to prevent the nation's gas reserves (the largest in Latin America) from being sold to a U.S. company, who planned on shipping the gas through a Chilean port (Dangl 2003).[5] Bolivia's Landless Movement called for land occupations, coca growers announced blockades of roads between Santa Cruz and Cochabamba, and the central labor confederation called for a general strike for September 30 (Hylton and Thomson 2007, p. 112). Through October, general strikes, civic strikes, marches, and various mobilizations continued.

Rather then continue with difficult negotiations with the central leaders of these demonstrations, the government turned to security forces, which killed at least sixty people and injured hundreds. In fact, there were cases of soldiers being tortured and killed by their superiors for refusing to shoot unarmed protesters, as well as instances of defectors from the military and police who joined the protesters (Dangl 2007, p. 147). The number of people who died during Sánchez's fourteen-month term was near the number of political killings that took place during Bolivia's military dictatorships, with some human rights activists viewing the deaths of civilians in October as unprecedented acts by a Latin American government since the end of the Cold War (Lehman 2006, p. 152). Despite these events, the U.S. embassy, the Organization of American States, and foreign petroleum companies continued to express their support for Sánchez and his continuation in office (Lehman 2006, p. 152; Dangl 2007, p. 125).

However, the popular anger in response to the deaths, coupled with resignations from his own cabinet and the refusal of the Bolivian army and police to engage in even more extensive violence against these protests, was too much for Sánchez to overcome. Jim Shultz, the director of the Democracy Center, an NGO based in Bolivia, argued that Sánchez de Lozada made too many demands of the military during this period: "Sánchez de Lozada would visit army headquarters and bribe military commanders to ensure their loyalty, but when he pushed for more repressive measures toward the population, the commanders simply refused, that signed the end of his presidency" (as quoted in Sánchez 2008). By October 15 there were reports of military units in different parts of the country refusing to obey their superiors and refusing to shoot at unarmed protesters, while military analysts concluded that military morale "is to the floor" (Wurgaft 2003). Sánchez de Lozada ultimately resigned and fled to Miami on October 17, 2003, and was replaced by his vice-president Carlos Mesa.

The end of the Sánchez de Lozada administration was a central event in the displacement of Bolivia's neoliberal policy coalition from control over the national state. Bolivia's armed forces aided his presidency in the face of police rebellions as well as in earlier protests, but clearly there were limits to how much they could be co-opted to buttress his government. Throughout the period of escalating antiglobalization protests, and even through the various struggles against coca growers, the armed forces remained divided and/or uncommitted to these ostensibly internal security threats. The Mesa administration would continue to reflect this tendency.

The government of Carlos Mesa (2003–5), contributed to briefly stabilizing the political situation, but his opposition to the nationalization of natural gas and the overall collapse in legitimacy of the dominant parties that had been in alliance with Sánchez led to continued confrontations with Bolivian social movements. This was reflected in another massive mobilization by social movements to close down the Bolivian Congress in 2005, with more than 50,000 people attempting to seize the center of La Paz in order to remove the Congress (The Internationalist 2005). The military remained internally divided between sectors sympathetic to the nationalist/populist politics of these movements and sectors sympathetic to the United States (Hylton and Thomson 2007, p. 120).

In April 2004 coup plans promoted by conservative groups within the military and civil society were uncovered. This alliance was fearful that Mesa would concede too much to pro-nationalization social movements. However, the coup failed to materialize, in part due to the opposition of nationalist members of the Bolivian armed forces (BBC Summary of World Broadcasts 2004; Gómez 2004). In fact, social movement leaders and groups demanded the support of the military. Evo Morales called for the army and the police to occupy the oil and gas fields, while representatives of the Bolivian Workers Central (COB) promoted an alliance with "patriotic" military officers and the support of an officer like "Hugo Chávez". The Miner Federation supported the activities of two army colonels, Julio Herrera and Julio César Galindo, who had offered to lead a civil-military junta in May 2005 under the banner of "New Generational" movement (The Internationalist 2005). In an interview with the newspaper *El Mundo* these soldiers asked that their military comrades from "the other line" not use violence to repress them or the social movements since they were seeking a peaceful transition. The two soldiers claimed that they had support from junior officers in all three of the military forces and proposed the nationalization of natural gas and oil resources, as well as the convocation of a constituent assembly. Ccsar and Herrera also questioned the character of Bolivia's democracy: "we live in a pseudodemocracy controlled by related groups. They have established a radical neoliberalism that has achieved misery. Our objective is a new democracy, true and pure, through the expression of the people in a constituent assembly" (Ibaibarriaga 2005). Their movement was ideologically supported by Jaime Solares, the head of the Bolivian Workers Central, who stated "whichever soldier that asks that Mesa, 'the sell-out,' leave is a patriot" (Ibaibarriaga 2005). Clearly calls for the military to intervene politically were direct challenges to traditional notions of civilian control, illustrating the priorities of important segments of Bolivian civil society. However, the military high command was uninterested in supporting such an undemocratic intervention.

Herrera and César went into hiding in 2005 for their acts of sedition. The commander in chief of the armed forces, Luis Aranda, promised that the officers would be punished to the fullest extent of the law and that "coup d'etat no longer exists in the Bolivian military's vocabulary"(Ibaibarriaga 2005). The high command denied any role in coup planning, but an associate of Evo Morales stated that "they didn't approach the right, instead they sought Evo's blessing. They wanted to stage a coup, but with the support of the social movement" (Lemoine 2006). This proposal was rejected by the Morales camp, which sought to obtain power through the electoral process. Although Herrera and César's call for a coup failed, Mesa ultimately resigned in June 2005 in the face of continuing protests and blockades. The military played a role in determining his successor, with General Aranda arguing on June 9 that "Congress must give the clearest possible expression of the will of the people," which contributed to the appointment of the head of the Supreme Court, Eduardo Rodriguez, over the conservative head of the Congress (Lemoine 2006).

Despite Aranda's support for Rodriguez, the interim president would dismiss him from his position within the high command. Aranda's dismissal was greeted with anger by a group of retired officers and their organization, Tradepa. Tradepa called for "a revolutionary, independent and humanist nationalism" and "the participation of the armed forces in national development" (Lemoine 2006). These ideals, combined with the actions of Aranda, as well as select junior officers, suggested that an ideological constituency existed within the serving and retired ranks sympathetic to nationalist politics and a developmentalist role for the armed forces. The administration of Evo Morales and his MAS party would go far to strengthening this approach during their government.

The Morales Presidency and Civil-Military Relations

Evo Morales won the December 2005 presidential election with 54 percent of the vote, an unprecedented margin in Bolivia's republican period. His popularity and connections with Bolivia's powerful social movements would allow him the space to begin the construction of a counterhegemonic bloc within the state. It also contributed to undermining efforts by his opposition to influence the armed forces against him and/or to mobilize a national movement to force him from power. The strongest opposition to Morales's policies of land reform and social redistribution rests within the wealthiest departments in eastern and southern Bolivia. Departments such as Tarija and Santa Cruz are where most of Bolivia's valuable natural gas is located, and political leaders in these departments have sought greater autonomy and control over their politics and the resources and land in their departments. These departments have also been the source of support for the market and neoliberal policies promoted by neoliberal policy coalitions in the past. The political and economic establishments within these departments have sought to frustrate Morales's nationalist/populist agenda through marches, boycotts, and the direct use of violence against Morales's supporters.

The tensions and divisions within the Bolivian armed forces that periodically emerged in the 1990s and early 2000s continued to be relevant. Just prior to Morales taking office, the head of the army, General Marcelo Antezana and defense minister Gonzalo Mendez were forced to resign by the interim president Rodriguez due to their allowing the United States to take and destroy twenty-eight surface-to-air missiles that the United States did not want in the hands of a leftist government (La Voz del Interior 2006). Morales wasted no time in purging the military of potential opponents and worked to re-organize its direction away from U.S.-assigned missions. Almost fifty-six generals and admirals were removed from the armed forces for their involvement in the ground-to-air missiles scandal (Sánchez 2006b).

His first defense minister, Walker San Miguel, had been an attorney and former head of Bolivia's bar association, as well as an academic with experience in administrative law (Bolivian Ministry of Defense 2008). San Miguel was committed to Morales's "new vision" for the military. This vision included the military's subordination to civilian authorities and a focus upon specific post-Cold War threats such as drug trafficking and terrorism, as well as new priorities such as the prevention of deforestation. The military has also been placed in charge of baking subsidized bread as well as distributing bonuses to school children and the elderly (Andean Information Network 2008). In addition, the country's national intelligence agencies within the military and the police were to be combined in a new national intelligence office in 2009, a change initiated by the Morales administration (BBC Monitoring Latin America 2008b). The military was to be included in the government's "macrodecisions" accompanying the democratic process and the government's decisions with a role in the country's development (BBC Monitoring Latin America 2006d). The military has been involved in different economic sectors, including chemical, mineral, and agricultural (La Razón 2009).

Regarding the country's development, the Morales administration proposed a series of plans and programs focused upon the "integral development" (*desarrollo integral*) of the nation. These plans included utilizing the armed forces in the improvement and expansion of infrastructure to improve domestic economic trade (*Plan "SINCALFA"*) as well as medical assistance to the poorest communities in the nation (*Plan "ASPIRINA"*). In addition, there were specific plans to assist municipal governments in disaster preparedness and rural communities in the production of foodstuffs (Ministerio de Defensa Nacional en Bolivia 2009). In August 2009 Defense Minister San Miguel claimed that the armed forces should be a "pillar of development," while the 2009 commander of the armed forces, Admiral José Luis Cabas, argued that the armed forces should "participate actively in national development" (La Razón 2009a; La Razón 2009b). In the swearing in of a new high command in January 2010 the military leadership openly stated their support of the changes promoted by Morales. The new commander of the army, General Alberto Cueto, argued that "to give birth to a new state we will make the changes necessary. We will modify ourselves in agreement with the government's plans" (La Razón 2010a). In the announcement of a new legislative proposal that would change the military's doctrine, Morales expressed his dream that Bolivia's armed forces be recognized internationally as "anti-capitalist." The new doctrine would be based on two pillars: equality between all Bolivians and the philosophy that all Bolivians should live well (La Razón 2010b).

This new vision also included reducing the military's ties to the United States. At the end of January 2006 the government proposed the dismantlement of Bolivia's Joint Task Force, a U.S.-supported and financed project that combined military/police units in coca eradication programs in Chapare (Arostegui 2006a; Chang 2006). Morales promoted individuals such as Wilfredo Vargas and Freddy Bersatti as commander in chief of the armed forces and commander of the army, respectively, individuals who openly expressed solidarity with Morales's "social revolution" and loyalty to the president (Ibaibarriaga 2007). Morales's defense advisor argued that "The [Bolivian] force for the fight against narco-trafficking has become an extension of the American [Drug Enforcement Administration], with all the risk that this implies for our national security. All our organs and institutions must return to government control" (Arostegui 2006a). The United States cut off military aid to specific units in response to the changes in government, including $500,000 from a U.S.-trained/funded elite counter-terrorism force after the Bolivian government appointed an individual to command the unit who the United States did not trust (Arostegui 2006b). In February 2008 Morales formally ended the long history of sending Bolivian officers/soldiers to the Western Hemisphere Institute for Security Cooperation (formerly the U.S. School of the Americas) because of its historical ties to dictatorships in Latin America (School of the Americas Watch 2008). Morales remarked that "we will gradually withdraw until there are no Bolivian officers attending the School of the Americas....They are teaching high ranking officers to confront their own people, to identify social movements as their enemies (as quoted in ¡Presente! 2008) In the case of Bolivia, Hugo Banzer had been trained there prior to his dictatorship, as well as generals implicated in the deaths of more than sixty people in the 2003 "Gas Wars" (School of the Americas Watch 2008). The ending of Bolivian military links with the Western Hemisphere Institute for Security Cooperation coincided with the dismissal of a U.S. diplomat following accusations of spying, as well as the dissolving of the Organization for Development of Police Research (ODEP), an intelligence unit funded by the U.S. State Department to battle narcoterrorism and terrorism (Arostegui 2008). The removal of suspect commanders, the appointment/promotion of supporters, and the reduction of Bolivia's links to the United States were coupled with weekly meetings Morales held with the high command to ensure their continued support (Ibaibarriaga 2007).

Morales also relied on his nationalist policies to maintain military solidarity. In May 2006 he signed a decree nationalizing the hydrocarbon sector, a policy popular with many in the military, utilizing the armed forces to help secure and occupy these national resources, taking control of fifty-three energy installations (Quiroga 2006). Hylton and Thomson argue that the use of the armed forces in this policy was "designed to cement ties with the military—one of the great enemies at times, but also great allies of past national political projects" (2007, p. 134). Morales committed to the armed forces that they would receive a portion of the profits from the oil and gas sector in order to modernize themselves (Sánchez 2006).

The government has stressed its national sovereignty to strengthen its position with the armed forces; however, it has also looked to the support from Cuba and Venezuela as well as other leftist Latin American governments to strengthen its control over the military. For example, Morales obtained the help of Cuban and Venezuelan intelligence teams to clear government offices of hidden microphones in order to frustrate possible U.S. intervention, as well as provide him with personal security (Arostegui 2006a, 2006b). In November 2006 Bolivia signed a military cooperation pact with Venezuela, as Venezuela provided technical assistance for military equipment, helped the Bolivian army build border posts, and improved its presence in the eastern lowlands of the country, regions where much of Morales's strongest opposition resided (Romero 2007a). In the first year of Morales's presidency Venezuela provided approximately $50 million in loans for Bolivia's military spending and over $120 million in overall general assistance, helping to offset declines in U.S. support (Romero 2007a; Romero 2007b). According to Douglas Pérez, an official in Venezuela's embassy in Bolivia, "no government had given the Bolivian military, since its democratic period (since 1982), support of this type or quantity, especially to improve the infrastructure and housing in which they live" (Ibaibarriaga 2007). Morales has even called for an "ALBA Armed Forces" so that the armed forces within this alliance "... can adopt new doctrines that are, of course, revolutionary and nationalistic; new doctrines whereby the armed forces are at the service of the peoples, fundamentally for dignity and sovereignty" (BBC Monitoring Latin America 2009).

However, this relationship has been used by some in the opposition and possibly foreign companies to gain military support for the removal of Morales from power. For example, Defense Minister Walker San Miguel claimed in February 2006 that "there are indications that a foreign multinational could be financing a slow and gradual, but systematic, process of destabilization" and that this multinational was working with the political opposition (Valdez 2006). In September 2006, retired General Antezana claimed that the armed forces were unhappy with "anti-democratic socialist absolutism" and its "Cuba-Venezuela orientation" of the Morales government, and that the military would need to "act" if politicians were unable to challenge the government (as quoted in Sánchez 2006). In late 2007 the opposition governor of Cochabamba and former army officer Manfred Reyes Villa called upon the armed forces to rise against the Morales reform process. Reyes Villa stated that "I call upon my comrades of the armed forces. You have been the guardians of democracy and today you must be the guardians of the sovereignty of this country. We cannot allow influence from abroad, with ideas from abroad" [in reference to the close relations between the Morales government and Venezuela] (Ibaibarriaga 2007).The commander in chief of the armed forces at the time, General Wilfredo Vargas, dismissed this demand and expressed his solidarity with Bolivia's "social revolution" and that the military "... only responds to their natural commanders" (Ibaibarriaga 2007) and "we have information that there exist coup movements. These are subjects that [are] handled by military intelligence, but the armed forces are not going to allow it" (Marirrodriga 2007).

In September 2008 the tensions between the regional opposition and the government reached a crisis point. In one specific instance, more than thirty Morales supporters were massacred by paramilitary actors allegedly organized and supported by the opposition governor of Pando during a period of widespread protest throughout opposition-held regions. The governor, Leopoldo Fernández, was arrested by the armed forces and held while the government investigated Fernández's role in the massacre (Chávez 2008). Venezuelan president Chávez angered many in the military when he accused the commander in chief of the armed forces, General Luis Trigo, of being sympathetic to the opposition and suggested that Venezuela would intervene if Morales was killed or overthrown. Chávez argued that "I'm not suggesting invading Bolivia," he said. "But we will not accept it," he said, referring to the possibility of a coup d'etat. "Bolivian oligarchy, just so you know. Gringo empire, just so you know. Bolivian soldiers who may be facilitating a coup, just so you know: we're not going to tolerate it, we're not going to accept it" (Bracci Roa 2008). General Trigo rejected such statements, stressing that Bolivia's armed forces would defend its national sovereignty, stating "To the president of Venezuela, Hugo Chavez, and to the international community we say that the [Bolivian] Armed Forces emphatically reject external interference of any nature, no matter where that interference may come from" (BBC Worldwide Monitoring. 2008).

Although regional actors such as Venezuela have potentially exacerbated divisions within the military, the response of the Union of South American Nations (UNASUR) to the September 2008 crisis illustrates the degree to which South America as a whole is prepared to condemn any type of coups. The UNASUR is a fledgling intergovernmental organization begun in 2004 with the signing of the Cuzco Declaration, committing South American governments to establishing regional integration comparable to the European Union (Suggett 2008b). Members of this organization met at the height of Bolivia's internal crisis in September 2008 and endorsed a statement that included the following:

- The UNASUR countries have expressed their "decided support for the constitutional government of Evo Morales" whose mandate was ratified by the majority of the Bolivian people in a recent referendum.
- The UNASUR members "reject any situation of civil coup attempt" or the rupture of the institutional order that could affect the territorial integrity of that country" (BBC Monitoring Latin America 2008c).

While these statements by themselves were not responsible for the survival of the Morales administration, they indicate the progress South America was making in operating outside of the institutional framework of the U.S.-dominated OAS to energetically criticize any effort to remove Morales unconstitutionally. During this political crisis, nationalist/populist and progressive governments were instrumental in organizing the meeting and in promoting solidarity with the Morales government.

Conclusion

In the case of civil-military relations in Bolivia, neoliberal policy coalitions successfully came and held state power for over two decades without the emergence of nationalist/populist factions within the military to prevent them from maintaining and exercising power. This was despite the history of nationalist/populist factions within the armed forces and despite the military's historical role in national development. These coalitions successfully eroded military prerogatives over military budgets, the defense ministry, and in the direction of national security strategy, specifically the military's increasing role in counterdrug operations. Factors internal and external to the conflicts within the Bolivian state and society were central to this outcome. Like Peru and Colombia, the Bolivian armed forces were increasingly oriented toward internal security threats and public order challenges, specifically the struggle first against coca farmers resisting U.S.-imposed crop eradication policies and second against an array of anticapitalist globalization actors within civil society. External to Bolivia were the requirements of transnational capital in the form of a leaner and more efficient state (pressuring Bolivian governments to reduce military expenditures) and the active support of the United States for economic reform as well as a larger role for the military in counterdrug policy. These processes helped to mitigate any potential challenges to neoliberal policy coalitions from within the armed forces, but as was pointed out earlier, they have not been successful in entirely eliminating these factions/elements within the military.

The government of Evo Morales, the quintessential "radical populist," has been able to draw upon remaining ideological sympathies within the armed forces as well as the assistance of Venezuela to strengthen military support for his nationalist/populist project. In contrast to Venezuela, neoliberal policy coalitions still retain a degree of regional authority and power. They have sought to influence the armed forces to join them in their fight, but thus far have been unable to move enough of the military to support their agenda. In addition, the links that the United States had established for decades with the Bolivian military are gradually being reduced, thus removing a potential lever the United States could use to destabilize the Morales government. The possibility of continued political control under Morales is dependent on his ability to advance the modernization of the military's equipment, ensure its benefits, and incorporate/co-opt those military factions sympathetic to a nationalist/developmentalist role to his political cal movement.

The Bolivian case illustrates again that the existence of neoliberal policy coalitions promoting the U.S. model of market democracies, coupled with internal security threats, are contributing factors to the erosion of military prerogatives in national policymaking. The case also demonstrates that this "progress" cannot be viewed as a static end-point given the social struggles/resistance that neoliberal economic policies have generated throughout the Andes. Nationalist/populist coalitions have been strong enough in the Bolivian case to achieve their aims, while sympathy from the armed forces has been critical to ensuring that no military coup is launched to disrupt this process. However, their ultimate success in establishing a counterhegemonic bloc requires incorporating the military politically to this economic and political agenda.

Conclusion

"How can a country consider itself to be a democracy that respects human rights when 80 percent of the population is subjected to the daily outrage of poverty and its terrible consequences? What type of democracy can be built upon illiteracy and the ignorance it breeds, malnutrition, unemployment and the other various plagues that often accompany the drama of poverty?"
— Venezuelan foreign minister Alí Rodríguez
at a special session of the Organization of
American States. February 23, 2005

"I do not conceive of socialism as anything but a profoundly democratic system, although not the democracy of the elites."
— Hugo Chávez, quoted in Jones 2007, p. 469

The existence of internal security threats in Peru, Colombia, and Bolivia did not lead to the military's expanded role in leadership selection or in public policymaking, but has contributed to conditions that have not only prevented military political intervention but also the *erosion* of military prerogatives. The two countries facing the gravest internal security threats since 1990 (even since 1980) have been Colombia and Peru, yet these two countries have gone the farthest in eroding military prerogatives and in strengthening civilian authority over the armed forces. While countries such as Venezuela and Ecuador have not had to face such difficult internal security challenges, they have maintained and/or expanded military prerogatives, specifically in economic and social policy.

This variation in military power has not corresponded with various institutionalist explanations. Military maintenance and expansion of prerogatives have taken place in countries in which the armed forces controlled democratic transitions (Ecuador) and in countries where civilian leaders were largely in control (Venezuela). The weakening and even collapse of party systems have taken place in all five countries, while the economic challenges of poverty, growth, and inequality face them all. Understanding the variation in military political intervention requires attention to how specific global variables have interacted with domestic conditions/institutions.

Globally, the expansion and promotion of low-intensity democracies by the United States, intergovernmental organizations, and international financial institutions have involved the promotion of a classical conception of civil-military relations. The model is in line with Huntington's version of "objective control" in which military power is to be subordinated to elected civilian authorities. Developmentalist roles, ownership of military-state industries, and a direct role in governing alongside civilian authorities or in influencing political/economic strategies are eschewed in this model for highly professional and efficient institutions dedicated primarily to security endeavors. Huntington wrote that "civilian control is undermined if they [the military] stray outside the military sphere..." and that objective civilian control requires military abstention from politics (1956, p. 678). Huntington's model of civil-military relations has been tied to the liberalization of economies, free trade, and the prioritization of electoral competition and liberal freedoms over socially equitable outcomes. However, these low-intensity democracies, in contrast to Huntington's classic model, have required a continuing role for internal security for these respective militaries. With the end of the Cold War and the disappearance of most guerrilla forces, internal and external security threats continue to be influenced by U.S. priorities, with illegal drugs, terrorism, and radical populism taking center stage as potential threats.

A reduced role for the armed forces in public policymaking and development with market economics has been considered a more effective set of institutions to establish the conditions necessary for capitalist stability and the investments of transnational corporations that are under potentially greater threat by military-dominated regimes. Military-dominated regimes represent a potential problem for capitalist investments because: (1) military governments have often been associated with the expansion of state intervention in the economy and/or expansion in state spending through military-owned companies, or increases in state spending on military resources; (2) military regimes can potentially generate radical opposition that sees no other alternative other than revolutionary change in the face of a closed/restricted political process; and (3) military regimes can be difficult for the business community to penetrate in order to shape policy, as was seen in the cases of Bolivia, Peru, and Ecuador during the 1970s.

The spread of capitalist globalization and low-intensity democracies globally has coincided in many countries with the emergence of the various ideological carriers of this political and economic agenda. Neoliberal policy coalitions often receive the support or the acquiescence of military factions oriented toward U.S. military doctrines and/ or sympathetic to U.S. foreign policy objectives. The military's orientation toward U.S. conceptions of security threats and civil-military relations, as well as the success of neoliberal policy coalitions, has been aided by the existence of internal security threats that have marginalized competing ideological factions within the military (though this influence was not as great in Bolivia). These internal security threats have also contributed to greater assistance from the United States and provided the necessary justification for the state or para-state repression of political opponents of capitalist globalization. In Colombia and Peru these domestic and external factors have been central to the erosion of military prerogatives since the late 1980s. In the case of Bolivia the extent of internal security threats was not as extensive; however, as in Colombia and Peru, neoliberal policy coalitions supported by the United States were able to make progress in reducing military prerogatives in the 1980s and 1990s. The factors that have been important to the erosion of prerogatives in these cases have been weak and/or nonexistent in the cases of Venezuela and Ecuador.

In neither Venezuela nor Ecuador have neoliberal policy coalitions been able to maintain power and/or establish a degree of policy continuity. Social movement pressures in Ecuador, specifically from organized/mobilized indigenous communities, as well as general repudiation of neoliberal economic policies by the Venezuelan population illustrated most starkly in the 1989 *Caracazo* have been central to resisting this agenda. In both cases nationalist/populist factions within the military have either directly/indirectly allied with anticapitalist globalization social movements and/or have taken the initiative in opposing neoliberal regimes. The development of these factions within the military was not tempered by the existence of significant internal security threats. These factions were also motivated by deteriorating economies despite the promises of market reform. Global actors have attempted in both cases to maintain a market democracy through linkages with the armed forces, threats of economic sanctions, and/or in supporting neoliberal/globalist policy sectors in civil society. However, they have

thus far been unable to prevent the coming to power of political movements seeking counterhegemonic models of politics, economics, and
civil-military relations. Even in the case of Bolivia, in which neoliberal
policy coalitions had held national power since 1985, anticapitalist globalization groups obtained national state power in 2005.

Democracy, Subjective Control, and Civil-Military Relations

Those governments that represent nationalist and populist reactions
against capitalist globalization have largely been viewed by the United
States, the mass media, and some Latin Americanists as representing
undemocratic politics and undemocratic civil-military relations. The
Venezuelan academic Miriam Kornblith argues that the Chávez administration aims to establish not a military government, but a "different
conception of democracy in which the classical institutions and rules of
representative democracy are of less and less importance, and in which
the army can be an important vehicle for presidential support" (2000, p.
70). Others have stressed the level of politicization and personal control
being pursued by Chávez, using his control over the armed forces to
control the public bureaucracy (Pion-Berlin and Trinkunas 2005, p. 17).
Both Rafael Correa in Ecuador and Evo Morales in Bolivia have been
accused of undermining democratic institutions and seeking solely the
means to maintain power and concentrate it in their hands. They have
also been accused of threatening democratic civilian control. Former
Ecuadorian defense minister Oswaldo Jarrín has warned of the increasing politicization of Ecuador's armed forces and the effort by the party
in government to dominate the military (phone interview, 10/22/08).

All three countries have written new constitutions that establish
mechanisms outside of traditional electoral channels to involve citizens in the day-to-day operations of government in forms of direct or
participatory democracy. The three governments have also called for
the democratization of other institutions outside simply political ones,
seeking to extend democratic control in the economic arena. They have
all in one form or another challenged how democracy has operated in
the past. This challenge has included returning (or continuing) civil-
military relations to a model in which the military is directly involved
in the economic and social development of the country and/or establishing entirely new forms of civil-military relations concomitant with
their nationalist/populist project, but under civilian authority.

This approach reflects a form of "subjective control" in which civilian groups in control of the state seek to "...persuade the military to identify with their particular interests, to adhere to their points of view, or both" (Lopez 2001, p. 91) or as Huntington described it "ensuring that the military leadership of the armies reflected the same interests, values, and outlook as the political leadership of society" (Huntington 1956, p. 677). This type of politicization runs contrary to traditional democratic models of civilian control and military professionalism.

In the case of the Andes, Colombia could be viewed as the least "politicized" case. However, the military has been a central force in maintaining and protecting the political objective of a neoliberal/globalist policy coalition in control of the national state. Most concretely, the military's role in directly and indirectly repressing and excluding those political actors that have emerged to resist capitalist globalization has been central. While Colombia has witnessed the increased involvement of civilian authorities in defense and security matters, this has corresponded with military human rights abuses that are beyond any abuses that have been committed in the other countries that I have examined. These abuses have largely targeted the popular sector and the poor, complementing the process of Colombia's integration into capitalist globalization. Thus, Colombia's "progress" in expanding civilian authority has not developed some type of apolitical institution, but has simply reinforced a political strategy of anti-Communist repression long held by the armed forces.

In countries such as Venezuela, Ecuador, and Bolivia there has been a commitment to expand the military's role in reducing poverty and economic inequality, objectives that can contribute to democratic and political stability. Of course, progress on these fronts is, in part, conditioned on the degree of policy autonomy and legitimacy that elites within and outside of these countries are willing to grant these governments. Disloyal oppositions in Venezuela and Bolivia in particular have contributed to undermining political stability within these respective nations. In all three cases this effort is part of a larger project to remake political and economic institutions in line with an often vague model of "Bolivarian Socialism." Thus, the military is being re-oriented from the ideological agenda set by the United States and globalist elites within these countries to embrace the agenda of these "radical populists."

The developmentalist and anti-poverty use of the military is in part a response to the failure of market or low-intensity democracies to address social and substantial outcomes of democracy. Latin America is the most unequal region in the world and became increasingly unequal during the 1980s and 1990s, the period of neoliberal economic reform (Karl 2000, pp. 154–5). Terry Lynn Karl writes that reductions in inequality may be central to democratic survival: "It is difficult for democratic institutions to function correctly or be maintained in a polity sharply divided by income and wealth, especially one that does little to redress this situation or, worse, actively exacerbates it" and that "inequality's pernicious undermining of democratic aspirations, institutions, and rules is the greatest threat facing democracy in the Americas today" (2000, pp. 155–6). Thus, could one argue that another consequence of politicizing the military behind a socially redistributive agenda, besides the potential for undermining civilian control, is the mitigation of a direct threat to the continuity of democratic governments? Isn't the proper question not whether the armed forces are being politicized or not, but to what end is this politicization being applied and whether civilian authorities are in control?

In the case of Venezuela, its program of social and educational *misiones*, in which the military has played an important role, has contributed to nearly three-quarters of Venezuelans receiving state support for health, education, housing, or food (Buxton 2007). Poverty and critical poverty have declined, and the World Bank has concluded that "Venezuela has achieved substantial improvements in the fight against poverty" (as quoted in Buxton 2007). According to *Latinobarómetro* polling, the percentage of Venezuelans satisfied with their political system increased from 32 percent in 1998 to over 57 percent in 2006 and Venezuelans (as well as Uruguayans) expressed the highest percentage of confidence in elections as the most effective means of promoting change in the country (Buxton 2007). Venezuelans were also the most politically active people than any other country surveyed that year.

Venezuela's model of "co-responsibility" in defending national security is often viewed by critics as the militarization of civil society. However, it is also consistent with a model of participatory democracy in which citizens become directly involved in the governing process beyond voting in elections. This is promoted in the 1999 constitution (Article 62) and is represented in the thousands of communal councils that have been given billions in government funds to directly address local needs in their own neighborhoods outside of formal political structures (Ellner 2008, pp. 127–8). A community leader in one of these communal councils in Lara stressed to me the extent that military involvement in his community had changed from repression and surveillance prior to Chávez to one that was committed to social projects and community improvements during the Chávez administration (interview, August

2007). Again and again in conversations and interviews that I had with Venezuelan community activists, unionists, or teachers during August 2007 and May 2008 the military's role expansion was viewed as a positive one that strengthened democracy. One leader of Afro-Venezuelan communities in Barlovento spoke of the repression and corrupt activities of the military prior to the election of Chávez (interview, May 2008). These political and economic successes are not to suggest that there are no democratic problems in Venezuela, but only to point out that most Venezuelans themselves do not view democracy under threat with the expansion of military prerogatives or increasing power within the executive. In addition, assessing the quality or potential survivability of democratic regimes on the basis of the level and extent of military prerogatives may lead analysts to overlook the potentially positive benefits to democracy of greater military power in a country's economic and social development. Table C.1 illustrates the variation in military power and democratic outcomes in the five countries.

Clearly, the governments of Venezuela and Ecuador (and increasingly Bolivia) seek to establish a developmentalist role for their armed forces, viewing this extension of military prerogatives not as a potential threat to democracy but as a collective process in which all institutions of the state are oriented to the development of the nation. This is especially the case given the large amount of resources dedicated to the military ensuring a degree of "dual usage" from the military security and development (Tee 2010, p. 7).[1]

The globalization of economic production, distribution, and politics represents central characteristics of our global system. Civil-military studies have largely been disconnected from this process, viewing civil-military relations through the lens of institutional interests, rules, organization, and doctrines within specific nation-states. It has been guided by a conception of elite democracy in which civilian control and eroded military prerogatives are viewed as central to democratic consolidation. The model of a professional military subordinated to civilian authorities and focused upon primarily security-related missions is a model concomitant with neoliberal conceptions of state behavior and modernization. It does not represent the "de-politicization" of the armed forces, but the direct politicization of the institution to the agenda of neoliberal policy coalitions. The failure of low-intensity democracy and "democratic" civil-military relations to obtain legitimacy in Venezuela, Ecuador, and Bolivia and the possibility of alternative models needs to be considered. The assumption that low-intensity or market democracies, and the corresponding civilian control, represent the

Table C.1   Military Prerogatives in the Andes, 1998–2010

	Level of Prerogatives	*Indicators*
Colombia	Low	– Civilian defense minister since 1991 – Civilian leadership over domestic intelligence, military budgets, and security strategies – Little to no role for military in economic or social policies
Peru	Low	– Civilian defense minister since 2001 – Civilian-initiated reforms of domestic intelligence, greater civilian authority over military budgets and security strategies – Little to no role for military in economic or social policy
Bolivia	Moderate	– Civilian defense minister throughout most of this period – Civilian and security services involved in administering domestic intelligence – Civilian leadership in security policies and military budgets – Growing role for military in economic and social policies
Ecuador	Moderate-High	– Civilian defense minister since 2007 – Civilian authority over military budgets and security strategies – Domestic intelligence largely under the purview of the military, but prerogative eroded in the Correa administration – Significant military role in the ownership of state companies and economic development
Venezuela	High	– Military defense minister throughout most of this period – Civilian authority over defense budgets and security strategies – Substantial role of military in economic and social policies

only legitimate model of democracy and civil-military relations needs to be challenged.

Future Research

Future research needs to address the degree to which the expansion of the military's prerogatives in economic or social development while maintaining civilian authority is detrimental to *all forms* of democratic politics and institutions as well as assess the extent that military political intervention in Latin America or in other regions of the world is related to larger national and global social struggles. This does not have to be at the expense of institutional analyses or represent some type of orthodox Marxist determinism that reduces all state behavior or internal relations as simply reflecting economic interests or the imperial dictates of the United States. Institutions do matter. The factional divisions/differences within the armed forces as well as their security responsibilities have been important to the variation that I have outlined earlier, but none of this is taking place within a vacuum. The context of these institutional issues, a state's societal and global environment, reflects a set of variables necessary to understanding the direction of civil-military relations.

Civil-military relations in regions such as the Southern Cone or Central America could be examined through this interactive model, assessing the extent that military prerogatives have shifted or changed with shifts in the power/influence of specific military factions, security threats, U.S. policies, and/or the outcome of societal struggles over the economic/political development of the nation. For example, to what extent does the size of the criminal threat of gangs in Central America vary, and how has this affected the strength of specific factions within the military and/or the level of repression against anti-capitalist globalization sectors in civil society? To what extent has past counterinsurgency wars narrowed the political space for legal political opposition and/or the strength of reformist/progressive factions within the military? Have U.S. aid and training policies cultivated enough support in these respective militaries to ensure their adherence to the civilian control associated with market or low-intensity democracies?

The recent case of Honduras is an interesting example in which a "populist" president and political ally of Hugo Chávez, Manuel Zelaya, was removed from power through a military coup on June 28, 2009. The coup was backed by a Honduran political and economic establishment generally supportive of Honduras's global integration as well as fearful of any potential changes toward a "radical populist" model. Although the Obama administration criticized the coup, it failed to implement effective sanctions against the coup government, while recognizing the November 2009 presidential elections organized by the coup government, which were condemned by many countries in Latin America. In fact, during Zelaya's exile, he met with presidents in

Argentina, Brazil, and Mexico, while Obama refused six opportunities to meet with him (Main 2010).

The Obama administration maintained the same antagonistic position against "radical populists" reflected during the Bush administration, tolerating and ultimately supporting this unconstitutional change in government. The military that removed Zelaya enjoyed relatively close ties with the United States, including the existence of the only U.S. base in Central America. As Army colonel Herberth Bayardo Inestroza remarked days after the coup, "'We fought the subversive movements here [in the 1980s] and we were the only country that did not have a fratricidal war like the others…It would be difficult for us, with our training, to have a relationship with a leftist government. That's impossible. I personally would have retired, because my thinking, my principles, would not have allowed me to participate in that" (as quoted in Robles 2009).

The conflict in Honduras, and the U.S. role in its outcome, reflects a deeper conflict over the extent that Honduras could shift away from a low-intensity democracy and capitalist globalization. The neoliberal elite allied with the armed forces and the United States effectively prevailed in this particular battle, though Honduran civil society in solidarity with Zelaya continued to organize in opposition to this elite's agenda in 2010. The interaction between political and factional conflict within a specific nation-state with global political/economic trends were (and are) relevant to understanding the variation in civil-military relations in the Andes and I suspect in other regions in Latin America. This broader perspective of these relations builds upon traditional institutionalist analyses while directly connecting the military to these societal and global processes.

NOTES

Introduction

1. A set of economic policies promoted by the United States and international financial institutions for more than three decades that include privatizations of state-owned enterprises, greater labor flexibility, financial and commercial deregulation, and the devaluation of currencies and reductions of tariffs.
2. The concept of "civil society" refers to a "set of social institutions, organizations, and associations that stand apart from the state" (Lim 2006, p. 164).
3. In describing the power structure of third-world governments in the post-Cold War era, Gills and Rocamora write that "the elites in the Third World—the oligarchies, the business community, and the military who serve U.S. and foreign interests (as well as their own)—are relied upon to control their local populations" (1992, p. 511).
4. Gills and Rocamora suggest that U.S. fears of nationalist movements long preceded the emergence of Chávez or Morales, arguing in their 1992 article that "...the primary threat to U.S. interests was not Communism, but rather any nationalistic regime responsive to popular demands for immediate improvement in standards of living and which therefore interfered with U.S. efforts to encourage private investment and repatriation of profits" (1992, p. 511).

1   Military Power and Capitalist Globalization

1. The relationship between low-intensity democracies and the interests of transnational corporations is reminiscent of a type of "social structure of accumulation" (SSA) in which a set of political and cultural institutions work to "mitigate and channel class conflict and stabilize capitalists' long-run expectations" (McDonough, Reich and Kotz 2010, p.2).
2. Prior to the Carter administration there had been progress in the U.S. Congress in giving attention to the importance of human rights in U.S. foreign policy, but it was not until the Carter administration that presidential power was mobilized behind this agenda (Mertus 2008, pp. 29–30).
3. Weinstein argued in a 1991 interview that "A lot of what we [NED] do today was done covertly twenty-five years ago by the CIA" (as quoted in Jones 2007, p. 304).
4. The emergence of the NED roughly coincided with important shifts in Reagan's foreign policy in Central America. The administration increasingly sought to curb the death squad activities of its military allies in El Salvador, in part due to pressures from a Democratic

Congress, but also as a result of arguments by key foreign policy advisers. In early 1984 a special commission established by the Reagan administration to examine its Central American policy (The Kissinger Commission) concluded that "we have a national interest in strengthening democratic institutions wherever in the hemisphere they are weak" (as quoted in Peceny 1999, p. 143).

5. In 2006 the United States Agency for International Development (USAID) argued on its website "Promoting Democracy and Good Governance" that "[e]stablishing democratic institutions, free and open markets, an informed and educated populace, a vibrant civil society, and a relationship between state and society that encourages pluralism, participation, and peaceful conflict resolution—all of these contribute to the goal of establishing sustainable democracies" (USAID 2006).

6. The U.S. SOUTHCOM is the unified combatant commands within the Department of Defense that is responsible for U.S. security in Latin America.

7. Between 1999 and 2003 the U.S. military trained more than 70,000 members of Latin American and Caribbean armed forces and police, and in 2003 Latin America represented 40 percent of U.S.-funded military trainees in the world (Barry 2005). In 2003 Colombia and Bolivia had the most trainees in Latin America, with Colombia having the most soldiers and police trainees (Barry 2005). Presently, Venezuela and Bolivia have stopped sending police or military personnel to the United States for training, while Ecuador has accused the Central Intelligence Agency of infiltrating Ecuador's domestic intelligence services within its armed forces (Lucas 2008; School of the Americas Watch 2004, 2008).

8. As will be shown in Chapter two, the Obama administration (2009–13) has in part responded to this "challenge" by completing a basing agreement with Colombia that will allow U.S. military personnel access to a larger number of military bases throughout the country (Carroll and MacAskill 2009).

9. "Lower middle-income" countries are classified with a gross national income (GNI) per capita of $826–$3,255 and "upper middle-income" countries as classified with a GNI per capita of $3,256–$10,065 (World Bank Group 2004).

2   The Erosion of Military Prerogatives: The Cases of Peru and Colombia

1. As quoted in *Political Violence and the Authoritarian State in Peru* by Jo-Marie Burt (2007, 202).

2. Voting turnout in the 2006 presidential election was 45 percent, approximately equal to the 2002 presidential election (Leech 2006).

3. His military regime represented the only military government in the 20th century as the armed forces had been largely subordinated to the leadership of dominant party leaders and often utilized to suppress domestic unrest.

4. The then-Defense Minister General Fernando Landazábal ordered members of the armed forces to contribute monies to the legal defense of the officers that had been accused (Human Rights Watch 1996).

5. The Department of National Planning (DNP) is the central agency that oversees the country's national budget.

6. Bedoya had represented a hard-line faction of the Colombian army during the Samper administration, critical of human rights conditions or efforts to prosecute military personnel accused of human rights violations.

7. Programs such as monies to subsidize the expansion of export crops complemented the vast majority of funds dedicated to Colombian security forces. In some cases the enterprises being approved for funding, such as palm oil plantations in Chocó, had been acquired through paramilitary violence and/or were controlled by paramilitary leaders themselves (Ballvé 2009).

8. An important illustration was the training of 4,000 Colombian soldiers by a U.S. counterinsurgency team between October 2002 and January 2003 to improve the Colombian army's ability to fight the FARC (Rochlin 2007, p. 46). In addition, improvements in military intelligence, mobility, and real-time information on guerrilla movements have been aided by greater access to U.S. technology and hardware (Ibid, 54–5).

9. Uribe's plans also included the recruitment of the civilian population, a peasant soldiers brigade, that would provide additional security for the communities that they lived in after receiving three months of military training (Rochlin 2007, p. 46). The aim was to train approximately 100,000 individuals by the end of 2006.

10. Between 2007 and 2009 fifty-nine leaders of different social movements, including movements representing the internally displaced and victims of human rights violations, had been assassinated, while the annual number of the internally displaced increased from approximately 200,000 in 2006 to more than 250,000 in 2009 (Romero and Arias 2009, pp. 7–8).

11. An antiguerrilla soldier in the Thirty-first Infantry Battalion referred to the process of "legalizing someone" (a "false positive") as a "daily affair" (Semana 2008).

12. APRA was able to penetrate the armed forces, enjoying the support of specific military factions, but these factions were generally undermined by anti-APRA factions from the late 1930s to the 1960s (García 1998, p. 480).

13. Rouquié suggests that the refusal of the United States to provide more effective weapons for the Peruvian armed forces in its counterinsurgency war, which forced Peru to turn to Europe for modern arms, contributed to the development of a nationalist conception within the military (1987, p. 145). This was coupled with sizable military purchases from the Soviet Union, with Peru being the only South American country during the 1970s to receive arms, as well as more than 100 Soviet military advisors (Federal Research Division 1989).

14. The government's takeover of the U.S. energy company International Petroleum Company was finalized early in Velasco's administration (Schneider 2007, p. 344).

15. Vásquez suggests that this change was largely a symbolic one, given that the defense minister remained a military officer: "...the only change that occurred was in the name of the ministry itself" (1996, p. 352).

16. One State Department cable on Aug. 23, 1990, detailed information from a Peruvian intelligence source, a former naval officer, who stated that the plan to carry out extrajudicial assassinations of suspected terrorists had "'the tacit approval of President Fujimori"'' (Romero 2009).

17. The use of military tanks to repress public protest over Fujimori's early austerity measures was an early example of overt state actions against anticapitalist globalization movements (Rochlin 2003, p. 67).

18. According to Peruvian president Alejandro Toledo, at least 10,000 Peruvians disappeared at the hands of state forces in the armed forces struggle against guerrilla insurgents (Rochlin 2003, p. 70).

19. The National Intelligence Service under Montesinos had almost 3,000 agents, but by 2004 the National Intelligence Council contained only 450 agents (Notisur 2004).

3   "Radical Populists" and Military Prerogatives in Venezuela and Ecuador

1. In fact, during the early 1960s the CIA penetrated parts of Ecuador's political and media establishment. For example, in 1961 both the second and third in presidential succession were receiving monies from the CIA while the policy discussions of the 1963–6 military regime were regularly monitored by the agency (Pineo 207, pp. 165–7).

2. Based on his extensive interviews with a majority of officers involved in different coups during the 1960s and 1972 (a total of eighty officers), Fitch finds that 22 percent held a developmentalist definition of the military role, while 63 percent possessed an "arbiter" conception of the military's role in Ecuadorian politics (Fitch 1986, p. 156).

3. These austerity policies complemented the "disciplining" of labor, including the repression of an October 1977 sugar workers strike that left 100 dead (Pineo 2007, p. 185).

4. In the early 1980s Ecuador's foreign debt equaled twice the amount of annual exports and increased from $5.8 billion in 1981 to $7.3 billion in 1983 (Pineo 2007, p. 194).

5. For example, Selverston-Scher's study of indigenous politics in the province of Bolivar refers to the "fraternal relationship" between the local military brigade and the indigenous group *Federación Campesina de Bolívar*, as the group often received food and shelter for their general assemblies (2001, p. 107).

6. Febres Cordero had been an important leader in the democratization process as well as a leading opponent of the previous administration of Oswaldo Hurtado. Hurtado had faced regular attacks from the business community that regularly sought the support of the military in removing Hurtado from office. The military's unwillingness to get involved, opposition from the United States, and divisions among business leaders undermined any progress in a coup against the Hurtado administration (Conaghan and Malloy 1994, pp. 132–4).

7. Bucaram's embrace of neoliberal economic policies followed a campaign in which he strongly criticized these economic strategies (Pineo 2007, p. 206).

8. In 1999 16 percent of the population was unemployed, while the underemployed reached 56 percent, with more than 70 percent of the population living in poverty (Gerlach 2003, p. 158).

9. Pérez Jiménez had led the UPM, but his movement had a falling out with the reformist government over its refusal to allow greater military participation in the government as well as its refusal to exile AD leader Rómulo Betancourt (Coronil 1997, p. 140).

10. Between August 2007 and August 2008 Venezuela held the fourth position behind Mexico, Saudi Arabia, and Canada as a source of oil for the United States (Energy Information Administration 2008).

11. This study classified 178 generals and admirals out of the total of 240 generals and admirals in Venezuela's armed forces (Manrique 2001, p. 330).

12. The "socialist factories" are joint ventures between the Venezuelan government and state companies from China and Iran to produce goods in strategic sectors such as foods, chemicals, machinery, and transportation, to be placed under the management of communal councils (Carlson 2008).

13. Rocio San Miguel, head of Citizen Control for Security, a think tank on security issues in Venezuela, concludes that this equals one-seventh of the 14,900 officers that existed in 2008 (Sanchez 2008).

4 Low-Intensity Democracy, Popular Resistance, and Military Power in Bolivia

1. As quoted in "Bolivia: 'We are here to serve the people, not capitalists'" (Fuentes 2010).

2. This included the policies of Colonel David Toro, who came to power in 1936 and expropriated Standard Oil of New Jersey's Bolivian properties in 1937, or the government of Col. Germán Busch, who promoted a progressive constitution in 1938 that guaranteed the right to organize unions, universal education, and nationalized subsoil rights. These challenges to elite interests would be frustrated by competing factions within the military in the 1940s (Worldmark Encyclopedia 2007, p. 69).

3. The revolution was led by a coalition of mine workers and peasants that supported MNR's uprising, which was sparked by an attempt by the military to prevent MNR's presidential candidate, Victor Paz Estenssoro, from taking office (Conaghan and Malloy 1994, p. 40).
4. Che Guevara would be killed by the Bolivian military in October 1967 after an almost year-long campaign to eradicate Guevara's guerrilla cell. A U.S.-trained elite battalion of Bolivian Rangers was the unit that tracked and ultimately extrajudicially executed Guevara.
5. Popular opposition was, in part, driven by continued resentment against Chile for taking away Bolivia's access to the coast after the War of the Pacific (1879–84).

Conclusion

1. Dongmin Lee finds that, despite over five decades in which the Chinese military has been directly involved in an array of nontraditional roles related to economic development, civilian supremacy has been maintained and the military's professional readiness as a fighting force has not been hampered (Lee 2010).

BIBLIOGRAPHY

Addicott, Jeffrey F. and Andrew M. Warner. 1994. Promoting the Rule of Law and Human Rights. *Military Review*, 74, 8, August.

Addicott, Jeffrey F. and Guy B. Roberts. 2001. "Building Democracies with Southern Command's Legal Engagement Strategy." *Parameters*. Vol.31, no.1, Spring: 72–85.

Aguero, Felipe. 1995. "Crisis and Decay of Democracy in Venezuela." In *Venezuelan Democracy Under Stress*, edited by Jennifer McCoy, et al, p.215–36. Miami: North-South Center.

Ahumada, Consuelo.2002. *Cuatro Años a Bordo de sí Mismo: La Herencia económica, social y política del gobierno de Andrés Pastrana*. Bogotá: El Ancora Editores.

Alberto Buttó, Luis. 2005. "Nuevo profesionalismo military de seguridad interna..." In Domingo Irwin and Frederique Langue, eds., *Militares y Poder en Venezuela*, 139–77. Caracas: Universidad Católica.

Ambrus, Steven. 2007. "Dominion of Evil." *Amnesty International Magazine*, Spring, Available at http://www.amnestyusa.org/Spring_2007/Dominion_of_Evil/page.do?id=1105393&n1=2&n2=19&n3=397; accessed April 10, 2007.

Amnesty International. 2008. " 'Leave us in Peace!' Targeting Civilians in Colombia's Internal Armed Conflict." Amnesty International Publications. Available at http://www.amnesty.org/en/library/asset/AMR23/023/2008/en/65b11bee-a04b-11dd-81c4-792550e655ec/amr230232008eng.pdf; accessed November 10, 2008.

———. 2004. "The Truth and Reconciliation Commission: a first step towards a country without injustice," *Amnesty International Website*, available at http://www.amnestyusa.org/document.php?lang=e&id=6E22AFDD4D87E7CB80256EEB00526B10; accessed Dec. 2, 2007.

———. 1999. "Peru: Legislation is not enough, Torture must be abolished in practice." *Amnesty International Website*. September. Available at http://www.amnesty.org/en/library/asset/AMR46/017/1999/en/dom-AMR460171999en.pdf; accessed June 10, 2008.

Amnesty International and the Fellowship of Reconciliation (FOR). 2008. Assisting units that commit extrajudicial executions. April. Available at http://www.forcolombia.org/sites/www.forcolombia.org/files/AIFORrptApr08.pdf; accessed June 1, 2008

Andean Information Network. 2008. "The Bolivian Armed Forces' Growing Mission." *Andean Information Network*, June 1. Available at http://ain-bolivia.org/index.php?option=com_content&task=view&id=119&Itemid=32; accessed November 1, 2008.

Angel Urrego, Miguel. 2001. "Social and Popular Movements in a Time of Cholera, 1977-1999." In Charles Bergquist, Ricardo Peñaranda, and Gonzalo Sánchez, eds., *Violence in Colombia, 1990-2000*, pp.171–8, Wilmington, DE: Scholarly Resources, Inc.

Arce, Moises and Paul T. Bellinger, Jr. 2007. "Low-Intensity Democracy Revisted." *World Politics*, 60, October:97-121.

Arostegui, Martin. 2008. "Spy Claims Strain Ties with U.S." *The Washington Times*, February 20. Lexis/Nexis.

———. "Evo Morales: A New Security Command for Bolivia." *Washington Times*, January 31. Lexis/Nexis.

———. 2006b. "U.S. Demands Return of Arms from Bolivia." *The Washington Times*, March 10. Lexis/Nexis.

Associated Press. 2008a. "Defense Chief: Ecuador Could Suspend Military Accords with the U.S." April 21, Lexis/Nexis.

———. "Bolivia Suspends U.S.-Backed Antidrug Efforts." *The New York Times*, November 1. Available at http://www.nytimes.com/2008/11/02/world/americas/02bolivia.html; accessed November 12, 2008

Avila Martínez, Ariel Fernando. 2009. "La Guerra contra las FARC y la Guerra de las FARC." Special Report, November: Corporación Nuevo Arco Iris.

Avilés, William. 2006a. *Global Capitalism, Democracy and Civil-Military Relations in Colombia*. Albany, NY: SUNY Press.

———. "Paramilitarism and Colombia's Low-Intensity Democracy." *Journal of Latin American Studies*, vol.38, no.2, May: 379–408.

Avritzer, Leonardo. 2006. "Civil Society in Latin America in the Twenty-First Century: Between Democratic Deepening, Social Fragmentation, and State Crisis," in Richard Feinberg, Carlos H. Waisman, and Leon Zamosc, eds., *Civil Society and Democracy in Latin America*, pp. 35–58, New York, NY: Palgrave Macmillan.

Baines, John. 1972. "U.S. Military Assistance to Latin America: An Assessment." *Journal of Interamerican Studies and Wortld Affairs*, vol. 14, no. 4 (Nov): 469–87.

Ballvé, Teo. 2009. "The Dark Side of Plan Colombia." *The Nation*, May 27th. Available online at http://www.thenation.com/doc/20090615/ballve/single; accessed June 24, 2009.

Barracca, Steven. 2007. "Military Coups in the Post-Cold War Era: Pakistan, Ecuador and Venezuela." *Third World Quarterly*, vol.28, no.1: 137–54.

Barrios Morón, Raúl and René Antonio Mayorga. 1994. *La cuestion militar en cuestion*. La Paz: Centro Boliviano de Estudios Multidisciplinarios.

Barry, Tom. 2005. "'Mission Creep' in Latin America—U.S. Southern Command's New Security Strategy." *IRC Americas Program Special Report*, July: 1–24.

BBC. 2008. "Ecuadorians Back New Constitution," September 29: Available at http://news.bbc.co.uk/2/hi/americas/7640704.stm; accessed Oct. 10, 2008.

———. 2003. "Prosecution Call for Peru's Guilty," BBC Website, available at http://news.bbc.co.uk/2/hi/americas/3190561.stm; accessed Aug. 3, 2007.

———. 2000. "Ecuador Coup Condemned." January 22. Available at http://news.bbc.co.uk/2/hi/americas/614434.stm; accessed June 5, 2007.

BBC Monitoring Latin America. 2009. "Bolivian leader proposes a unified ALBA bloc military force." *Los Tiempos*, November 11. Lexis/Nexis.

———. 2008a. "Ecuador Reorganizing Military, Police Intelligence Services." *El Comercio Website*, Quito, Ecuador. May 6: Lexis/Nexis.

———. 2008b. "Bolivia Government to Restructure Intelligence Service." *La Razón*, Bolivia, November 12: Lexis/Nexis.

———. 2008c. "Chilean President Reads UNASUR Declaration in Support of Bolivia." Television Nacional de Chile, Santiago, Sept. 16: Lexis/Nexis.

———. 2007. "Ecuador defense minister says armed forces to have greater 'social focus'." *El Universo*, Guayaquil, Ecuador. January 23: Lexis/Nexis.

———.2006a. "Ecuadorian Indigenous Confederation Condemns "dictatorial" state of emergency." *CONAIE Website*, Ecuador. March 23: Lexis/Nexis.

————. 2006b. "Ecuador to take 'multidimensional' approach to security-defense minister." *El Comercio Website,* Quito, Ecuador. August 22: Lexis/Nexis.

————. 2006c. "Ecuadorian Defense Minister Heard of his Resignation by Phone." *El Comercio Website,* Quito, Ecuador, August 31: Lexis/Nexis.

————. 2006d. "Bolivia's Military to Gain New Role, "Vision" under Morales." *La Razón,* Bolivia, September 13: Lexis/Nexis.

————. 2005. "Ecuador Must Update its Defense Policy, Minister Says." *El Comercio Website,* Quito, Ecuador. Aug.30: Lexis/Nexis.

BBC Summary of World Broadcasts. 2004. "Coup Rumours Overshadow Bolivian President's Trip to Argentina." *La Prensa Website,* La Paz, Bolivia, April 25: Lexis/Nexis.

————. 2002. "Andean Countries Agree to Reduce Military Spending in Andean Charter for Peace." *El Diario, Bolivia.* June 21: Lexis/Nexis.

————. 2000a. "Gallup Poll Shows only 22 percent of Population Back Peace Process." *Radio Cadena Nacional,* October 14: Lexis/Nexis.

————. 2000b. "New President Stresses Government's Democratic Credentials." *ABC Website,* Madrid. November 30: Lexis-Nexis.

————.1999a. "Government Bill to Modernize Armed Forces." *Radio Cadena Nacional,* Bogotá, Colombia. March 4: Lexis/Nexis.

————. 1999b. "President Mahuad Announces Military Budget Reduction." *El Comercio,* January 26: Lexis/Nexis.

————. 1987. "Ecuador Kidnapping of President and Release of Vargas Pazzos." *Radio Quito,* January 19: Lexis/Nexis.

BBC Worldwide Monitoring. 2008. "Bolivian Armed Forces Chief 'Rejects' Venezuelan Military Force." *La Razón,* Bolivia, Sept. 13: Lexis/Nexis.

Bergquist, Charles, Ricardo Peñaranda and Gonzalo Sánchez G. 2001. *Violence in Colombia.* Wilmington, Delaware: SR Books.

Bigler, Gene E. 1982. "Professional Soldiers and Restrained Politics in Venezuela." In Robert Wesson, ed., *New Military Politics in Latin America,* 175–96. New York: Praeger.

Bigwood, Jeremy. 2006. U.S. meddling in Peruvian Presidential Race? *Upside Down World,* March 15. Available at http://upsidedownworld.org/main/content/view/227/1/ Accessed February 2, 2008.

Blair, Dennis. 2010. "Annual Threat Assessment of the U.S. Intelligence Community for the Senate Select Committee on Intelligence." Statement for the Record, February 2, Washington, D.C.

Blair-Trujillo, Elsa. 1993. *Las Fuerzas Armadas.* Bogotá: CINE

Bolivian Ministry of Defense. 2008. "Ministro de Defensa Nacional." Available at http://www.mindef.gov.bo/index.php?option=com_content&view=article&id=56&Itemid=83; accessed October 1, 2008.

Bonilla, Adrian. 2006. "U.S. Andean Policy, the Colombian Conflict, and Security in Ecuador." In *Addicted to Failure: U.S. Security Policy in Latin America and the Andean Region,* edited by Brian Loveman, p. 103–29. Lanham: Rowman and Littlefield.

Bowman, Kirk. 2002. *Militarization, Democracy and Development: The Perils of Praetorianism in Latin America.* University Park, PA: Penn State University Press.

Bracci Roa, Luigino. 2008. "Chávez Denounces Bolivian Commanders's Inaction and Asks Bolivian Soldiers to Remain Loyal to Evo." *Radio Mundial,* Available at http://www.radiomundial.com.ve/yvke/noticia.php?11608; accessed Sept. 18, 2008.

Bradley, Theresa. 2007. "Venezuela's Chávez calls for Greater Role for Communal Councils." *Venezuelanalysis,* June 21. Available at http://www.venezuelanalysis.com/news/2461; accessed November 1, 2008.

Brinkley, Douglas. 1997. Democratic Enlargement: The Clinton Doctrine. *Foreign Policy*, 106, Spring: 110–27.

Bruneau, Thomas and Harold Trinkunas. 2006. Democratization as a Global Phemomenon and its Impact on Civil-Military Relations. *Democratization* 13, 5, December: pp.776–90.

———. 2008. "Global Trends and Their Impact on Civil-Military Relations." In *Global Politics of Defense Reform*, Edited by Thomas Bruneau and Harold Trinkunas, pp. 3–19. New York, NY: Palgrave.

Bruneau, Thomas C. 2005. "Civil-Military Relations in Latin America: The Hedgehog and the Fox Revisted" *Revista Fuerzas Armadas y Sociedad*, vol.19, no.1–2: pp. 111–31.

Bruneau, Thomas. 2006. "Ecuador: The Continuing Challenge of Democratic Consolidation and Civil-Military Relations." *Strategic Insights*, vol.5, no.2, February: http://www.ccc.nps.navy.mil/si/2006/Feb/bruneauFeb06.asp.

Burggraaf, Winfield and Richard Millett. 1995. "More than Failed Coups." In *Lessons of the Venezuelan Experience*, edited by Louis W. Goodman, et al, p. 54–78. Washington, D.C.: Woodrow Wilson Center Press.

Burt, Jo-Marie and Philip Mauceri. 2004. "Introduction," in Jo-Marie and Philip Mauceri, eds., *Politics in the Andes*, pp. 1–14, Pittsburgh: University of Pittsburgh Press.

Burt, Jo-Marie and Coletta Youngers. 2010. "Peruvian Precedent: The Fujimori Conviction and the Ongoing Struggle for Justice." *NACLA*, vol.43, no.2, March/April: 6–8.

Burt, Jo-Marie. 2004. "State Making Against Democracy," in Jo-Marie and Philip Mauceri, eds., *Politics in the Andes*, pp. 247–268, Pittsburgh: University of Pittsburgh Press.

———. 2006. "State-Society Relations in Urban Peru, 1950–2000" in Paul Drake and Eric Hershberg, eds., *State and Society in Conflict: Comparative Perspectives on Andean Crisis*, pp. 220–56, Pittsburgh: University of Pittsburgh Press.

———. 2007. *Political Violence and the Authoritarian State in Peru: Silencing Civil Society*. New York: Palgrave Macmillan.

Bush, George. 1990. Statement on Signing the International Narcotics Control Act, 1990–November 21, 1990. *The American Presidency Project*, Available at http://www.presidency.ucsb.edu/ws/index.php?pid=19084 Accessed June 10, 2008.

Bustamante, Fernando. 1989. "The Armed Forces of Colombia and Ecuador in Comparative Perspective." In *Democracy Under Siege: New Military Power in Latin America* edited by Augusto Varas, p. 17–33. New York: Greenwood.

———. 1998. "Democracy, Civilizational Change and the Latin American Military." In *Fault Lines of Democracy in Post-Transition Latin America* edited by Felipe Agüero and Jeffrey Stark, p. 345–70. Miami, FL: North-South Press.

———. 1999. "Las FF.AA ecuatorianos y la coyuntura politico-social de fin de siglo." In *Control civil y fuerzas armadas en las nuevas democracies latinoamericanas*, edited by Rut Diamint, 339–62. Buenos Aires: Universidad Toruato di Tella and Nuevohacer.

———. 2003. "La crisis de la institucionalidad de la defensa en el Ecuador."In *El control democratico de la defensa en la region andina*, edited by Comisión Andina de Juristas, 95–111. Lima, Peru: Comisión Andina de Juristas.

Buxton, Julia. 2007. "The deepening of Venezuela's Bolivarian Revolution." *OpenDemocracy*, March 5. Available at http://www.opendemocracy.net/democracy-protest/deepening_revolution_4592.jsp; accessed September 10, 2008.

Call, Charles. 1991. *Clear and Present Dangers: The U.S. Military and the War on Drugs in the Andes*. Washington, D.C.: Washington Office on Latin America.

Canadian Press, The. 2008. "The Peru's Shining Path Guerrillas on the rise again." June 2. Available at http://www.cicte.oas.org/Rev/en/About/News/2008/CICTEpercent20News percent2014-2008-I.pdf Accessed June 30, 2008.

BIBLIOGRAPHY

Carlson, Chris. 2008. "Venezuela Advances Project for 'Socialist Factories.'" *Venezuelanalysis*, June 10: http://www.venezuelanalysis.com/news/3538; accessed November 12, 2008.

Carroll, Rory and MacAskill, Ewen. 2009. "Outcry in South America over U.S. Military Base Pact." *The Guardian*, August 27: Available at http://www.guardian.co.uk/world/2009/aug/27/anger-america-colombia-bases-deal; Accessed January 30, 2010.

Center for Democracy and Governance. 1998. "Civil-Military Relations: USAID's Role," *Center for Democracy and Governance-Technical Publication Series*, July: Washington, D.C.: U.S. AID.

Center for Hemispheric Defense Studies (CHDS). 2008a. "Brief History of CHDS." http://www.ndu.edu/chds/index.cfm?secID=15&pageID=91&lang=EN&type=section (accessed Aug. 20, 2007).

———. 2008b. "Bio of General (Ret.) R. Oswaldo Jarrín Roman." http://www.ndu.edu/chds/docUploaded/OswaldoJarrín.html (accessed Aug.20, 2008).

Center for International Policy. 2006a. "Just the Facts-E-IMET, Expanded International Military Education Training," *Center for International Policy Website*, Available at: http://ciponline.org/facts/eimet.htm; Accessed Jan.5, 2006.

———. 2003. Limitations on Assistance to Security Forces (The "Leahy Law"). *Just the Facts*. Available at http://www.ciponline.org/facts/leahy.htm; Accessed May 30, 2008.

———. 1999. Colombia Fires a General While Washington Plans New Military Aid. September 17. Available at www.ciponline.org/04.htm; Accessed February 9, 2000.

Chang, Jack. 2006. "New Bolivian President Quickly Comes Under Fire." *The Philadelphia Inquirer*. Jan. 30. Lexis/Nexis.

Chávez, Franz. 2008. "Bolivia: Governor Arrested for 'Porvenir Massacre.'" *Inter-Press Service*, September 16. Available at http://www.ipsnews.net/news.asp?idnews=43893; accessed December 10, 2009.

Chillier, Gaston and Laurie Freeman. 2005. "Potential Threat: The New OAS Concept of Hemispheric Security." *Washington Office of Latin America-Special Report*, July. Available at http://www.wola.org/media/Potentialpercent20threatpercent20security_lowres.pdf; accessed July 21, 2009.

CIA. 1999. "Armed Groups Filling Power Vacuum in Rural Areas," *Senior Executive Intelligence Brief, Top Secret*, 3 pp. CIA declassification release under FOIA, August 2004. Available at http://www.gwu.edu/~nsarchiv/NSAEBB/NSAEBB166/index.htm; accessed February 20, 2010.

Clayton, Lawrence A. 1999. *Peru and the United States*. Athens, GA: University of Georgia Press.

Cleaves, Peter S. and Henry Pease García. 1986."State Autonomy and Military Policy Making." In J. Samuel Fitch and Abraham Lowenthal, eds. *Armies and Politics in Latin America*, 335–56. New York: Holmes Meier.

Clinton, William. 1996. "A National Security Strategy of Engagement and Enlargement." February (The White House). Available at http://www.fas.org/spp/military/docops/national/1996stra.htm; accessed June 23, 2009.

Clunan, Anne. 2008. "Globalization and the Impact of Norms on Defense Restructuring." In Thomas Bruneau and Harold Trinkunas, eds. *Global Politics of Defense Reform*, 21–48. New York, NY: Palgrave.

Cochrane, Allan and Kathy Pain. 2004. "A Globalising Society?" in David Held, ed., *A Globalizing World? Culture, Economics and Politics*, 5–46. New York: Routledge.

Colombia Reports. 2009. "Disappointing outlook on Human Rights in Colombia: UN Rapporteur." June 18. Available at http://colombiareports.com/colombia-news/news/4618-disappointing-outlook-on-human-rights-un-rapporteur.html; accessed June 22, 2009.

Colombian Government. 2001. "Colombian Government Briefing Document on National Security Law, July 23. Available at the Center for International Policy's website: http//www.ciponline.org/Colombia/01072301.htm.

Comercio, El. 2006. "Los militares limitarán sus inversiones." Dec. 21. http://www.elcomercio.com/solo_texto_search.asp?id_noticia=53499&anio=2006&mes=12&dia=21   (accessed Aug. 20, 2008).

Comisión Andina de Juristas. 2002a. "Cronología Ecuador, mayo del 2002." May 2 and May 23, http://www.cajpe.org.pe/cronolog/Mayoec6.htm (accessed Aug. 20, 2008).

Comisión Andina de Juristas 2002b. "Cronología Ecuador, abril del 2002." April 12. http://www.cajpe.org.pe/cronolog/Abrilec6.htm (accessed Aug. 20, 2008).

Comisión Intereclesial de Justicia y Paz. 2009. "Derecho de petición al Presidente Uribe sobre seguimiento del DAS contra Justicia y Paz." Available at http://colombia.indymedia.org/mail.php?id=103365; accessed March 10, 2010.

Conaghan, Catherine. 2008. "Ecuador: Correa's Plebiscitary Presidency." *Journal of Democracy,* vol.19, no.2, April: 46–60.

Conaghan, Catherine, James Malloy, and Luis A. Abugattas. 1990. "Business and the 'Boys': The Politics of Neoliberalism in the Central Andes." *Latin American Research Review,* vol.25, no.2: 3–30.

Conaghan, Catherine and James Malloy. 1994. *Unsettling Statecraft.* Pittsburgh, PA: University of Pittsburgh Press.

CONAIE. 1998. "CONAIE's view on some key concepts." January. Available at http://conaie.nativeweb.org/conaie11.html, accessed Oct. 15, 2008.

Concha Sanz, Tomás E. 2003. "Fiscalización y transparencia del presupuesto asignado a la defense. Algunas anotaciones sobre el caso de Colombia." In Comisión Andina de Juristas eds., *El Control Democratico de la Defensa en la Region Andina,* 183–204. Lima, Peru: Embajada de Finlandia.

Congressional Budget Office. 1994. "The Andean Initiative," March. Available at http://www.cbo.gov/ftpdoc.cfm?index=4885&type=0; accessed Dec. 10, 2007.

Constable, Pamela. 1992. Peruvian leftists squeezed in president's power play. *The Boston Globe,* October 11. p. 4. Lexis/Nexis.

Cooper, Marc. 2002. "The Coup that Wasn't." *The Nation,* September 11. Available at http://www.thenation.com/doc/20020506/marccooper; accessed January 5, 2009.

Coronil, Fernando. 1997. *The Magical State.* Chicago: University of Chicago Press.

Council on Foreign Relations. 2004. *Andes 2020: A New Strategy for Colombia and the Region.* January. New York: Council on Foreign Relations Press.

Cox, R.W. 1981. "Social Forces, States and World Orders," *Millenium: Journal of International Studies* 10 (2): 126–55.

———. 1987. *Production, Power and World Order.* New York: Columbia University Press.

Crabtree, John. 2000. "Populisms Old and New: The Peruvian Case." *Bulletin of Latin American Research,* 19: 163–76.

Crandall, Russell, Paz, Guadalupe and Riordan Roett, eds. 2005. *The Andes in Focus: Security, Democracy and Economic Reform.* Boulder, CO: Lynne Rienner.

Dangl, Benjamin. 2007. *The Price of Fire: Resource Wars and Social Movements in Bolivia.* Oakland, CA: AK Press.

Dangl, Benjamin. 2003. "Bolivia's Gas War." *ZNET,* September 24. Available at http://www.zcommunications.org/bolivias-gas-war-by-ben-dangl; accessed July 10, 2009.

Darío Restrepo, Javier. 2009. "All the President's Spies." *Inter-Press Service,* June 13. Available at http://www.ipsnews.net/news.asp?idnews=47210; accessed March 8, 2010.

Dávila, Andrés. 1998. *El Juego del Poder: Historia, Armas, y Votos.* Santafé de Bogotá: Uniandes, CEREC.

———. 1999. "Ejército regular, conflictos irregulares: la institucion militar en los ultimos quince años." In *Reconocer la Guerra para Construir la Paz*, ed. Malcolm Deas and María Victoria Llorente, 283–346. Bogotá: CEREC.

Department of the Air Force, U.S. 2009. "Military Construction Program: Fiscal Year 2010 Budget Estimates," Justification Data Submitted to Congress, May 2009. Available at http://www.justf.org/files/primarydocs/091104pal.pdf; Accessed February 20, 2010.

Desch, Michael. 1999. *Civilian Control of the Military: The Changing Security Environment*. Baltimore, MD: Johns Hopkins University Press.

DeShazo, Peter Tanya Primiani and Phillip McLean. 2007. *Back from the Brink*. CSIS Report, November. Available at http://www.csis.org/media/csis/pubs/071112-backfromthebrink-web.pdf. Accessed March 10, 2008.

Diamint, Rut. 1998. "Responsables ante la defense." In Rut Diamint, ed., *Argentina y la seguridad internacional*, pp. 13–14. Santiago, Chile: FLASCO.

Dietz, Henry. 1992. "Elites in an Unconsolidated Democracy: Peru during the 1980s." in John Higley and Richard Gunther, eds., *Elites and Democratic Consolidation in Latin America and Southern Europe*. New York, NY: Cambridge University Press.

Dominguez, Jorge. 1997. *Technopols: Freeing Politics and Markets in the 1990s in Latin America*. College Park: Penn State University Press.

Drake, Paul and Eric Hershberg, eds. 2006. *State and Society in Conflict : Comparative Perspectives on Andean Crises*. Pittsburgh, PA : University of Pittsburgh Press.

El Economista.es. 2007. "Contraloría reclama eficacia en el gasto en seguridad y Defensa," August 10, 2007, Online at: http://www.eleconomista.es/empresas-finanzas/noticias/260502/08/07/Contraloria-reclama-eficacia-en-el-gasto-en-seguridad-y-defensa.html; accessed February 1, 2008.

Economist, The. 2000. "Ecuador's Post-Coup Reckoning." January 29. Lexis/Nexis.

———. 2003. "Spying on the Spies." October 11. Lexis/Nexis.

———. 2006. 'Arms, votes and the man; Venezuela and the United States ' February 11. Lexis/Nexis.

Ejército Nacional Republica de Colombia. 2007. With Satisfaction the Army Commander receives the United States Certification. April 11. Available at http://www.ejercito.mil.co/index.php?idcategoria=190833; Accessed June 20, 2008.

Ellner, Steve. 2008. *Rethinking Venezuelan Politics*. Boulder: Lynne Rienner.

Encyclopedia of World Biographies. 2005–2006. "Hugo Banzer Suárez." Available at http://www.bookrags.com/biography/hugo-banzer-suarez/; accessed February 28, 2010. New York: Thomson Gale.

Energy Information Administration. 2008. "Crude Oil and Petroleum Imports Top 15 Countries." U.S. Department of Energy. Available at http://www.eia.doe.gov/pub/oil_gas/petroleum/data_publications/company_level_imports/current/import.html; accessed October 20, 2008.

Estellano, Washington. 1994. "From Populism to the Coca Economy in Bolivia." *Latin American Perspectives*, Issue 83, vol.21, no.4, Fall:34–45.

EUROMONEY.2005 "Andean: World Bank and Ecuador Kiss and Make Up." Nov. Lexis/Nexis.

Evans, Michael. 2005. "Paramilitaries as Proxies:Declassified Evidence on the Colombian Army's Anti-guerrilla 'allies'." *The National Security Archive*, October 16. Available at http://www.gwu.edu/~nsarchiv/NSAEBB/NSAEBB166/index.htm; accessed February 20, 2010.

Faux, Jeff. 2006. *The Global Class War*. Hoboken, NJ: John Wiley and Sons, Inc.

Federal Research Division. 1989. *Soviet Union: A Country Study*. Washington, D.C. Available at http://www.country-data.com/cgi-bin/query/r-12696.html; accessed February 20, 2010.

Fertyl, Duroyan. 2005. "Ecuador: People Drive Out the People." *Green Left Weekly*, April 27. Available at http://www.greenleft.org.au/2005/624/34863; accessed July 4, 2009.

Fitch, J. Samuel. 1979. "The Political Consequences of U.S. Military Aid to Latin America." *Armed Forces and Society*, 5, 3: 360–86.

————. 1993. "The Decline of US Military Influence in Latin America." *Journal of Interamerican Studies and World Affairs*, vol.35, no.2, Summer:1–49.

————. 1998. *The Armed Forces and Democracy in Latin America*. Baltimore: Johns Hopkins University.

————. 2001. "Military Attitudes toward Democracy in Latin America: How Do We Know if Anything Has Changed?" in David Pion-Berlin, ed., *Civil-Military Relations in Latin America*, 59–87. Chapel Hill: University of North Carolina Press.

————. 2003. "The Armed Forces and Society in South America: How Similar? How Different?" Paper presented at the Sixth Annual Research and Education in Defense and Security Studies, Oct. 28–31, Santiago, Chile.

————. 2005. "Post-Transition Coups: Ecuador 2000." *Journal of Political and Military Sociology*, 33, 1, Summer: 39–58.

Fleishman-Hillard. 2008. "Thought Leadership From Around the Globe." Retrieved online http://www.fleishman.com/client-solutions/international-advisory-board.html; accessed April 19, 2008.

Forero, Juan. 2002. New Role for the U.S. in Colombia: Protecting a Vital Oil Pipeline. *New York Times*, October 4: A4, A6

————. 2004. "Documents Show C.I.A. Knew of a Coup Plot in Venezuela." *New York Times*, December 3. Lexis/Nexis.

————. 2005. "Ecuador's Leader Flees and Vice-President Flees." *The New York Times*, April 21. Available at http://www.nytimes.com/2005/04/21/international/americas/21ecuador.html ?pagewanted=print&position=; accessed July 4, 2009.

————. 2006. "The (American) Selling of the (Bolivian) President, 2002." *The New York Times*, February 26. Lexis/Nexis.

Freedom House. 2004. "Peru" *Freedom in the World*. Available at http://www.freedomhouse. org/template.cfm?page=22&year=2004&country=3007; accessed March 10, 2007.

Fuentes, Fred. 2010. "Bolivia: We are here to serve the people, not capitalists." *Green Left Weekly*, January 29. Available at www.greenleft.org.an/node/43098; accessed August 24, 2010.

Fujimori on Trial. 2008. Gen. Robles Claims Fujimori had Direct Command of Colina Detachment through National Intelligence Service. May 8. Available at http://fujimorion-trial.org/?p=317 Accessed June 15, 2008.

Fundación Libertad, Democracia y Desarollo. 2004. "The Budget for State Security in Bolivia-2004." Santa Cruz. Available at http://www.hacer.org/pdf/BoliviaLASED.pdf; accessed 9/16/2008.

Gamarra, Eduardo A. and James M. Malloy. 1988. *Revolution and Reaction: Bolivia, 1964-1985*. New Brunswick: Transaction Publishers.

————. 1996. "Bolivia: Revolution and Reaction." In *Latin American Politics and Development*, edited by Howard J. Wiarda and Harvey Kline, p.305-325. Boulder: Westview.

García Linera, Alvaro. 2006. "State Crisis and Popular Power." *New Left Review*, 37, Jan/Feb: 73–85.

García, José. 1998. "Peru and Bolivia." In *Latin America: Its Problems and Its Promise*. Edited by Jan Knippers Black, 475–96. Boulder, CO: Westview Press.

Gerlach, Allen. 2003. *Indians, Oil, and Politics: A Recent History of Ecuador*. Wilmington: Scholarly Resources Press.

Gibbs, Terry and Gary Leech. 2009. *The Failure of Global Capitalism: From Cape Breton to Colombia and Beyond.* Sydney, Nova Scotia, Canada: Cape Breton University Press.

Gill, Stephen. 1994. *Gramsci, Historical Materialism and International Relations.* New York: Cambridge University Press.

Gills, Barry, Joel Rocamora, and Richard Wilson. 1993 *Low Intensity Democracy. Political Power in the New World Order.* London: TNI/Pluto Press.

Gills, Barry and Joel Rocamora. 1992. "Low intensity democracy." *Third World Quarterly,* vol.13, no.3: 501–23.

Gilly, Adolfo. 2005. "The Emerging 'Threat' of Radical Populism." *NACLA,* vol. 39, no.2, Sep/Oct: 37–45.

Gindin, Jonah. 2005. "Chavistas in the Halls of Power, Chavistas on the Street." *NACLA,* vol 38, no.5, March.

Giraldo Gustavo, G. Gallon. 1991. *Derechos Humanos y Conflicto Armado en Colombia.* Bogotá: Comisón de Juristas Andinas.

Giraldo, Javier. 1996. *The Genocidal Democracy.* Monroe, ME : Common Courage Press.

Global Security. 2005. "Ecuador: Fall of Gutiérrez Exemplifies Andean 'Instability.'" April 27. http://www.globalsecurity.org/military/library/news/2005/04/ wwwh50428.htm (accessed Aug. 20, 2008).

Golinger, Eva. 2004a. "Declassified Documents Back Venezuelan President's Claim of U.S. Aid to Opposition Groups." *Venezuelanalysis,* February 10. http://www.venezuelanalysis.com/news/351 (accessed Feb. 10, 2006).

———. 2004b "U.S. Gave Cash to Anti-Chavez Groups." *People's Weekly World,* September 16.

Golinger, Eva. 2006. "CIA Announces New Mission in Venezuela and Cuba." *Venezuelanalysis. com,* August 19. Available at http://www.venezuelanalysis.com/news/1897; accessed July 11, 2009.

Gómez, Luis. 2004. "Coup d'Etat Plot, Exposed, Shakes Bolivia." *The Narco News Bulletin,* April 18. Available at http://www.narconews.com/Issue33/article957.html; accessed September 27, 2008.

González Casanova, Pablo. 1988. *Los militares y la politica en America Latina.* Mexico City: OCEANO.

Goshko, John M. 1992a. "Bush: U.S. to Urge Pressure on Peru." *The Washington Post,* April 11, 1992, A20. Lexis/Nexis.

———. 1992b. "U.S. Pulls Out GIs Training Peruvians in Narcotics Fight." *The Washington Post,* April 15: A27, Lexis/Nexis.

Gott, Richard. 2000. *In the Shadow of the Liberator: Hugo Chávez and the Transformation of Venezuela.* New York: Verso Press.

Graham, Carol. 1994. "Introduction." In Joseph Tulchin and Gary Bland, eds., *Peru in Crisis,* 1–22. Boulder: Lynne Rienner.

Gramsci, Antonio. 1971. *Selections from the Prison Notebooks of Antonio Gramsci,* trans. by Q. Hoare and G. Nowell Smith. New York: International.

Grandin, Greg. 2006. "The Wide War: How Donald Rumsfeld Discovered the Wild West in Latin America." *Mother Jones,* May 8. Available at http://www.motherjones.com/politics/2006/05/latin-america-and-wide-war; accessed May 21, 2009.

Gutiérrez, Francisco. 2003. "El escenario colombiano," in Comision Andina de Juristas (eds.) *El control democratico de la defensa en la region andina,* 79-91. Lima, Peru: Embajada de Finlandia.

Guzmán, Gustavo. 2003. "Goni y las FFAA: Del desprecio al amor."*Pulso doc Bolivia,* August 23. Available at www.comunidadboliviana.com.ar/shop/detallenot.asp?notid=302; accessed September 16, 2008.

Gutiérrez, Lucio. 2001. "Un país para todos los ecuatorianos-Entrevista con el Coronel Lucio Gutiérrez." In Heinz Dietrich, ed. *La cuarta via al poder*, 152–69. Bogotá:Ediciones desde abajo.

Hallinan, Conn. 2002. "U.S. Shadow Over Venezuela." *Foreign Policy in Focus*, April 17. http://www.fpif.org/commentary/2002/0204venezuela2.html (accessed 1/5/07)

Harnecker, Marta. 2003a. "The Venezuelan Military: The Making of an Anomaly," *Venezuelanalysis.com*, Oct. 20, www.venezuelanalysis.com/articles.php?artno=1040; (accessed Aug. 26, 2006).

———. 2003b. "Interview with President Chávez: The Military in the Revolution and the Counter-Revolution." *Venezuelanalysis*, Oct. 20, www.venezuelanalysis.com/articles.php?artno=1039; (accessed Aug. 26, 2006).

Harris, Jerry. 2005. "To Be or Not To Be: The Nation-Centric World Order Under Globalization," *Science and Society*, vol. 69, No.3, July: 320–40.

Hartlyn, Jonathan. 1985. "Producer Associations, The Political Regime, and Policy Processes in Contemporary Colombia." *Latin American Research Review*, vol.20, no.3: 111–38.

Harvey, David. 2005. *The New Imperialism*. New York, NY: Oxford University Press.

Haste, Paul. 2007. Polo Democrático's Challenge to Colombia. *Dissident Voice*, October 2. Available at http://www.thirdworldtraveler.com/Colombia/Polo_Democratico.html; accessed June 15, 2008.

Haugaard, Lisa, Gimena Sánchez-Garzoli, Adam Isacson, John Walsh and Robert Guitteau. 2008. "A Compass for Colombia Policy," http://justf.org/files/pubs/081022comp.pdf; Center for International Policy, Latin American Working Group Education Fund, U.S. Office on Colombia and Washington Office on Latin America. Accessed October 30, 2008.

Hayes, Monte. 2006. "Left-Leaning Candidate Surges in Peru." *Associated Press*, January 14. Lexis/Nexis.

Healy, Sean. 2001. "Ecuador: Unrest Forces Presidential About Face." *Green Left Weekly*, February 14. Available at http://www.greenleft.org.au/2001/436/26719; accessed July 4, 2009.

Hearn, Kelly. 2006. García See Chile as His Economic Example. *The Washington Times*, June 8: A13, Lexis/Nexis.

Held, David. 2006. *Models of Democracy, 3rd Edition*. Cambridge: Polity Press.

Hellinger, Daniel. 2006. "Venezuela." In Harry E. Vanden and Gary Prevost, eds. *Politics of Latin America*, 468–95. New York: Oxford University Press.

Heraldo, El. 2009. "Evo quiere ampliar ALBA a fuerzas armadas." July 19. Available at http://www.elheraldo.hn/Ediciones/2009/07/19/Noticias/Evo-quiere-ampliar-ALBA-a-fuerzas-armadas; accessed February 10, 2010.

Hristov, Jasmin.2009. *Blood and Capital: The Paramilitarization of Colombia*. Athens, OH: Ohio University Press.

Humala Tasso, Antauro. 2001. *Ejercito peruano: milenarismo, nacionalismo y etnocacerismo*. Lima, Peru: OSREVI E.I.R.L.

Human Rights Watch. 2010. "Paramilitaries Heirs." *Human Rights Watch Report*, February 3. Available at http://www.hrw.org/en/reports/2010/02/03/paramilitaries-heirs-0; accessed June 20, 2010.

———. 2006. "World Report 2007: Peru," Available at http://hrw.org/englishwr2k7/docs/2007/01/11/peru14887.htm; accessed June 6, 2007.

———. 2005. "Smoke and Mirrors: Colombia's Demobilization of Paramilitary Groups." *Human Rights Watch Report*, vol. 17, no.3, August.

———. 2004. "Bolivia. Ruling Holds Military Accountable for Rights Abuses." Available at http://www.hrw.org/en/news/2004/05/06/bolivia-ruling-holds-military-accountable-rights-abuses; accessed December 20, 2009.

———. 1996. *Colombia's Killer Networks- The Military-Paramilitary Partnership and the United States.* New York: Human Rights Watch. p.12

Hunter, Wendy.1997a. *Eroding Military Influence in Brazil.* Chapel Hill: University of North Carolina Press.

———. 1997b. "Continuity or Change? Civil-Military Relations in Democratic Argentina, Chile, and Peru." *Political Science Quarterly,* 112, 3: 453–75.

———. 1996. *State and Soldier in Latin America.* Peaceworks 10: United States Institute of Peace, October. Available at http://www.usip.org/pubs/peaceworks/pwks10.html; accessed February 10, 2005.

Huntington, Samuel. 1956. "Civilian Control and the Constitution." *American Political Science Review,* vol.50, no.3, September: 676–99.

Hylton, Forrest and Sinclair Thomson. *Revolutionary Horizons: Past and Present in Bolivian Politics.* New York: Verso Press.

Ibaibarriaga, Mercedes. 2005. "Oficiales rebeldes del Ejercito boliviano." *El Mundo,* May 27. Lexis/Nexis.

———. 2007. "Tension en Bolivia." *El Pais,* Dec. 9. Lexis/Nexis.

Instituto de defensa legal. 1990. *Peru 1989, en la espiral de violencia.* Lima.Instituto de defensa legal.

International IDEA. 2005. Ambassador Allan Wagner-Biographies of Speakers. *International IDEA.* Available at http://www.idea.int/about/anniversary/bios.cfm. accessed July 8, 2008.

International Crisis Group. 2002. "Colombia's Elusive Quest for Peace." *Latin America Report,* no.1. March 26. Bogotá/Brussels.

———. 2003. "Colombia: President Uribe's Democratic Security Policy." *Latin America Report,* no.6. November 13. Bogotá/Brussels.

———. 2004. "Colombia's Borders: The Weak Link in Uribe's Security Policy," *Latin America Report,* no.9. Sept.23.

———. 2007. "Ecuador: Overcoming Instability?" *Latin American Report,* no.2, August 7.

———. 2008. "Latin American Drugs II: Improving Policy and Reducing Harm." *Latin America Report,* no.26, March 14.

Internationalist, The. 2005. "Coup Threats, Rightist Maneuvers vs. Calls for 'Workers to Power.'" June, Available at http://www.internationalist.org/boliviaexplodes0506.html; accessed 9/14/08.

Isacson, Adam. 2004. "The U.S. Military in the War on Drugs." In Collett Youngers and Eileen Rosin, eds. *Drugs and Democracy in Latin America,* 15-60. Boulder: Lynne Rienner.

———. 2009a. "Integrated Action." *Plan Colombia and Beyond Blog.* May 26, Available at http://www.cipcol.org/?p=873; accessed June 22, 2009.

———. 2009b. "These killings were carried out in a more or less systematic fashion by signicant elements within the military." *Plan Colombia and Beyond Blog,* June 18, available at http://www.cipcol.org/; accessed June 22, 2009.

Isikoff, Michael 1992. "Bush, Latin Leaders Agree to Stepped-Up Drug Fight." *The Washington Post,* February 28: A2, Lexis/Nexis.

Jacome, Francine. 1999. "Las relaciones civico-militares en Venezuela." In *Control Civil y fuerzas armadas en las nuevas democracies latinoamericanas,* edited by Rut Diamint, 401–32. Bueno Aires: Nuevohacer.

Jaime Cisneros, Luis. 2001. Peru's President-Elect Chooses Government. *Agence France Presse.* July 27. Lexis/Nexis.

James, Deborah. 2006. "U.S. Intervention in Venezuela: Clear and Present Danger." *Global Exchange,* January. Available at http://www.globalexchange.org/countries/americas/venezuela/USVZrelations1.pdf; accessed July 11, 2009.

Janicke, Kiraz. 2010. "Venezuela Creates Peasant Militias, Enacts Federal Government Council." *Venezuelanalysis.com*, February 22. Available at http://venezuelanalysis.com/news/5150; accessed March 3, 2010.

Jones, Bart. 2007. *Hugo!: The Hugo Chávez Story from Mud Hut to Perpetual Revolution.* Hanover, NH: Steer Forth Press.

———. 2004. "U.S. Funds Aid Chávez Opposition." Venezuelanalysis, April 2. http://www. venezuelanalysis.com/analysis/448 (accessed June 1, 2007).

Juárez, Carlos E.1994. "Trade and Development Policies in Colombia: Export Promotion and Outward Orientation, 1967–1992." In *Economic Development Under Democratic Regimes-Neoliberalism in Latin America* edited by Lowell S. Gustafson, 51-79. Westport, CT: Praeger

———. 1996. " Politics and Economic Policy in Colombia." Paper presented at the American Political Science Association meeting, San Francisco.

Just the Facts. 2008a. "Military and Police Aid, All Programs." *Center for International Policy*, http://justf.org/All_Grants_Country (accessed July 25, 2008).

———. 2008b. "U.S. Military and Police Trainees Listed BY Country, All Programs." *Center for International Policy*, http://justf.org/All_Trainees_Country (accessed July 25, 2008).

Justice for Colombia. 2009. "ITUC: Colombia is World's Most Dangerous Place for Trade Unionists." June 11. Available at http://www.justiceforcolombia.org/?link=newsPage& story=751; accessed June 27, 2009.

Karl, Terry Lynn. 1990. "Dilemmas of Democratization in Latin America." *Comparative Politics* 23, no. 1: 1–21.

———. 2000. "Economic Inequality and Democratic Instability." *Journal of Democracy*, 11, 1: 149–56.

Kirk, Robin. 2003. *More Terrible than Death.* New York: Public Affairs.

Kornblilth, Miriam. 2000. "Venezuela." In *The Crisis of Democratic Governance in the Andes*, edited by Cynthia Arnson, 68-72. Washington, D.C.: Woodrow Wilson International Center for Scholars.

Kozloff, Nikolas. 2006. *Hugo Chávez-Oil, Politics, and the Challenge to the U.S.* New York: Palgrave.

La Razón. 2009."El entorno condiciona a la fuerza militar." Available at http://www.la-razon. com/versiones/20090807_006812/nota_244_857713.htm; accessed January 15, 2010.

La Voz del Interior. 2006."Cupula militar entra en crisis por la destitucion del jefe del Ejercito." January 23. Lexis/Nexis.

Lama, Abraham. 2001. Historic Chance to Depoliticize the Armed Forces. *IPS-Inter Press Service*, October 5. Lexis/Nexis.

Lander, Luis and Margarita López-Maya.2002. "Venezuela's oil reform and Chavismo," *NACLA*, 36,(1): 21-23.

Latin American Regional Reports. 2007. "Chavez defends new doctrine for the armed forces." Oct. 11. Lexis/Nexis.

Latin American Weekly Report. 2003. "Military Industries." June 10.

———. 2002. Reshuffle Creates Rift with Ruling Party. January 22:39.

———. 2000. Peru's New Government Moves to Eradicate the Montesinos Legacy. November 28: 553–4.

Laurienti, Jerry M. 2007. *The U.S. Military and Human Rights Promotion: Lessons from Latin America*. Westport, CT: Praeger.

Leal-Buitrago, Francisco. 2006. *La Inseguridad de la Seguridad: Colombia 1958-2005.* Bogotá: Planeta.

———. 2002. *La seguridad nacional a la deriva.* Bogotá: Universidad de los Andes, CESO.

————. 1994. *El Oficio De La Guerra- La Seguridad nacional en Colombia*. Tercer Mundo Editores: Bogotá, Colombia.

Leal-Buitrago, Francisco and León Zamosc, eds.1990. *Al filo del caos : crisis política en la Colombia de los años 80*. Bogotá, Colombia : Instituto de Estudios Políticos y Relaciones Internacionales : Tercer Mundo Editores

Ledebur, Kathryn. 2003. "Coca Conflict Turns Violent." *Washington Office on Latin America*, February 1. Available at http://www.wola.org/index.php?option=com_content&task=view p&id=525&Itemid=2; accessed July 19, 2009.

————. 2005. "Bolivia: Clear Consequences." In *Drugs and Democracy in Latin America: The Impact of U.S. Policy,* edited by Colletta Youngers and Eileen Rosin, pp. 143–84. Boulder: Lynne Rienner.

————. 2010. "Bolivian Armed Forces Block Investigation of Dicatorship Deaths." *Andean Information Network*, February 17; Available at http://ain-bolivia.org/2010/02/bolivian-armed-forces-block-investigation-of-dictatorship-deaths/; accessed March 6, 2010.

Lee, Dongmin. 2010. "The Chinese Military as a Modernization Agent." Paper presented at the Western Political Science Association Conference, March 31–April 2, San Francisco, CA.

Leech, Gary. 2007. Two Perspectives from the Colombian Left. *Colombia Journal*, July 12. Available at http://www.colombiajournal.org/colombia260.htm; Accessed June 1, 2008.

————. 2006. "Uribe Victory Likely to Lead to Increased Repression." *Colombia Journal*, Available at http://www.colombiajournal.org/colombia236.htm; accessed June 22, 2009.

Lehman, Kenneth. 2006. "A 'Medicine of Death'? U.S. Policy and Political Disarray in Bolivia, 1985–2006." In *Addicted to Failure: U.S. Security Policy in Latin America and the Andean Region*, edited by Brian Loveman, p.130–68. Boulder: Rowman and Littlefield.

————. 1999. *Bolivia and the United States: A Limited Partnership*. Athens: University of Georgia.

Lemoine, Maurice. 2006. "Bolivia: the military plan and wait." *Le Monde diplomatique*, February. Available at http://mondediplo.com/2006/02/08bolivia; accessed 12/2/07.

Lim, Timothy. 2006. *Doing Comparative Politics*. Boulder, CO: Lynne Rienner Press.

Lopez, Ernesto. 2001. "Latin America: Objective and Subjective Control Revisted." In David Pion-Berlin, ed. *Civil-Military Relations in Latin America*, 88–107. Chapel Hill: University of North Carolina Press.

Lopez Molina, Alberto. 2005. *Democracia y militares, crisis y arbitraje*. Quito:Editorial El Conejo.

López Maya, Margarita.2004. "Hugo Chávez Frías: His Movement and his Presidency." In *Venezuelan Politics in the Chávez Era* edited by Steve Ellner and Daniel Hellinger, 73–92. Boulder: Lynne Rienner.

Loveman, Brian. 2006. "U.S. Security Policies in Latin America and the Andean Region, 1990–2006." In Brian Lovemen, ed., 1–52, *Addicted to Failure*. Lanham, MD: Rowman and Littlefield.

Lucas, Kintto. 2008. "Ecuador: 'CIA Infiltration' Charges Prompt Shake-Up in Armed Forces." *Inter-Press Service*, April 10. Available at http://ipsnews.net/news.asp?idnews=41945; accessed July 26, 2009.

Mahoney, James and Dietrich Rueschemeyer. 2003. *Comparative Historical Analysis in the Social Sciences*. New York: Cambridge University Press.

Main, Alexander. 2010. "'A New Chapter of Engagement': Obama and the Honduran Coup." *NACLA*, January/February, vol.43, Issue #1: 15–21.

Mainwaring, Scott. 2006. "The Crisis of Representation in the Andes." *Journal of Democracy*, 17, no.3, July:13–27.

Mainwaring, Scott and Timothy R. Scully. 1995. "Introduction."In *Building Democratic Institutions: Party Systems in Latin America*, Edited by, Scott Mainwaring and Timothy R. Scully, 1–34. Stanford, CA: Stanford University Press.

Mainwaring, Scott, Ana María Bejarano, and Eduardo Pizarro Leongómez, eds. 2006a. *The Crisis of Democratic Representation in the Andes*. Standord, CA.: Stanford University Press.

———. 2006b. "The Crisis of Democratic Representation in the Andes: An Overview." In *The Crisis of Democratic Representation in the Andes*, edited by Scott Mainwaring, Ana María Bejarano and Eduardo Pizarro Leongómez, 1–44. Stanford, CA: Stanford University Press.

Manrique, Miguel. 2001. "La participación política de las Fuerzas Armadas venezolanas en el system politico (1998-2010)." In *Las Fuerzas Armadas en la región andina*. Edited by Martin Tanaka, 305–36. Lima: Comisión Andina de Juristas.

Manwaring, Max. 2005. "Venezuela's Hugo Chávez, Bolivarian Socialism, and Asymetric Warfare." *Strategic Studies Institute*, October. Available at *http://www.strategicstudiesinstitute. army.mil/pdffiles/PUB628.pdf*; accessed November 10, 2008.

Mares, David. 1998. "Civil-Military Relations, Democracy and the Regional Neighborhood." In David Mares, ed. *Civil-Military Relations: Building Democracy and Regional Security in Latin America, Southern Asia, and Central Europe*, 1–24. Boulder, CO: Westview Press.

———. 2001. "Latin American Economic Integration and Democratic Control of the Military: Is there a Symbiotic Relationship?" in *Civil-Military Relations in Latin America*. Edited by David Pion-Berlin, 223–45. Chapel Hill: The University of North Carolina Press.

María Vidal, Ana. 1993. *Los decretos de guerra*. Lima: IDS.

Marks, Thomas A. 2007. "A Model Counterinsurgency: Uribe's Colombia (2002–2006) vs FARC." *Military Review*, March–April: 41–56.

Marirrodriga, Jorge. 2007. "Evo Morales mima al Ejército." *El Pais*, December 3. Lexis/Nexis.

Martz, John. 1987. *Politics and Petroleum in Ecuador*. New Brunswick: Transaction Books.

———. 1996. "Ecuador." In *Latin American Politics and Development* edited by Howard J. Wiarda and Harvey Kline, p. 326–40. Boulder, CO: Westview Press.

———. 1998. "Venezuela, Ecuador and Colombia." In *Latin America:Its Problems and Its Promise*. Edited by Jan Knippers Black, 455–74. Boulder, CO: Westview Press.

Mauceri, Philip. 1996. *State Under Siege: Development and Policymaking in Peru*. Boulder, CO: Westview Press.

McClintock, Cynthia. 2006. "An Unlikely Comeback in Peru." *Journal of Democracy*, vol.17, no.4, October:95–109.

McClintock, Cynthia and Fabián Vallas. 2003. *The United States and Peru*. New York, NY: Routledge.

McClintock, Michael. 1992. *Instruments of Statecraft: U.S. Guerrilla Warfare, Counterinsurgency, and Counterterrorism, 1940–1990*. New York: Pantheon Books.

McDonough, Terrence, Michael Reich, and David M. Kotz. 2010. "Introduction: Social Structure of Accumulation Theory for the 21st Century". In *Contemporary Capitalism and Its Crises* edited by Terrence McDonough, Michael Reich, and David M. Kotz, pp. 1-19. New York: Cambridge University Press.

McSherry, J. Patrice. 2000. "Preserving Hegemony: National Security Doctrine in the Post-Cold War Era," *NACLA-Report on the Americas*, Nov/Dec:26–34.

———. 1998. "The Emergence of Guardian Democracy." *NACLA*, 32, 3 (Nov/Dec): 16–24.

Mercopress. 2007. "Ecuador to repair roads system with funds to repay creditors." Feb. 27. http://ecuador-rising.blogspot.com/2007/03/ecuador-to-repair-roads-system-with.html (accessed Aug. 21, 2008).

Mertus, Julie A. 2008. *Bait and Switch: Human Rights and U.S. Foreign Policy, 2nd Edition*. New York, NY: Routledge.

Miles, Marc A., Edwin J. Feulner, and Mary Anastasia O'Grady. 2004. *2004 Index of Economic Freedom*. Washington, D.C.: The Heritage Foundation and *The Wall Street Journal*.

The Military Balance, 1995–1996. 1995. London: International Institute for Strategic Studies.

Ministerio de Defensa Nacional en Bolivia. 2009. *Planes y programas de cooperación al desarrollo integral.* Available at http://www.mindef.gov.bo/index.php?option=com_content&view=article&id=45&Itemid=87; accessed July 26, 2009.

Ministerio de Defensa Nacional-República de Colombia. 2008. Política integral de DDHH y DIH. Available at http://www.mindefensa.gov.co/descargas/Documentos_Home/Politica_DDHH_MDN.pdf Accessed May 29, 2008.

Mitchell, Christopher. 1977. *The Legacy of Populism in Bolivia.* New York: Praeger.

Molina Flores, Col. Alberto. 2005. *Democracia y Militares: Crisis y Arbitraje.* Quito: Editorial El Conejo.

Müller Rojas, Alberto. 2007. "A View from Inside the Military." Interview with retired General Muller Rojas, *Venezuelanalysis,* July 9: http://www.venezuelanalysis.com/analysis/2488; accessed July 10, 2008.

Murillo, Mario. 2008a. "History Repeats Itself for Indigenous Communities Under Attack in Colombia." *NACLA,* October 15: Available at http://nacla.org/node/5106; accessed October 20, 2008.

———. 2008b. "The Final Offensive for the Free Trade Agreement is a Stark Contrast to other Developments in the Hemisphere." *Colombia Journal,* September 15th. Available at http://www.colombiajournal.org/colombia294.htm; accessed June 27, 2009.

Myers, David. 1996. "Venezuela." In *Latin American Politics and Development* edited by Howard Wiarda and Harvey Kline, 227–69. Boulder: Westview Press.

Naim, Moises. 1993. *Paper Tigers and Minotaurs.* Washington, D.C.: Carnegie Endowment.

Nash, Nathaniel C. "Army Unrest Stirs Bolivia, the Land of Coups. (Foreign Desk)." *New York Times* 3 June 1992. *General OneFile.* Web. 6 Mar. 2010.

National Endowment for Democracy. 2006. "Democracy Projects Database," http://www.ned.org/dbtw-wpd/textbase/projects-search.htm; accessed March 3, 2006.

———. 2010. "Statement of Principles and Objectives." Available at http://www.ned.org/publications/statement-of-priniciples-and-objectives; accessed March 16, 2010.

Navarro, Elias. 2008. "Nos maltrataron y amenazaron de muerte." *La República Online,* October 24: http://www.larepublica.com.pe/content/view/251886/483/; Accessed October 28, 2008.

New York Times. 1984. "Bolivia Arrests 100 in Attempted Coup; Denies Cocaine Link." July 3. Lexis/Nexis.

———. 1992. "Risky Realism in Peru." April 21: A22.

———. 1999. "Ecuador to get IMF Loan, August 28. Lexis/Nexis.

———. 2000a. "Days of Rebellion End With Ouster of Ecuador Leader." January 22. Available at http://www.nytimes.com/2000/01/22/world/day-of-rebellion-ends-with-ouster-of-ecuador-leader.html; accessed July 4, 2009.

———. 2000b. "Ecuador's Endangered Democracy." Editorial. January 25. Available at http://www.nytimes.com/2000/01/25/opinion/ecuador-s-endangered-democracy.html; accessed July 4, 2009.

Norden, Deborah. 2001. "The Organizational Dynamics of Militaries and Military Movements: Paths to Power in Venezuela." in David Pion-Berlin, ed. *Civil-Military Relations in Latin America,* 108–34. Chapel Hill: University of North Carolina Press.

Nordlinger, Eric. 1977. *Soldiers in Politics: Military Coups and Governments.* Englewood Cliffs, NJ: Prentice-Hall.

North, Liisa. 2004. "State Building, State Dismantling, and Financial Crises in Ecuador." In Jo-Marie Burt and Philip Mauceri, eds. *Politics in the Andes,* 187–206. Pittsburgh: University of Pittsburgh Press.

Noticias Uno. 2010. "Rafael García dice que desde el DAS se traficaba." Available at http://www.noticiasuno.com/noticias/das-sigue-chuzando.html; Accessed March 10, 2010.

NotiSur. 2004. "Peru: President Alejandro Toledo Dissolved Intelligence Service." April 30th.

Nunez, Elizabeth. 2006. "Civil Soldiers: they call it 'co-responsibility'." *New Internationalist*, June: http://findarticles.com/p/articles/mi_m0JQP/is_/ai_n16619197; accessed October 10, 2008.

Nuñez, Nelson.2006. "Qué viene con el gobierno de izquierda en Ecuador." *Analitica.com*, Dec. 1: http://www.analitica.com/va/internacionales/opinion/6368849.asp (accessed 8/22/08).

Obando, Enrique.2006. "U.S. Policy Toward Peru: At Odds for Twenty Years." In Brian Loveman, ed., 169–196, *Addicted to Failure*. Lanham, MD: Rowman and Littlefield.

———. 1998a. "Civil-Military Relations in Peru, 1980–1996." In Steve J. Stern, ed., *Shining and Other Paths*, pp. 385–410. Durham, NC: Duke University Press.

———. 1998b. "Fujimori and the Military." In John Crabtree and Jim Thomas, eds., *Fujimori's Peru*, pp.192–208, London: Institute of Latin American Studies.

———. 1994. The Power of Peru's Armed Forces. In Joseph S. Tulchin and Gary Bland, eds. *Peru in Crisis*, pp.101–24, Boulder, CO: Lynne Rienner Publishers.

———. 1992. La seguridad interna en la actual coyuntura. In Eduardo Ferrero Costa, ed. *Proceso de retorno a la institucionalidad democratica en Peru,* pp. 93–104, Lima: CEPEI.

Ocando, Casto. 2009. "Venezuelan Military Targets Chávez Critics in Its Ranks." *The Miami Herald*, June 10. Available at http://www.miamiherald.com/583/story/1088373.html; accessed June 8, 2009.

O'Donnell, Guillermo. 1973. *Modernization and Bureaucratic-Authoritarianism. Studies in South American Politics*. Berkely, CA: University of California Press.

Organization of American States. 2006. "The OAS and Free Trade." Available at http://www.oas.org/key_issues/eng/KeyIssue_Detail.asp?kis_sec=15; accessed April 20, 2007.

Orias Arredondo, Ramiro. 2005. "Bolivia: Democracy Under Pressure." In *The Andes in Focus,* edited by Russell Crandall, Guadalupe Paz, and Rioran Roett, pp. 45–65. Boulder: Lynne Rienner.

Ortiz, Román D. 2005. "Las relaciones civiles-militares en Colombia: control democrático de las fuerzas armadas en el contexto de un conflicto interno." In José A. Almeda, ed., *Democracias frágiles . las relaciones civiles-militares en el mundo iberoamericano*, pp. 573–92, Valencia, Spain: Editorial Tirant Lo Blanch.

Otárola Peñaranda, Alberto. 2003. "El proceso de reforma del Ministerio de Defensa y el rol de las Fuerzas Armadas para la consolidación democrática. El caso peruano." In Comisión Andina de Juristas, ed., *El control democratico de la defense en la region andina: scenarios para una integración civil-militar,* pp. 165–80, Lima, Peru: Embajada de Finlandia.

Oxhorn, Philip. 2006. "Conceptualizing Civil Society from the Bottom Up: A Political Economy Perspective." In Richard Feinberg, Carlos H Waisman and Leon Zamosc, eds., 59–86, *Civil Society and Democracy in Latin America*, New York, NY: Palgrave Macmillan.

Páez, Angel. 2009. "Peru: Spying on Social Movements." *Inter-Press Service News*, March 12. Available at http://ipsnews.net/news.asp?idnews=46090; accessed July 8, 2009.

Palmer, David. 1996. "Peru: The Enduring Authoritarian Legacy," in *Latin American Politics and Development*, eds Howard Wiarda and Harvey Kline, Boulder: Westview Press, 4th ed, 200–26.

———. 1994. "Commentary," in *Peru in Crisis: Dictatorship or Democracy?*, eds.Joseph Tulchin and Gary Bland, Boulder: Lynne Rienner Press, 133–6.

Pardini, Lydia and Raylsiyaly Rivero. 2008. "Plan Ecuador: Practical Ideas or Lofty Ideals?" *Council on Hemispheric Affairs*, August 18: http://www.coha.org/2008/08/plan-ecuador-practical-ideas-or-lofty-ideals/; accessed November 2, 2008.

Pearce, Jenny. 1990. *Colombia-Inside the Labyrinth.* London: Latin America Bureau.

Pearson, Tamatha. 2008. "Coup Plot Against Chavez Disclosed on Venezuelan TV." *Venezuelanalysis,* September 11: http://www.venezuelanalysis.com/news/3786; accessed October 15, 2008.

Peceny, Mark. 1995. *Democracy at the Point of Bayonets.* University Park, PA: The Pennsylvania State University Press.

Peeler, John. 1992. "Elite Settlements and Democratic Consolidation: Colombia, Costa Rica, and Venezuela." in John Higley and Richard Gunther (eds.), *Elites and Democratic Consolidation in Latin America and Southern Europe,* 81–112. New York:Cambridge University Press.

Peruvian Times. 2008. "Antauro Humala begins trial for 2005 assault on police station." March 28. Available at http://www.peruviantimes.com/antauro-humala-begins-trial-for-2005-assault-on-police-station/; accessed June 22, 2009.

———. 2009. "Death toll rises in aftermath in clash between police and indigenous protesters in Peru's northern Amazon." Available at http://www.peruviantimes.com/death-toll-rises-in-aftermath-of-clash-between-police-and-indigenous-protesters-in-perus-north-amazon-jungle/; accessed June 22, 2009.

Petras, James and Henry Veltmeyer. 2005. *Social Movements and State Power.* New York: Pluto Press.

Petras, James and Morris Morley. 1992. *Latin America in the Time of Cholera.* New York, NY: Routledge.

Pineo, Ronn. 2007. *Ecuador and the United States: Useful Strangers.* Athens: University of Georgia Press.

Pion-Berlin, David. 1997. *Through Corridors of Power.* College Park: Pennsylvania State University Press.

———. "Civil-Military Intervention." In David Pion-Berlin, ed., *Civil-Military Relations in Latin America,* pp. 135–60, Chapel Hill, NC: University of North Carolina Press.

———. 2005. "Political Management of the Military." *Military Review,* 85, 1 (Jan–Feb): 19–32.

Pion-Berlin, David and Harold Trinkunas. 2007. "Attention Deficits: Why Politicians Ignore Defense Policy in Latin America," *Latin American Research Review,* 42, no.3: 76–199.

———. 2005. "Democratization, Social Crisis and the Impact of Military Domestic Roles in Latin America." *Journal of Political and Military Sociology,* vol.33, no.1 (Summer): 5–24.

Pizarro, Eduardo. 1996. *Insurgencia sin revolución.* Bogotá : Tercer Mundo Editores.

———. 1995. "La reforma military en un contexto de democratizacion política," in F. Leal Buitrago (ed.) *En Busca de la estabilidad perdida,* pp. 159–208, Bogotá: Tercer Mundo Editores.

Porch, Douglas. 2008. "Civil-Military Relations in Colombia." In Thomas Bruneau and Harold Trinkunas (eds.) *Global Politics of Defense Reform,* 127–54, New York: Palgrave.

Premo, Daniel. 1989. "The Politics of Civilian Rule in Colombia." In *From Military to Civilian Rule,* ed. Constantine Danopoulos, 98–126, New York: Routledge.

¡Presente! 2008. "Bolivia says no!" *¡Presente!,* Spring. Available at http://www.soaw.org/presente/images/pdf/Spring2008.pdf; accessed Julu 21, 2009.

Quintana, Juan Ramón. 2005. "Militares y politicos en Bolivia." In *Democracias Frágiles: Las Relaciones Civiles-Militares en el Mundo Iberoamericano,* edited by José Antonio Olmeda Gómez, p. 391–462. Madrid: Tirant lo Blanch.

Quintana, Juan Ramón and Raul Barrios. 1999. "Las relaciones civiles-militares en Bolivia: una agenda pendiente." In *Control Civil y Fuerzas Armadas en las Nuevas Democracias Latinoamericanos,* edited by Rut Diamint, p. 223–64. Buenos Aires: Grupo Editor Latinoamericano.

Quiroga, Alberto. 2006. "Bolivian President Nationalizes Natural Gas Sector." *National Post*, May 2. Lexis/Nexis.

Quiroga, Diego. 2010. "Algunos interrogantes sobre la politíca seguridad democratic." *Cien días*, August, no.70. Available at http://www.cinep.org.co/node/1049; accessed August 20, 2010.

Ragin, Charles. 1987. *The Comparative Method*. Berkeley : University of California Press.

Ramírez Lemus, María Clemencia and Kimberly Stanton, John Walsh. 2005. Colombia: A Vicious Circle of Drugs and War. In Colletta Youngers and Eileen Rosin (eds.) *Drugs and Democracy in Latin America*, 99–142, Boulder, CO: Lynne Rienner.

Ramirez, Franklin. 2001. "¿Campos hegemónicos emergentes?" In *Las fuerzas armadas en le region andina*, edited by Martin Tanaka, p. 347–62. Lima: Comisión Andina de Juristas.

Razón, La. 2009a. "Están subordinadas a la autoridad civil." Available at http://www.la-razon.com/versiones/20090807_006812/nota_244_857714.htm; accessed March 13, 2010.

———. 2009b. "El entorno condiciona a la fuerza militar." Available at http://www.la-razon.com/versiones/20090807_006812/nota_244_857713.htm; accessed March 13, 2010.

———. 2010a. « FFAA cambiarán la doctrina para los nuevos oficiales. » January 25. Available at http://www.la-razon.com/versiones/20100125_006983/nota_249_943091.htm; accessed March 13, 2010.

———. 2010b. « Las FFAA alistan una ley para cambiar su doctrina. » Available at http://www.la-razon.com/versiones/20100129_006987/nota_247_945577.htm; accessed March 13, 2010.

Red de Seguridad y Defensa de América Latina. 2008. "Bolivia. Ley Orgánica de las Fuerzas Armadas de la Nación 'Comandantes de la Independencia de Bolivia.'" Available at http://atlas.resdal.org/Archivo/d0000286.htm; accessed November 12, 2008.

Reuters. 2008. "Years after Slaughter, Peru Opens Giant Burial Pit." May 29. Available at http://www.reuters.com/article/latestCrisis/idUSN29317645; accessed May 29, 2008.

Richani, Nazih. 2001. *Systems of Violence*. Albany: SUNY Press.

———. 2005. "Multinational Corporations, Rentier Capitalism, and the War System in Colombia." *Latin American Politics and Society*, vol. 47, no.3, Fall: 113–44.

Rivera, Fredy. 2001. "Democracia minimalista y 'fantasmas' castrenses en el Ecuador Contemporáneo."In *Las fuerzas armadas en le region andina*, edited by Martin Tanaka, pp. 194–225. Lima: Comisión Andina de Juristas.

———. 2004. "Partidos, Fuerzas Armadas y crisis institucional en tiempos de incertidumbre." In *El control democrático de la defense en la región andina*, 151–161. Lima: Comisión Andina de Juristas.

Rivera, Fredy and Franklin Ramírez Gallegos. 2005. "Ecuador: Democracy and Economy in Crisis." In *The Andes in Focus* edited by Russell Crandall, G. Paz and R. Roett, pp. 121–50. Boulder, CO: Lynne Rienner.

Roberts, Kenneth. 2003. "Social Polarization and the Populist Resurgence in Venezuela." In *Venezuelan Politics in the Chávez Era* edited by Steve Ellner and Daniel Hellinger, pp. 55–72. Boulder: Lynne Rienner.

———. 2007. "Latin America's Populist Revival." *SAIS Review*, vol. XXVII, no. 1, Winter–Spring: 3–15.

Robinson, William I.1996. *Promoting Polyarchy: Globalization, U.S. Intervention, and Hegemony*. New York: Cambridge University Press.

———. 1996b. "Globalization, the world system, and 'democracy promotion' in U.S. foreign policy," *Theory and Society* 25 (No. 5):615–65.

———. 2008. *Latin America and Global Capitalism*. Baltimore, MD: Johns Hopkins University Press.

Robles, Frances. 2009. "Top Honduran Military Lawyer: We Broke the Law." *The Miami Herald*, July 3. Available at http://www.miamiherald.com/news/americas/story/1125872.html; accessed August 2, 2009.

Rochabrun, Guillermo. 1996. "The Enigmas of Fujimori." *NACLA*, July/August.

Rochlin, James. 2007. *Social Forces and the Revolution in Military Affairs*. New York: Palgrave.

———. 2003. *Vanguard Revolutionaries in Latin America: Peru, Colombia and Mexico*. Boulder, CO: Lynne Rienner Press.

Rohter, Larry. 1999. "Colombia Is Reeling, Hurt by Rebels and Economy." *New York Times*, July 18: Section 1, pg.3. Lexis/Nexis.

———. 2000a. "Ecuador Shifts Control to No.2 Man." *The New York Times*, January 23. Available at http://www.nytimes.com/2000/01/23/world/ecuador-coup-shifts-control-to-no-2-man.html?pagewanted=2; accessed July 4, 2009.

———. 2000b. "Ecuador's Coup Alerts Region to Resurgent Military." January 30. Available at http://www.nytimes.com/2000/01/30/world/ecuador-s-coup-alerts-region-to-a-resurgent-military.html?pagewanted=2; accessed July 4, 2009.

Romero, Carlos. 1998. "Las relaciones entre Venezuela y Estados Unidos durante la presidencia Clinton." In Andrés Franco, ed. *Estados Unidos y los países Andinos 1993-1997*, 141–72. Bogotá: Centro Editorial Javeriano.

Romero, Mauricio and Angélica. 2009. "Paramilitares, neo-paramilitares y afines: crecen sus acciones criminales ¿Qué dice el gobierno?" Special Report, November: Corporación Nuevo Arco Iris.

Romero, Simon. 2009. "Cocaine Trade Helps Rebels Reignite War in Peru." *New York Times*, March 17. Available at http://www.nytimes.com/2009/03/18/world/americas/18peru.html; Accessed June 22, 2009.

———. 2009. "Peru's Ex-President Is Convicted and Given 25 Years for Killings and Other Abuses." *The New York Times*, April 8. Lexis/Nexis.

———. 2008. "Ecuador's Leader Purges Military and Moves to Expel American Base." *New York Times*, April 21. Lexis/Nexis.

———. 2007a. "Bolivia Leader Lets Venezuela Send Soldiers, Angering Foes." January 9. Lexis/Nexis.

———. 2007b. "Venezuela Rivals U.S. in Aid to Bolivia." *New York Times*, Feb. 23. Lexis/Nexis.

Rouquié, Alain. 1987. *The Military and the State in Latin America*. Berkeley: University of California Press.

Rosales Ferreyros, Cecilia. 2007. Ministros se defienden de críticas en su contra. *El Comercio.com*. December 22. Available at http://www.elcomercio.com.pe/edicionimpresa/Html/2007-12-22/ministros-defienden-criticas-su-contra.html; accessed June 25, 2008.

Rospigliosi, Fernando. 2000. *Montesinos y las Fuerzas Armadas*. Lima: IEP.

———. 1999. "Política y autoritarismo en las fuerzas armadas peruanas," in Rut Diamint (ed.), *Control civil y fuerzas armadas en las nuevas democracies latinoamericanas*, pp.433-466. Buenos Aires: Universidad Torcuato Di Tella, Nuevo Hacer.

Rothkopf, David. 2008. *Superclass*. New York, NY: Farrar, Straus and Giroux.

Rubio, Marcial. 1994. "Commentary," in Joseph Tulchin and Gary Bland (eds.), *Peru in Crisis: Dictatorship or Democracy?*, pp. 129–31. Boulder: Lynne Rienner Press.

Ruhl, J. M. 1981. "Civil-Military Relations in Colombia: A Societal Explanation." *Journal of Interamerican Studies and World Affairs*, 23, no.2 (May): 123–46.

Sachs, Jeffrey. 2000. "Shock Therapy Applied to Bolivia." *Commanding Heights*, Interview, June 15. Available at http://www.pbs.org/wgbh/commandingheights/shared/minitextlo/int_jeffreysachs.html#7; accessed September 21, 2008.

Safford, Frank and Marco Palacios. 2002. *Colombia: Fragmented Land, Divided Society*. New York, NY: Oxford University Press.

Salazar, Milagros. 2008. "Peru: Indigenous Organizations Aim for the Presidency." *Upside Down World*, May 29. Available at http://upsidedownworld.org/main/content/view/1309/76/; accessed March 20, 2009.

Salinas, Carlos. 1997/1998. "The Washington Update: A Hell of a Ride." *Colombia Bulletin*, 2, no.3 (Winter): 32–6.

Samper, Ernesto. 2000. *Aquí estoy y aquí me quedo*. Bogotá : El Ancora Editores.

Sánchez, Alex. 2006a. "The Next Domino? Ollanta Humala, Presente!" *Council on Hemispheric Affairs*, January 4. Available at http://www.coha.org/2006/01/the-next-domino-ollanta-humala-presente/; accessed October 10, 2008.

————. 2006b. "The Grounds for Bolivia's New Military Bases." *Council on Hemispheric Affairs*, October 18. Available at http://www.coha.org/2006/10/the-grounds-for-boliviapercente2-percent80percent99s-new-military-bases/; accessed October 3, 2008.

————. 2008. "Bolivia's Military: It's a Difficult Life, but Certainly There is no Sign of an Impending Coup." *Council on Hemispheric Affairs*, November 5. Available at http://www.coha.org/2008/11/boliviapercentE2percent80percent99s-militaryitpercentE2percent80-percent99s-a-difficult-life-but-no-sign-of-a-military-coup-yet/; accessed on July 26, 2009.

Sanchez, Fabiola. 2008. "Dissenting military officers say they've been pushed aside in Venezuela under Chávez." *San Diego Union Tribune,* June 28. Available at http://www.signonsandiego.com/news/world/20080628-1202-venezuela-dividedmilitary.html; accessed June 2, 2009.

Sandoval, Luis. 2009. "Historia del Polo Democrático Alternativo." *Polo Democrático Alternativo Website*, Available at http://www.polodemocratico.net/-Estatutos-plataforma-y-; accessed June 22, 2009.

Sanger, David. 2001. "Bush Links Trade with Democracy at Quebec Talks." *New York Times*, April 22: section 1, pg.1. Lexis/Nexis.

Santa Cruz, Arturo. 2007. "Election Monitoring and the Western Hemisphere Idea." In Thomas Legler, Sharon F. Lean and Dexter S. Boniface, eds. *Promoting Democracy in the Americas*, 133–51. Baltimore, MD: Johns Hopkins Press.

Schneider, Ronald. 2007. *Latin American Political History*. Boulder: Westview Press.

School of the Americas Watch. 2008. "Bolivian Military Withdraws From Controversial US Army Training School." Press Release, February 19th.

————. 2004. "Venezuela Ceases All Training of Soldiers at the School of the Americas." March 2: http://www.venezuelanalysis.com/news/384; Accessed October 10, 2008.

Schulte, Elizabeth. 2003. "Mass Strikes Brings Peru to Standstill." *Socialist Worker.org*, June 6, Available at http://socialistworker.org/2003-1/456/456_12_Peru.shtml; accessed June 22, 2009.

Selmeski, Brian. 2002. Democracy, Economic Development and the Ecuadorian Armed Forces. Available at http://www.cda-acd.forces.gc.ca/bolivia/engraph/publications/research/sup-porting/doc/selmeski_ee_paper.pdf accessed June 2, 2005.

Selverston-Scher, Melina. 2001. *Ethnopolitics in Ecuador*. Miami: North-South Press.

Semana. 2008. "Mi hermano fue un falso positivo." October 25. Available at http://semana.com/noticias-nacion/hermano-falso-positivo/117023.aspx; accessed January 1, 2009.

Shaw, Carolyn M. 2003. "Limits to Hegemonic Influence in the Organization of American States." *Latin American Politics and Society*, Fall: 59–92.

Shiefer, Carsten and Heinz Dieterich. 2006. "Weighty Alternatives for Latin America: Discussion with Heinz Dieterich." *MRZINE*, July 2, available at http://mrzine.monthlyreview.org/2006/schiefer070206.html; accessed June 15, 2010.

Sklair, Leslie. 2002. *Globalization: Capitalism and its Alternatives*. New York: Oxford University Press.

Smith, Steve. 2000. "U.S. Democracy Promotion: Critical Questions." In Michael Cox, G. John Ikenberry and Takashi Inoguchi, eds., *American Democracy Promotion*, 63–84. New York, NY: Oxford University Press.

Solidarity Center, The. 2006. *Justice for All: The Struggle for Worker Rights in Colombia*. Washington, D.C.: American Center for International Labor Solidarity.

Solimano, Andrés. 2005. "Political Instability, Institutional Quality and Social Conflict in the Andes." In Andrés Solimano, ed., *Political Crises, Social Conflict and Economic Development: The Political Economy of the Andean Region*, 15–44. Northampton, MA: Edward Elgar.

Solingen, Etel. 1998. *Regional Orders at Century's Dawn*. Princeton: Princeton University Press.

Stallings, Barbara. 1992. International Influence on Economic Policy: Debt, Stabilization, and Structural Reform. In Stephan Haggard and Robert Kaufman, eds. *The Politics of Economic Adjustment: International Constraints, Distributive Politics, and the State*. Princeton: Princeton University Press.

Stepan, Alfred. 1988. *Rethinking Military Politics*. Princeton: Princeton University Press.

———. 1986. "The New Professionalism of Internal Warfare and Military Role Expansion." In Abraham Lowenthal and J. Samul Fitch, eds. *Armies and Politics in Latin America*, 134–50. New York: Holmes and Meier.

Stockholm International Peace Research Institute. 2009. "Military Expenditure Database." Available at http://www.sipri.org/databases/milex; accessed March 14, 2010.

STRATFOR. 2005. "Ecuador: Is Palacio Looking for an Exit?" *STRATFOR Global Intelligence Review*, August 9. Available at http://www.stratfor.com/ecuador_palacio_looking_exit; accessed July 4, 2009.

Suggett, James. 2008a. "Venezuelan Military and Civilians Test-Run Defense Operations." June 10: http://www.venezuelanalysis.com/news/3542; accessed October 20, 2008.

———. 2008b. "South American Nations Form New Regional Grouping: UNASUR." *Venezuelanalysis*, May 24. Available at http://www.venezuelanalysis.com/news/3488; accessed Sept. 18, 2008.

Tate, Winifred. 2007. *Counting the Dead: The Culture and Politics of Human Rights Activism in Colombia*. Berkeley, CA: University of California Press.

Teresa Romero, Maria. 2002 "U.S. policy for the promotion of democracy: the Venezuelan case." In *Democracy and Human Rights in Latin America*, edited by Richard Hillman, John A. Peeler, and Elsa Cardozo Da Silva, p. 103–24. Westport: Praeger.

Tickner, Arlene. 2003. "Colombia and the United States: From Counternarcotics to Counterterrorism." *Current History* (February): 77–85

Time. 1965. "Colombia: General Unrest." February 12. Available at http://www.time.com/time/magazine/article/0,9171,840536,00.html; accessed March 30, 2010.

Toscano, Denys. 2005. "Relaciones Ecuador-Estados Unidos: Periodos presidenciales de Abdalá Bucaram y Fabián Alarcón." In *Las relaciones Ecuador-Estados Unidos en 25 años de democracia (1979–2004)*, edited Javier Ponce Leiva, p. 113–38. Quito: Flacso.

Traub, James. 2010. "Does Obama Have His Own Freedom Agenda or Not?" *Foreign Policy*, February 24. Available online at http://www.foreignpolicy.com/articles/2010/02/24/does_obama_have_his_own_freedom_agenda; accessed March 30th, 2010.

Treaster, Joseph. 1989. Rebels Step up Killings in Peru to Disrupt Election. *The New York Times*, October 26. Available at http://query.nytimes.com/gst/fullpage.html?res=950DEED9133DF935A15753C1A96F948260; accessed June 15, 2008.

Trinkunas, Harold. 2005. *Crafting Civilian Control of the Military in Venezuela: A Comparative Perspective*. Chapel Hill, NC: University of North Carolina Press.

Trinkunas, Harold. 2001. "Crafting Civilian Control in Argentina and Venezuela." In David Pion-Berlin, ed. *Civil-Military Relations in Latin America*, 161–193. Chapel Hill: University of North Carolina Press.

United States Agency for International Development. 2008. Latin America and the Caribbean: Economic and Social Database. Available at http://qesdb.cdie.org/lac/index.html; accessed June 3, 2008.

———. 2006. "Democracy and Governance." Available at http://www.usaid.gov/our_work/democracy_and_governance/; accessed January 10, 2007.

———. 2005. "Transition Initiatives," Available at http://www.usaid.gov/our_work/cross-cutting_programs/transition_initiatives/focus/civmil.html; Accessed May 2, 2006.

———. 2003. Final Evaluation of OTI's Program in Peru. Available at http://www.usaid.gov/our_work/cross cutting_programs/transition_initiatives/country/peru/rptFinal.pdf. Accessed June 2, 2008.

United States Department of Defense. 1992. "Document: Peru-Military Unease Growing." December 23. *National Security Archive.* Available at http://www.gwu.edu/~nsarchiv/NSAEBB/NSAEBB37/. Accessed March 8, 2010.

United States Embassy in Peru. 2000. "U.S. Embassy Cable: The State of the Military on the Eve of the Elections." April 7. *National Security Archive,* Available at http://www.gwu.edu/~nsarchiv/NSAEBB/NSAEBB72/index2.htm; accessed March 8, 2010.

United States Institute for Peace. 2004. "Civil Society Under Siege in Colombia," Special Report: February, no.114. Internet: http://www.usip.org/pubs/specialreports/sr114.html; accessed May 5, 2006.

U.S. State Department. 2000. Peru, Country Report on Human Rights Practices for 1999. February 23. Available at http://www.state.gov/g/drl/rls/hrrpt/1999/398.htm. Accessed July 5, 2008.

———. 2005. "Background Note: Peru," December. Internet: www.state.gov/r/pa/ei/bgn/35762.html; Accessed February 18, 2006.

Universo, El. 2006. "Nueva ley entra a delimiter el campo de acción de las Fuerzas Armadas." Dec. 26. http://archivo.eluniverso.com/2006/12/26/0001/8/8F5971D222684603A97112A683DCC08D.aspx

Urrutia, Miguel.1994. "Colombia." In *The Political Economy of Policy Reform,* ed. John Williamson, 285–315, Washington, D.C.: Institute for International Economics.

Valdivieso, Jeanneth. 2006. "Ecuador Names 1st Female Defense Chief." *Washington Post,* December 27, http://www.washingtonpost.com/wp-dyn/content/article/2006/12/27/AR2006122701366.html; accessed Aug.21, 2008.

Valencia, León. 2009. "La seguridad democratic en crisis" In *¿El declive de la seguridad democratic?* Special Report, November: Corporación Nuevo Arco Iris.

Varas, Augusto,ed. 1989. *Democracy Under Siege: New Military Power in Latin America.* New York: Greenwood Press.

Valdez, Carlos. 2006. "Bolivian Minister Backs Claim of Corporate Conspiracy against President." *Associated Press*, February 9. Lexis/Nexis.

Vásquez, George. 1996. "Peru," in Constantine Danopoulos and Cynthia Watson (eds.) *The Political Role of the Military*, 338–63. Westport, CT: Greenwood.

Villamizar, Andres. 2003. *Fuerzas militares para la guerra.* Bogotá: Fundación Seguridad y Democracia.

Vivas, Fernando. 2008. Un nuevo militarismo. *El Comercio.com.* January 17. Available at http://www.elcomercio.com.pe/edicionimpresa/Html/2008-01-17/un-nuevo-militarismo.html. Accessed July 2, 2008.

Wagner, Allan. 2005. "The Role of Integration in Strengthening Democracy: The Andean Case." Paper presented at the Conference "Building Democracy Across Borders" organized by IDEA International. Stockholm, June 10.

Washington Office on Latin America. 2010. "Arms-R-Us: South America Goes Shopping-A WOLA Report on South American Defense Expenditures." Available at http://www.wola. org/images/stories/Security%20Policy/arms%20r%20us%20-%20south%20america%20 goes%20shopping.pdf; accessed March 14, 2010.

Webber, Jeffery R. 2007a. "Empire's Island in a Sea of Struggle." *International Viewpoint: News and Analysis from the Fourth International,* January 2007, http://www.internationalviewpoint. org/spip.php?article1198.

Weekly News Update on the Americas. 2005. "Reservists Seize Police Post." *World War 4 Report,* Available at http://www.ww4report.com/perumiltaryrevolt; accessed June 24, 2009.

Wiarda, Howard. 2003. *The Soul of Latin America.* New Haven: Yale University Press.

Williams, Marc Eric. 2005. "U.S. Policy in the Andes: Commitments and Commitment Traps," in Russell Crandall, Guadalupe Paz and Riordan Roett (eds.), *The Andes in Focus. Security, Democracy and Economic Reform,* 151–72. Boulder, CO: Lynne Rienner.

Willis Garcés, Andrew. 2009. "Colombia: Struggling for Autonomy and Justice in the Face of State Repression." *Upside Down World,* February 25. Available at http://upsidedownworld. org/main/content/view/1737/61/; accessed March 20, 2009.

Wilpert, Gregory. 2007. *Changing Venezuela by Taking Power.* New York: Verso Press.

Wilson, Scott. 2002a. "Acting Leader of Venezuela Steps Down." *Washington Post,* April 14. Lexis/Nexis.

———. 2002b. "Clash of Visions Pushed Venezuela Toward Coup."*Washington Post,* April 21. Lexis/Nexis.

Wolpin, Miles. 1975. "External Political Socialization as a Source of Conservative Military Behavior in the Third World." In Kenneth Fidel, ed., *Militarism in Developing Countries,* 259–82. New Brunswick: Transaction Books.

World Bank. 2010. "Data File-Latin America and the Caribbean 2010." Available at http:// web.worldbank.org/WBSITE/EXTERNAL/COUNTRIES/LACEXT/0,,contentMDK :22117191~pagePK:146736~piPK:146830~theSitePK:258554,00.html; accessed March 1, 2010.

WorldEconomicForum.2008."TheGlobalCompetitivenessReport,2008–09."Availableathttp:// www.weforum.org/en/initiatives/gcp/Globalpercent20Competitivenesspercent20Report/ index.htm; accessed June 10, 2008.

Worldmark Encyclopedia of the Nations. 2007 [electronic resource]. Edited by Timothy L. Gall and Jeneen M. Hobby. Detroit, MI: Thomson Gale.

Wurgaft, Ramy. 2003. "Un país sumido en el caos." *El Mundo,* October 15. Lexis/Nexis.

Yashar, Deborah.1999. "Democracy, indigenous movements, and the postliberal challenge in Latin America." *World Politics,* vol.52, no.1: 76–104.

Youngers, Colletta. 2004. "Collateral Damage: The U.S. "War on Drugs" and Its Impact on Democracy in the Andes." In Julie Marie-Burt and Philip Mauceri (eds.), *Politics in the Andes: Identity, Conflict and Reform,* pp. 126–43, Pittsburgh: University of Pittsburgh Press.

Zelaya, Cesar. 2005. "Sobre la insurgencia nacionalista contra el gobierno de Toledo." *La Fogata-Digital,* Available at http://www.lafogata.org/05latino/latino1/peru1_0701.htm; accessed June 24, 2009.

Zibechi, Raúl. 2005a. "South America's New Militarism." *IRC Americas Program Special Report,* July 18: 1–8.

Zibechi, Raúl. 2005b. "The Other Colombia, the One of Hope: Militarism and Social Movements," *Counterpunch*, March 5/6. Internet: http://www.counterpunch.org/zibechi03052005.
html; accessed May 5, 2006.

———. 2008. "Colombia: Social Conflict Replaces Warfare." *Upside Down World*, December
11. Available at http://upsidedownworld.org/main/content/view/1623/61/; accessed March
20, 2009.

INDEX

Alarcon, Fabian, 92
Alston, Philip, 63
Alvarado, Velasco, Juan, 37, 65–6, 78, 86, 107
American International Group, 29
American Political Foundation, 27
Andean Community, 31–2, 79, 97
Andean Corporation of Promotion, 40
Andean Parliament, 40
Andean Regional Initiative, 137
Andean Trade Preference Act (ATPA), 31, 132
Andean Trade Preferences and Drug Eradication Act (ATPDEA), 138
Andean Tribunal of Justice, 40
Antezana, Marcelo, 142, 146
Anticapitalist globalization movements, 5–8, 11–12, 32, 33–4, 36, 39, 44, 49, 61, 78, 80, 84, 90, 92, 97, 106, 111, 122–4, 134–6, 140, 144, 148, 153–4, 159
Anti-Communism, 109, 125–7
Antineoliberal movements, *see* Anticapitalist globalization movements
Aranda, Luis, 141–2
Aráoz, Flores, Ántero, 79
Arias, Francisco, 107–8, 110
Aruilera, Roldós, Jaime, 87
Argentina, 35, 116
Ayala, Turbay, Cesár, Julio, 48

Baduel, Isaias, Raúl, 118
Bank of the South, 22
Bantz, Craddock, 33
Banzer, Hugo, 126–7, 130–1, 136–7, 144
Barco, Virgilio, 51–2
  Decree 1150, 51
Bedoya, Harold, 53–4
Belaunde, Fernando, 65–7
Bermúdez, Morales, Francisco, 66
Bersatti, Freddy, 144
Betancur, Belisario, 48
Bolivarian Alternative for the Americas (ALBA), 22, 80, 121, 145
Bolivia, 1–2, 4–5, 7–14, 16, 30–1, 33–4, 36–40, 80, 91, 93, 99, 116, 123, 123–54, 157, 158
Bolivian Congress, 126, 160
Bolivian Workers Central (COB), 140–1
COFADENA, 127, 131
Confederacion de Empresarios Privados de Bolivia (CEPB), 128, 134
Democratization, 128–9
February 2003 protests, 117, 138–9
Gas Wars, 138–42
Movement Toward Socialism, 136
Movimiento Nacionalista Revolucionario (MNR), 120, 125–6, 129–30
Nationalization, 141, 145

Bolivia—*Continued*
 National Democratic Action Party
  (AND), 129–31
 Plan Verde, 69–70
Borja, Rodrigo, 90
Botero, Fernando, 52
Bucaram, Abdalá, 92, 98
Bucarám, Assad, 87
Bush, H.W., George, 30, 50, 132, 137
Bush, W. George, 27, 57

Cabas, Luis, José, 143
Caldera, Rafael, 110
Campesino Association of the Cimitary
 River Valley (ACVC), 63
Carmona, Pedro, 114–15, 116–17, 120
Carter, Jimmy, 25–6
Carvajal, Leonardo, 120
Center for Hemispheric Defense Studies
 (CHDS), 29, 100
Center for Inter-American Relations, 26
Chávez, Hugo, 9, 33, 38, 83, 107, 111–15,
 117–21, 146
 Lands Law, 111
 Organic Hydrocarbons Law, 111
Chile, 76, 99, 116, 134–5
Clinton, Bill, 27, 55
Cohen, William, 28–9
Cold War, 26, 51, 85, 109, 143, 152
 U.S. National Security Doctrine, 31,
  46, 125, 127
Colombia, 1–2, 3, 5, 7, 9, 10–11, 30,
  35–6, 38–40, 43–64, 81, 83, 91, 93,
  99, 102, 105, 110, 114–16, 123–4,
  136–7, 148, 151, 153, 155, 158
 Association of Indigenous Councils of
  Northern Cauca (ACIN), 63
 Bolivian Paramilitaries, 46–50, 54–5,
  57–8, 61–3
 Bolivian Paramilitary demobilization,
  61–2, 66
 Colombian Congress, 53
 Colombian Supreme Court, 62
 Conservative Party, 45, 47

Coordinating Center for Integrated
 Action (CCAI), 59
Counterinsurgency, 36, 44–7, 49–51,
 57, 59
Defense Forces of Colombia (AUC),
 49–50, 59, 62
Department of Administrative
 Security (DAS), 52, 62
Department of Planning, 52
Human rights violations, 30, 48–51,
 53–4, 57–63
Import Substitution Industrialization,
 104, 110
Liberal Party, 45, 47
Muerte a Secuestradores (MAS), 48
National Army of Liberation (ELN),
 44, 46, 59
National Defense and Security
 Law, 55
National Front (1958–1986), 45, 47
National Popular Action (ANAPO), 47
Union Patriotica, 49
Cordero, Febres, Leon, 89
Correa, Rafael, 9, 33, 34, 99, 100–3
Counterhegemony, 33, 35–8, 84,
 117–21, 135, 142, 149, 154
Counterinsurgency, 1–2, 6, 11, 36,
 44–7, 49–51, 57, 59, 64–5, 67, 71,
 80, 85, 105, 159
Counternarcotics, *see* U.S. Drug War
Cueto, Alberto, 143

Da Silva, Paul, Gerald, 78
Danino, Robert, 76
de Lozada, Sanchez, 131, 133–4, 136–40
de Rincon, Ramirez, Lucia, Marta, 59
de Mola, Loret, Aurelio, 76
Declaration of Cartagena, 30–1
Defense Ministerial of the Americas,
 28, 29
del Castillo, Jorge, 79
del Rio, Alejo, Rito, 54
Democracy Promotion, 8, 18, 21, 25–7,
 31, 44, 71–3, 80, 109, 111, 115, 124

Democratization, 25–8, 66, 74, 87,
128, 154
Developmentalist/state-led model, 8,
22–3, 26, 37, 39, 66–7, 80, 81, 84,
86, 88, 101, 103, 106, 108, 110,
127, 134–5, 142
Drug Cartels, 13, 30, 50–1
Cali Cartel, 54
Medellin Cartel, 49–50
Duran-Ballen, Sixto, 90

Ecuador,1–2, 3, 5, 6, 9–10, 13–14, 16–17,
26, 33–4, 35–8, 40–1, 83–103,
121–3, 152–5, 158
2000 coup, 6, 94–6
Coordinated Social Movements
(CSM), 92
Democratization, 87
Directorate of Industries, 86
Ecuadorian Congress, 90
Guayaquil Chamber of Industry, 90
Indigenous population, 89, 91–2, 97
National Confederation of
Ecuadorian Indians (CONAIE), 34,
89–92, 94–5, 97–8, 100, 122
Nationalization, 90–1
Petroecuador, 102
United Workers Movement, 92
Esguerra, Alfonso, 52
Estenssoro, Paz, Victor, 130, 134

False positives, 63
FARC (Fuerzas Armadas
Revolucionarios de Colombia), 5,
44, 46, 53, 56–9, 64
FEDECAMARAS, 114–15, 117, 120
Fernandez, Leopoldo, 146
Figueroa, Mata, Carlos, 119
Fleishman-Hillard, 28
Free Trade Area of the Americas,
32, 138
Frechette, Myles, 54
Fuerzas Armadas Revolucionarios de
Colombia, see FARC

Fujimori, Alberto, 17, 43, 68–75, 77–8,
94–5, 114
Decree 746, 70–1
Decree 752, 70

Galindo, César, Julio, 141
Gallardo, José, 94
García, Alan, 66, 68–9, 72, 75, 79–80
Gaviria, César, 51–2, 54, 59, 96
Gutiérrez, Lucio, 83, 93, 95, 97–8, 100

Hegemony, 23–5, 120, 125
Heritage Foundation, 38–9
Herrera, Julio, 141
Hill, James, 9
Hommes, Rudolph, 52
Huaman, Adrian, 67
Humala, Antauro, 78
Humala, Ollanta, 78–9
Human Rights Violations, 3, 12, 30,
48–9, 54, 57, 63, 73–4, 129, 137, 139
Human Rights Watch, 61–2

Ibarra, Velasco, María, José, 86
Inter-American Development Bank, 32
Interamerican Dialogue, 21, 100, 107
International Monetary Fund, 21 24, 32,
58, 67, 70, 72, 88, 94, 131
Iran, 37

Jarrín, Oswaldo, 99–101
Jiménez, Pérez, Marcos, 104

Lara, Rodríguez, 86–7
Larriva, Guadalupe, 101
Latin American Free Trade
Association, 79
Leahy Law, 28, 54
Leftist movements, see Populist
movements
Leyva, Camacho, Luis, 47
Linowitz Report, 26
Lloreda, Rodrigo, 53
Llosa, Vargas, Mario, 69

Low-intensity democracy, 2–3, 6, 9–11, 23–6, 32, 34, 39–40, 44, 64, 74, 81, 84, 87, 109, 111

Mahuad, Jamil, 83, 93–7
Martinez, Leopoldo, 120
McCaffrey, Barry, 28
Mendez, Gonzalo, 142
Mendoza, Carlos, 94, 96, 113
Mesa, Carlos, 140–1
Meza, García, 128–9
Military professionalism, 25, 77, 155
Millán, Fernando, 54
Molina, Carlos, 116
Montesinos, Vladamir, 70–1, 73–4
Morales, Evo, 5, 8, 33, 36, 39, 80, 124, 136, 137–8, 142–8
 Plan ASPIRINA, 143
 Plan SINCALFA, 143
Movimiento Bolivariano 200
 see Bolivarian Revolutionary
 Movement (MBR-200) (Venezuela)

Nationalist movements, *see* Populist movements
Neoliberal Policy Coalitions, 2, 5–9, 11, 21–2, 36, 39–40, 44–5, 52, 81, 84, 111, 121–4, 129, 131, 134–5, 140, 142, 147–8, 153–4, 157
Noboa, Gustavo, 96–7, 99, 121
Novoa, Ruiz, 47

Obama, Barak, 27, 60, 63, 159–60
Organization of American States (OAS), 31–2, 72, 96, 98, 147
Organization of the Petroleum Exporting Countries (OPEC), 85
Ortiz, Benjamin, 94
Ovando, Alfredo, 126

Palacio, Alfred, 98–9, 100
 Civil Service and Administrative Career Law, 99–100
Paniagua, Valentín, 75
Paramilitaries, 14, 46–50, 54–5, 57–8, 61–3, 66, 119, 146

Pardo, Rafael, 48, 51
Pastrana, Andrés, 53, 55, 57–9
Pazzos, Llosa, Carlos, Juan, 79
Pazzos, Vargas, Frank, 89–90
Pérez, Andres, Carlos, 13, 106–10
Peru, 1–3, 5, 7, 9, 11–14, 16–17, 30, 35–45, 57, 64–83, 86, 91, 93–5, 107, 114, 116, 123–4, 136, 148, 151, 153, 158
 ALBA Houses, 80
 American Popular Revolutionary Alliance (APRA), 65, 68
 Center for Higher Military Studies (CAEM), 65–6
 Center for International Human Rights, 76
 Colina Group, 72, 74
 Defense Ministry Law, 76
 Democratization, 66–7
 Human rights violations, 30
 Internal security threat, 44, 80–1
 National Intelligence Council (CNI), 75
 National Intelligence Service (SIN), 70–1, 74–6
 Peruvian Congress, 67, 71–2, 75–7
 Peruvian Judiciary, 71
 Plan Verde, 69–70
 Political and Strategic Studies Institute, 73
 Revolutionary Government of the Armed Forces, 65
 Shining Path guerilla movement, 5, 13, 44, 57, 67–9, 72–4, 77, 79–90
 Truth and Reconciliation Commission, 68
 Tupac Amaru Revolutionary Movement (MRTA), 44, 67
Petro, Gustavo, 64
Pinilla, Rojas, Gustavo, 45, 47
Pizarro, Rebeiz, Gabriel, 47
Polo Democrático, 63–4
Ponce, Javier, 103
Popular Action Party, 65

Populist movements, 2–3, 6, 8–11, 21–2, 30, 32–3, 35–7, 29, 44, 46, 64–8, 78, 80, 84–5, 88, 90–1, 95, 102, 107, 110, 113, 115, 122–6, 133, 135, 140–2, 145, 147, 148–9, 152–4
Poveda, Mendoza, Carlos, 96
Poveda, Ramírez, 116

Rangel, Vicente, Jose, 112
Raymond, Jr., Walter, 27
Reagan, Ronald, 27, 90
Reich, Otto, 116
Richarson, Bill, 56
Rocha, Manuel, 137–8
Romero, Peter, 96
Romero, Rincon, Lucas, 116
Russia, 37, 120

Salcedo, Francisco, 119
Samper, Ernesto, 52–4
San Miguel, Walker, 143, 146
Sandoval, Wellington, 102
Santiago Commitment, 31
Santos, Daniel, 138
Santos, Manuel, Juan, 59
Schultz, Jim, 139
Solares, Jaime, 141
South American Defense Council, 37, 121

Tapias, Fernando, 53
Toledo, Alejandro, 75–80
Torres, José, Juan, 126
Tovar, Valencia, Alvaro, 47
Trigo, Luis, 146
Trilateral Commission, 26

Union of South American Nations (UNASUR), 147
United Nations, 21
United States, 3, 5, 7–9, 12, 14, 17–19, 21, 24, 30–2, 35, 37, 39, 54, 61, 66, 81, 94, 96–7, 99–102, 105, 109, 119–22, 124–6, 129, 131–3
Defense Cooperation Agreement, 60

Foreign Policy, 17–19, 26–9, 56–8, 92–3, 116, 153
International Military Education Training (IMET), 29, 77
International Narcotics Control Act, 50
Military aid, 9, 19, 29–30, 46–7, 50–1, 55–6, 57, 59, 71, 77, 85–6, 91–3, 115–16, 126, 144
National Endowment for Democracy, 27, 73, 77, 115
National Security Council, 27, 39
Office of Transition Initiatives, 77, 115
Plan Colombia, 50, 55–7, 60, 98
Plan Ecuador, 102
U.S. Agency for International Development (USAID), 27, 47, 72, 77, 115, 116, 120
U.S. Army Special Warfare, 47, 126
U.S. Central Intelligence Agency, 27, 55, 74
U.S. Congress, 28–9, 50, 54, 56–7, 137
U.S. Department of Defense, 29, 100
U.S. Drug War, 13, 28, 30–1, 50–1, 55–7, 93, 102, 105, 124–5, 132–3, 137, 144
U.S. Foreign Policy, 9, 18, 26–7, 60, 90–1, 116, 153
U.S. House Armed Services Committee, 33
U.S. International Military Education Training (IMET), 29, 120
U.S. Southern Command (U.S. SOUTHCOM), 9, 28, 59, 73
U.S. State Department, 51, 55, 74, 144
U.S. Treasury, 32
Western Hemisphere Institute of Security Cooperation (School of the Americas), 29, 33, 108, 116, 120, 144
Uribe, Álvaro, 43, 53, 58–64
Uribe, Montoya, Mario, 60

Vargas, Wilfredo, 144, 146
Velasco, Vasquez, Efrain, 116

Venezuela, 1–3, 5, 6, 9–11, 13–14, 16–17,
    34, 36–7, 38, 40, 80, 83–5,87, 89,
    91, 93, 95, 97, 99, 101, 103–22
    1992 coup, 6, 71, 83
    1999 Constitution, 112–13,
        118–19, 156
    April 2002 Coup, 113–22
    Bolivarian Revolutionary Movement
        (MBR–200), 107–8, 117
    Bolivarian Socialism, 34, 117, 155
    Caracazo, 34, 36, 107–8, 153
    Christian Democratic Party (COPEI),
        104, 110
    Confederation of Venezuelan Workers
        (CTV), 114
    Democratic Action Party (AD),
        103–4, 129
    Democratic Coordinator (CD), 113–14
    Import Substitution Industrialization,
        22, 104, 110
    Instituto de Altos Estudios de la
        Defensa Nacional (IAEDEN), 112
    Ley Orgánica de las Fuerzas Armadas
        de la Nación, 99, 118, 132, 134
    Plan Bolivar, 112–13
    Punto Fijo Pact, 104–5, 109
    Presidential Committee for
        Communal Power, 113
    Revolutionary Party of Venezuela
        (PRV), 107
    Union Patriotica Militar, 103
    Venezuelan Congress, 105
Villa, Reyes, Manfred, 146

Wagner, Allen, 79
Waisman, David, 76
Washington Consensus, 18, 88
Watson, Alexander, 69
Weinstein, Allen, 27
Wilhelm, E., Charles, 29
World Bank, 21, 24, 31–2, 51, 70
World Social Forum, 22
World Trade Organization, 21, 32

Yarborough, William, 47

Zamora, Paz, 132
Zuazo, Siles, Hernan, 129